Discovering Organizations

Discovering Organizations

Robin Burrow

OXFORD
UNIVERSITY PRESS

Great Clarendon Street, Oxford, OX2 6DP,
United Kingdom

Oxford University Press is a department of the University of Oxford.
It furthers the University's objective of excellence in research, scholarship,
and education by publishing worldwide. Oxford is a registered trade mark of
Oxford University Press in the UK and in certain other countries

© Oxford University Press 2025

The moral rights of the author have been asserted.

All rights reserved. No part of this publication may be reproduced, stored in a retrieval system,
transmitted, used for text and data mining, or used for training artificial intelligence, in any form or
by any means, without the prior permission in writing of Oxford University Press, or as expressly
permitted by law, by licence or under terms agreed with the appropriate reprographics rights
organization. Enquiries concerning reproduction outside the scope of the above should be sent
to the Rights Department, Oxford University Press, at the address above.

You must not circulate this work in any other form
and you must impose this same condition on any acquirer

Published in the United States of America by Oxford University Press
198 Madison Avenue, New York, NY 10016, United States of America

British Library Cataloguing in Publication Data

Data available

Library of Congress Control Number: 2024948047

ISBN 978-0-19-284746-1

Printed in the UK by
Bell & Bain Ltd., Glasgow

Links to third party websites are provided by Oxford in good faith and
for information only. Oxford disclaims any responsibility for the materials
contained in any third party website referenced in this work.

The manufacturer's authorised representative in the EU for product safety is Oxford University Press España S.A. of El Parque Empresarial San Fernando de Henares, Avenida de Castilla, 2 – 28830 Madrid (www.oup.es/en or product.safety@oup.com). OUP España S.A. also acts as importer into Spain of products made by the manufacturer.

Contents

Detailed Contents	vii
Tables	xi
Photos	xiii
Case Studies	xv
Research Insights	xvii
Preface	xix
Acknowledgements	xxv
1. Humans and Organizations	1

PART 1: THE BIG FOUR

2. Public Organizations	17
3. Private Organizations	45
4. Informal Organizations	75
5. Criminal Organizations	105

PART 2: HOW ORGANIZATIONS WORK

6. Record-Keeping, Rules, and the Invention of Bureaucracy	139
7. Formality, Rationality, and Organizations	173
8. Power, Control and the Motivation to Work	205
9. Resistance and the Informal Side of Organizations	236
Index	267

Detailed Contents

Tables xi
Photos xiii
Case Studies xv
Research Insights xvii
Preface xix
Acknowledgements xxv

1. Humans and Organizations 1
   1.1 Introducing organizations 1
   1.2 An "organized" species 2
   1.3 The origins of organization 4
   1.4 The rise of altruism 6
   1.5 Introducing Part 1: The Big Four 9
   1.6 Introducing Part 2: How Organizations Work 11
   References 13

PART 1: THE BIG FOUR

2. Public Organizations 17
   2.1 Introduction 17
   2.2 What are public organizations? 18
   2.3 Why learn about public organizations? 19
   2.4 The first public organizations in history 20
   2.5 Why not everyone thinks public organizations are the best thing since sliced bread 27
   2.6 Summary 33
   References 42

3. Private Organizations 45
   3.1 Introduction 45
   3.2 What are private organizations? 46

3.3	Why learn about private organizations?	47
3.4	The first corporations	51
3.5	Why we love corporations	54
3.6	Why not everyone thinks corporations are the best thing since sliced bread	56
3.7	Introducing the concept of Marxism	56
3.8	Summary	62
	References	73

4. Informal Organizations — 75

4.1	Introduction	75
4.2	What are informal organizations?	76
4.3	Why learn about informal organizations?	79
4.4	Extremely informal organizations in focus	80
4.5	Semi-formal organizations in focus	84
4.6	Why informal organizations matter	87
4.7	Summary	91
	References	99

5. Criminal Organizations — 105

5.1	Introduction	105
5.2	What are criminal organizations?	106
5.3	Why learn about criminal organizations?	107
5.4	How criminal organizations work	108
5.5	The rule of 21	110
5.6	Cooperation in criminal organizations	114
5.7	Ritualized fraternity and cooperation in criminal organization	115
5.8	Violence and cooperation in criminal organizations	120
5.9	Summary	123
	References	133

PART 2: HOW ORGANIZATIONS WORK

6. Record-Keeping, Rules and the Invention of Bureaucracy — 139

6.1	Introduction	139
6.2	What is bureaucracy?	140
6.3	Where do you find bureaucracy?	143

6.4 Where did bureaucracy come from?	144
6.5 Why we love a good bureaucracy	151
6.6 The flaws in the system	152
6.7 Summary	160
References	170

7. Formality, Rationality, and Organizations — 173

7.1 Introduction	173
7.2 Theoretical foundations	174
7.3 Manufacturing and the birth of modern rational factories	176
7.4 Rationality and the post-industrial services economy	188
7.5 Summary	193
References	201

8. Power, Control, and the Motivation to Work — 205

8.1 Introduction	205
8.2 Theoretical foundations	206
8.3 Motivating the workforce	207
8.4 Summary	224
References	232

9. Resistance and the Informal Side of Organizations — 236

9.1 Introduction	236
9.2 Theoretical foundations	237
9.3 Forms of resistance	244
9.4 A few final points	251
9.5 Summary	252
References	260

Index — 267

Tables

3.1	Types of private organization	47
5.1	Major Yakuza crime syndicates, 2001	128
6.1	The key characteristics of a bureaucracy	142
7.1	The principles of Taylorism	187
7.2	The principles of Fordism	187

Photos

4.1	Gold Rush in the Peruvian Amazon	77
5.1	Full Body Tattoo Suit (Anton Kusters)	117
5.2	Hands (Anton Kusters)	117
5.3	Office of the Kobe Yamaguchi-gumi in Awaji, Japan	127
6.1	The Ishango Bone (discovered in the Democratic Republic of Congo)	146
6.2	Sumerian clay tokens c 8000 BCE	147
6.3	Sumerian engraved tokens c 4000 BCE	148
6.4	Sumerian bullae c 3250 BCE	148
6.5	Sumerian cuneiform writing c 3000 BCE	149
6.6	Pre-flight checklist for the Boeing B17 "flying fortress"	167
6.7	WHO Safe Surgery Checklist	168
7.1	A Harappan Brick	178
7.2	Persian vertical windmills on the Irano-Afghan Border	179
7.3	The Arsenal of Venice (Venice, Italy) from 1797 map by Gian Maria Maffioletti	180
7.4	Lombe's silk throwing mill Derby (UK)	182
7.5	Evans' flour factory	184

Case Studies

Case Study:	The Edu-factory	36
Case Study:	The corporation that ruled a country	65
Case Study:	Poverty, microfinance, and extremely informal organizations	94
Case Study:	The Japanese Yakuza	126
Case Study:	The World Health Organization Surgical Safety Checklist	163
Case Study:	McLove	196
Case Study:	The greatest experiment of all time?	227
Case Study:	What people do when resistance is risky	255

Research Insights

Research Insight:	Bearing the burden of austerity	35
Research Insight:	ExxonMobil and the great climate cover-up	65
Research Insight:	An underground business	93
Research Insight:	How organized criminals infiltrate mainstream organizations	126
Research Insight:	A checklist that saves lives	163
Research Insight:	Normalized lying at work	196
Research Insight:	Motivation, Venetian-style	226
Research Insight:	Beyond the hidden/public resistance divide: How bloggers defeated a big company	255

Preface

This is a book about organizations. It is about how we humans work together and get things done in more or less purposeful and systematic ways. It's a critical book. It's also, I hope, an optimistic book. Our capacity for organization is quite remarkable. I think the organizations we build are among our greatest achievements, even if they don't always feel like it.

My aim in writing this book is to help people better understand the organizations that surround them and how they work. The way I've approached this ambition is by starting at the literal beginning—with where, when, and why we humans started to get organized, and the sort of organizations we established. This is "Chapter 1," and its content is drawn heavily from archeology and anthropology.

The four chapters that follow are dedicated to what I see as the main forms of organization that exist in the world today. I'm calling them the "Big Four," because I think it sounds grand. For me, the big four comprises: (1) public, (2) private, (3) informal, and (4) criminal organizations. Each of these types of organization gets a chapter to themselves, in Part 1 of the book.

In each of the "Big Four" chapters I go back to basics. I have a crack at explaining what public, private, informal, and criminal organizations are, and why I think people should learn about them. In the case of public and private organizations, I also say a bit about their history—about the concept of a corporation, for example, and the competing ways we can make sense of and evaluate what they do. This provides a segue into wider social and political issues relating to organizations. You can follow these up if you want. There are lots of references there you can use.

In the "Big Four" section of the book, the chapter on public organizations comes first. It begins with the earliest evidence we have of community-run organizations in neolithic Syria. For many people, it'll seem quite weird to go this far back in history. I do it to try and connect the reader with the basic idea of a public organization. That is, with the idea of organizing for the greater [public] good. There is also a bit about the origins of the modern bureaucratic state, in the short-lived, but incredibly impressive, Chinese Qin empire. The chapter finishes with the neoliberal critique of state institutions and a case study based on Peter Fleming's "Dark academia" (Fleming, 2020, 2021). It's a proper page turner.

The chapter on private organizations begins with an introduction to the concept of a corporation and its ancient Roman origins. The chapter ends with the Marxist critique of the capitalist system. In between I talk about the quirky ideas that underpin and distinguish corporations (what makes them so special), and why we love (and hate) them so much. This chapter's case study takes aim at the East India Company, and why you really don't want companies in charge of countries. The chapters on informal and criminal organizations contains material that you won't find in any other textbook (I checked). I cover them because if you're serious about understanding the organized world, you simply can't ignore them. Just because an organization isn't legally registered (or have classic bureaucratic structures), doesn't mean they don't matter. In fact, I actually think these organizations should be studied first. Informal organizations in particular.

To elaborate very briefly: I've included a chapter on informal organizations for several reasons, but principally because, most people on this planet will never hold a contract of employment in a formal organization at any point in their life (Perry et al., 2007). For them, the world of formal organizations is an alien one (Alcock, 2018).

Criminal organizations get a chapter because they're also everywhere, and they're pretty important. You don't have to be a detective to see this. You also won't find criminal organization in any other textbook on organization studies. In fact, the field of organizational studies in its entirety has virtually nothing to say about criminal organizations. To write this chapter I had to borrow heavily from adjacent fields, such as criminology. It took ages.

In Part 2 of the book, I shift away from the principal forms of organizations that define our world, and focus more explicitly on how organizations work. To my own discredit, I lean towards the organizational mechanics of formal public and private organizations—largely because there is a ton of research in this area. To simplify things I focus on what I see as the four most critical concepts in organization studies (broadly defined). The four chapters that make up Part 2 of this book cover: (1) bureaucracy, (2) rationalized systems of organization, (3) power and motivation, and (4) resistance to control. Each of these topics gets their own chapter, and together they make up Part 2 of this book.

You'll see another radical departure from other textbooks when you get to Part 2. Since I was an undergraduate, I've been frustrated with just how weird the content of many textbooks is. My frustrations have been validated in recent years by the growing amount of research showing that aspects of what is contained in popular textbooks is actually highly problematic (see Bridgman, Cummings, & Ballard, 2019; Cummings, Bridgman, Hassard, & Rowlinson, 2017; Hassard, 2012). The problems are multifaceted, but one big one is that currently many textbook authors tend to present things in a very distorted way. In some cases the stories they tell about organizations are largely fictional. They uncritically reproduce myths that have little historical basis or accuracy. These textbooks do little justice to either the genesis of foundational ideas, or to our understanding of how organizations actually work. It's crazy stuff.

Rather than reproduce the now well-engrained narrative I've done something different. I've attempted an elementary form of conceptual history (as in Koselleck & Presner, 2002)—thanks to Steve Cummings at Victoria University of Wellington (New Zealand) for introducing me to this. In essence, I've simply taken practices that define how modern organizations work and tried to trace their history. I've looked at who invented what, where, when, and why. For example, in the chapter on bureaucracy, my starting point isn't the great Max Weber (who I have absolutely no problem with), but a 5,000-year-old Mesopotamian brewery and the fledgling logo-syllabic script of a man called Kushim. In the case of rationalized systems of organization, my starting point isn't the self-celebrating Henry Ford and his marvelous production assembly line, but a curiously extinct, remarkably uniform civilization from the Indian subcontinent. In the chapter on motivation, my starting point isn't the Hawthorne studies, but the demise of slavery in Europe and the "enlightened" search for more humane ways of achieving social progress.

What this approach enables me to do is tell what I think is a better, more plausible story about organizations. It enables me to talk about organizations as something we humans do, and have done for a very, very long time. And it enables me to (re)attribute some of history's biggest organizational innovations to people who lived and worked in places outside of Europe and North America. This way I can bring in the contributions of Iranians, Iraqis, Chinese, Indians and everyone else, and showcase their largely ignored contributions to our modern, organized world.

For me, the historical dimension of this book is its principal and most important distinguishing feature. Another is the relatively unorthodox way I've gone about writing it. The style I've gone for is pretty informal. You might like it, you might not. Either way, my aim was to try and distinguish this book from the incredibly dull alternatives that are out there. Textbooks in particular have this unique ability to deaden interesting topics and make them utterly boring and impenetrable. It's really quite remarkable. I've literally had more fun reading the small print on my mortgage, than the textbooks I read as part of this project. As a consequence, I've had a go at writing differently. I hope you find this book slightly less onerous to read than all the rest.

The last thing I want to emphasize is that I don't consider this to be a definitive account of organizations in any way, shape, or form. It's just my own take on things. It's my attempt at what Cummings et al. (2017) would call "a new history" of organizations. This book is certainly not perfect; however, it is an attempt to celebrate the glorious, quirky details that make up the story of human organization. I hope you'll find that story interesting.

Robin Burrow
York, 2025

References

Alcock, G. (2018). *KasiNomic Revolution: The Rise of the African Informal Economy South Africa*. Cape Town: Jonathan Ball Publishers.

Bridgman, T., S. Cummings, & J. Ballard. (2019). Who built Maslow's pyramid? A history of the creation of management studies' most famous symbol and its implications for management education. *Academy of Management Learning & Education* 18(1), 81–98.

Cummings, S., T. Bridgman, J. Hassard, & M. Rowlinson. (2017). *A New History of Management*. Cambridge: Cambridge University Press.

Fleming, P. (2020). Dark academia: Despair in the Neoliberal Business School. *Journal of Management Studies* 57(6), 1305–1311. doi: https://doi.org/10.1111/joms.12521

Fleming, P. (2021). *Dark Academia: How Universities Die*. London: Pluto Press.

Hassard, J. S. (2012). Rethinking the Hawthorne Studies: The Western Electric research in its social, political and historical context. *Human Relations* 65(11), 1431–1461.

Koselleck, R. & T. S. Presner. (2002). *The Practice of Conceptual History: Timing History, Spacing Concepts*. Red Wood City: *Stanford University Press*.

Perry, G. E., O. Arias, P. Fajnzylber, W. F. Maloney, A. Mason, & J. Saavedra-Chanduvi. (2007). *Informality: Exit and Exclusion*. The World Bank.

Acknowledgements

I worked on this book intensively for almost two years, and less intensively for at least three years prior to that. In that time I've racked up a long list of people to acknowledge. These are people who have been extremely generous with their help, support, advice, encouragement, comments, critique, and all the rest. They are not responsible for the content of this book. That responsibility is mine alone, along with any errors, omissions, or misrepresentations it may contain.

I am profoundly grateful to my old employer (Cardiff University) who granted me the research leave I needed to finish this project. I'm particularly grateful to Tim Edwards for his huge support and encouragement. Also to Sarah Gilmore, another staunch supporter and steadfast friend.

Thanks and acknowledgment also go to the 11 reviewers of my initial proposal, the 8 reviewers of my initial chapters, and the 5 reviewers of the final manuscript. I would also like to thank my editors at Oxford University Press. In particular, Nicola Hartley, who enthusiastically shared my vision for this book from the start, and skilfully navigated its commission. I'm also grateful to Kelly Lewars, who took over from Nicola, and did a fantastic job of pushing the book to its completion.

I am also very grateful to Martin Parker and Rachel Williams, who corresponded with me right at the very start of this project. Each read, commented on, and challenged my initial book proposal in different ways. Similarly Chris Grey whose generous comments and kind encouragement helped to allay my considerable anxieties about trying to do such a different project.

Thanks are also due to the fantastic Todd Bridgman, Steve Cummings, Peter Fleming, Davide Nicolini, David Jones, Yuan Huang, James Wallace, Mike Marinetto, Toma Pustelnikovaite, Jukka Rintamäki, Marcus Gomes, and Maja Korica.

I am also grateful to the representatives of the National Trust at Powis Castle, who generously opened the Robert Clive collections for me, and took the time to talk with me about his role in the East India Company.

Particular thanks must also go to Anton Kusters, for taking the time to talk with me about his incredible ethnography with the Yakuza clans of Japan. Anton kindly allowed us to use the photos he took during his assignment with the Yakuza in the Criminal Organizations chapter of this book. I am profoundly grateful to him for that.

Similarly, I'm profoundly grateful to G. G. Alcock, for talking with me at length about his autoethnographic work in the African informal economy, and his book *Kasinomics: The African Informal Economies and the People who Inhabit them*.

I am also very grateful to Bev and Jo who were fantastic hosts in Queenstown (New Zealand), where I finished the final manuscript.

Lastly, eternal thanks are due to the ever-great Claire Talbot, for everything.

Special Thanks

I would also like to extend special thanks to those instructors, both named and anonymous, who took the time to offer thoughtful reviews of this title as it developed.

Rebecka Arman, University of Gothenburg

Karen Boll, Copenhagen Business School

Constantin Ciachir, University of Surrey

Adelien Decramer, Ghent University

Pippa Denny-Gelder, University of Lincoln

Gail Greig, University of St. Andrews

John Healy, Trinity College-Dublin

Rima Hussein, Northumbria University

Alan Johnston, York St John University

Deborah Kerfoot, Keele University

Maja Korica, Professor at the Institut d'Économie Scientifique et de Gestion, University in France

Allan Lee, University of Exeter

Zoltan Lippenyi, University of Groningen

Sideeq Mohammed, University of Kent

Yaqub Paul Murray, Royal Agricultural University

Stephen Perkins, London Metropolitan University

Jiachen Shi, University of Leeds

Joana Vassilopoulou, Brunel University

Xanthe Whittaker, Leeds University Business School

1
Humans and Organizations

1.1 Introducing organizations

If you look up the word "organization(s)" in the Oxford English Dictionary you'll see a reference to something called "structure." Also to things like "systematic ordering or arrangement" and to "the condition of being organized." Intriguing? Possibly. Annoyingly vague? Most definitely.

When we talk about organizations we are generally referring to the ways people cooperate with one another and get things done. An organization really isn't any more complicated than that. For sure, organizations *can* be complicated. However if you look at what an organization actually is, you'll see it's basically just people cooperating with each other. Organizations are all about people working together and doing things in more or less purposeful and systematic ways.

We often talk about organizations in tangible terms. We talk about ***the*** organization. Or, about ***an*** organization. I do it throughout this book. However an organization isn't really a tangible thing. This is quite a difficult idea to get your head around. The hard reality though, is that an organization isn't anything you can touch, pick up, or carry around with you. It's a concept. A figment of our impressive human imagination.

Crazy stuff, surely? Not really. Consider this: can you touch an organization? Can you touch the organization that published this book, for example? What would you touch? For sure Oxford University Press has buildings, computers, desks, and all the rest. But is that the organization? Of course not. These things are not Oxford University Press. They are really important, but they're just the tools that enable people to work together to publish books.

The effects of the COVID-19 pandemic beautifully illustrate the intangibility of organizations. When the virus hit, organizations all around the globe were forced to morph into virtual entities. The organization I worked for at the time (Cardiff University) did this almost overnight. On Tuesday 24 March 2020, I was in my office. I sat in meeting rooms, bought a burrito from the canteen, and collected books from the library. On Wednesday 25 March, everything was shut. By the 27 March, the car park was chained, my access card deactivated, and my students had disappeared into cyberspace.

Although I couldn't see my colleagues or shake hands with them, the university did not cease to exist. We had to rapidly reorganize everything, but the university continued to function. Classes were taught online. Exams were sat remotely. Essays were marked on iPads. Degrees were awarded on Zoom. All this happened through the collaborative efforts of people from their bedrooms, kitchens, and dining rooms, using whatever technology was available. This is the very essence of what an organization is: it is people collaborating together.

1.2 An "organized" species

Our ability to organize ourselves in complex ways is one of the cornerstones of our success as a species. I'm not alone in thinking this. As Seabright (2010) points out, humans' capacity to establish and run sophisticated organizations is unprecedented in the animal kingdom. There are strong arguments that we humans have survived and achieved all that we have partly because of this ability.

Today, virtually everything we do involves an organization of one form or another. We enter the world in an organized way, with the help of midwives, doctors, and hospitals. We also leave it in an organized way, with the help of carers, funeral homes, religious ceremonies, and lawyers. Our lives, and the societies we live in are stuffed full of organizations of every type imaginable.

To really get this point, try thinking about something you do that doesn't involve an organization. It's hard. You'd probably interacted with a whole bunch of organizations before you'd even got out of bed.

Take my morning, for example. Before I bounced out from under the bed sheets, I'd caught up with friends on Instagram, read the news, checked my email, sold something on eBay, and talked to a guy in Chile. So, I'd connected with Meta, Apple News, Microsoft, and eBay—four different organizations. Even the time I set my alarm involved an organization. I don't want to be at work by 9 am, but the organization that pays me starts early, so I fit in with that. It seems only fair.

As you read this book, one thing you'll see is that organizations are not "modern" inventions. The simple reality is that organizations have existed in one way or another for tens of thousands of years, probably longer. There was also no great epiphany or Newtonian moment when some brainiac came up with the idea of an organization. The truth is that we've been organizing ourselves for ages. At some points in our history, we've done it quite well and at other times less so.

This might seem like a weird thing for me to say. The reality though is that humanity's organizational history is not one of linear progression. We didn't figure out the basics, and then smoothly progress to today's spectacularly complex organizations. The pathway that led us to the organizations we have now was a long, twisting, and bumpy one.

Consider this: in 550 BCE, the Achaemenid Persians were reading and responding to consistently formatted, folded, and sealed letters from people over 2,600 km away. Those letters were just seven days old (Briant, 2002). Imagine the organization required to achieve that. We're talking standardized documents, 2,600 km, 550 BCE. As I write these words, I'm still waiting for a package my brother couriered to me two months ago. It still hasn't arrived. I think FEDEX should have a chat with the Achaemenid Persians.

Now think about the Pyramids in Giza, Egypt. Built about 4,500 years ago, they are one of the greatest monuments ever made. Not only are they massive, and architecturally impressive, but no other man-made structure in existence is more accurately aligned to true north (Spence, 2000). Also think about the Great Wall of China. Built in 7th century BCE onwards, it measures more than 6,000 km and is the largest man-made structure in existence (Waldron, 1990).

Now think about the organizations that built these structures. Think about the planning, logistics, scale, and sophistication of the organizations required to build these vast, complex structures thousands of years ago. This was not the work of "bored savages" (Graeber & Wengrow, 2021). It was something altogether more sophisticated.

1.3 The origins of organization

The origins of our ability to organize ourselves in complex ways has a fascinating history. It's not clear precisely how we developed this capacity. However, archeologists and anthropologists currently believe it emerged out of a series of evolutionary developments that occurred about 75,000 to 90,000 years ago. These developments probably occurred in a place not far from Port Elizabeth in South Africa (Singer & Wymer, 1982)—which, incidentally, is where my dad was born.

What happened near Port Elizabeth was that we developed new cognitive and linguistic abilities that enabled us to cooperate with one another very effectively. Here there are two important points to note. First, there is actually evidence of human cooperation as far back as 250,000 years ago, and in multiple different locations around the world (McBrearty & Brooks, 2000). However, the point 75,000 to 90,000 years ago in South Africa is significant because this is when and where we have evidence of a fundamental shift in *how* we were cooperating with each other.

The second point to note relates to the evidence we have of human cooperation. This evidence is almost certainly biased ***against*** civilizations that lived in the equatorial regions of the world (MacGregor, 2011). In the tropics, any artefact not made of stone would have decayed long before any intrepid, mosquito-bitten archeologist could discover it. What this means is that most of what we know about our ancient history is based on artefacts found in places where things don't decay quickly—from the dry deserts of Iraq, Iran, Syria, India, and Egypt. This is not to say that what we know is wrong, just that it is probably only part of the story.

It is also worth keeping in mind that when it comes to our ancient history there are very few certainties. We're talking about a period in our history from which very, very little evidence of human life remains. The few artefacts that do remain are fragmented, confusing and must be enthusiastically interpreted. That is vigorously analyzed, endlessly discussed, debated, wrapped in layers and layers of conjecture, and often quite shaky theorizing. Interpretations change, and it's worth keeping that in mind as you read this book—particularly when I'm talking about the dim and distant past.

All that said, from the evidence we have it seems that up until 75,000 to 90,000 years ago we humans would only cooperate in relatively simple ways. Like other "social" species such as ants, termites, and beavers, we generally only cooperated with genealogical kin (blood relations) and in a quite limited way (Kappeler & Van Schaik, 2006). We cooperated if it was fundamental to our survival and if we got more out than we put in. So, we cooperated to hunt big animals because the rewards were higher, and the risks were lower than doing it alone. This is *mutualistic* cooperation and prior to 75,000 to 90,000 years ago it was the principal basis upon which early organizations worked.

The crucial change was this: we developed the ability to cooperate with people who were not genealogical kin (blood relations) and for reasons that extended beyond mutual benefit (Bowles & Gintis, 2013, p. 196). We started cooperating with relative and complete strangers and began to do so even when we didn't get much in return. You could say we started to care less about ourselves and more about others. You could even say we started to be nice to each other. This is *altruistic* cooperation, and we started doing it about 75,000 years ago.

The reason why altruism is so significant is because it runs against the logic of survival. It shows that people would cooperate for reasons that extend beyond their own selfish interests. Crucially, that people will reduce their own life chances so that another may benefit. So, altruism mattered because it improved social security. More people who were more willing to put more effort into supporting each other meant that more of us survived. When survival was the only game in town, altruism meant that we got much better at it. This is visible in the archeological record, which shows that groups made up of altruistic cooperators started to outcompete groups made up of mutualistic cooperators. Survival of the fittest had turned into survival of the most cooperative.

Social security is only part of the reason why the emergence of altruistic behavior was such a big deal. In some respects, it's not even the main story. Wolves and humpback whales also exhibit altruistic behavior (Mech & Boitani, 2010; Pitman et al., 2017). So what was different with us? The answer is that we also developed cognitive and linguistic abilities that enabled us to shape individual and collective behavior in ways that supported group cohesion and coordination. In particular, we developed the ability to exert power and influence over one another, and in ways that were far more complex than direct physical force (e.g., bashing someone with a big stick).

So not only were we altruistic, but we also worked out how to manipulate one another. What we figured out was how to reward people for their altruism and discourage individualistic behavior (Rand & Nowak, 2013). Thus through systems of reward and punishment we increased the prevalence of altruism, binding groups together through shared principles, values, and beliefs about what is right and wrong. This is what makes us unique in the animal kingdom. It is also what enables us to establish and run organizations in all sorts of different shapes and sizes.

1.4 The rise of altruism

Currently, we are settling on three main reasons why altruistic social preferences supporting cooperation outcompeted (and continue to outcompete) unmitigated and amoral self-interest. These are broadly as follows:

1.4.1 Protection, reward, and altruism

First, we developed ways of protecting people who were altruistic from people who were greedy and wanted to exploit them. Think about this in the context of modern organizations. For example, a group of people working together on a project. In competitive contexts there is a risk that group members will want to put in as little effort as possible but realize as big a return as possible. We all know someone who wants to do no work but get all the credit; however, the best outcome for the group is for every member to contribute as much effort as possible. It's a bit of a cliché, but the basic point of working together is that more can be achieved collectively than by people working alone.

What we developed all those years ago was the ability to encourage people to cooperate generously and to punish those who took out more than they put in. We learnt to do things like allocate valuable resources (such as food and information) to altruistic collaborators, and to shun, ostracize, and even execute "free-riders" (Bowles & Gintis, 2013, p. 5).

Think about this in the context of students working together on a group assignment. The same basic scenario exists. It's unlikely you'll execute lazy members, but you will leverage the same basic mechanisms to maintain peoples' investment in the project. Groups find ways of protecting and rewarding those who contribute (such as by awarding a higher share of the grade), while at the same time punishing those who don't.

Think about it. Do you still talk to the person who made no effort in your last group assignment? Did you call out their failure to contribute to your lecturer, make a point of it in your team's *WhatsApp* or *WeChat* group. Did you complain to a friend? The capacity to influence behavior in these kinds of ways was one of the abilities we developed.

1.4.2 Socialization, behavioral norms, and altruism

The second reason why altruistic social preferences started to outcompete self-interest was that we developed elaborate systems of socialization through which altruistic behavioral norms were taught to people alongside systems of reward and punishment. So, we learnt how to teach others what it meant to be part of our group, but also to teach them how "right" and "wrong" behaviors would (and should) be rewarded and punished. The crucial point is this: establishing behavioral norms is one thing, systematically policing them is quite another.

Our ability to do both of these things—establish rules and police them—is hugely important in the context of organizations (see Barker, 2001). Again, think about this in the context of a group of students working on an assignment. It is one thing to have a chat at the start of the assignment and make a plan for how you're going to work together. It's quite another to systematically police what you've agreed and make sure everyone does it. Groups that are able to do both—establish norms *and* police them—are more likely to be successful. These groups will be more focused, cohesive and cooperative, and free riding will be better policed.

1.4.3 Competition, dominance, and altruism

The third reason why altruistic social preferences started to outcompete self-interest was related to competition between groups for resources. Here the simple reality is that cooperative groups were able to exert greater influence within a particular territory. They could encroach on the territory and resources of their less cooperative neighbors, and simply take over. The effect this had was to disseminate cooperative behaviors. Groups that were good at cooperating may have taught less effective groups how to work with one another. Alternatively less cooperative groups may have just died out.

Time for some more caveats. First, the shift towards altruistic cooperation was a gradual one. It wasn't the case that one day our ancestors didn't cooperate altruistically, and the next day they did. Rather, altruism actually emerged quite slowly and only became a preferred way of behaving within a community quite gradually. Think thousands of years, rather than days and months.

The second caveat is that just because altruistic behavior became more common, it does not mean that our ancestors all suddenly became unbearably nice to each other. By any standard, tribal communities (much like society today) could be extremely brutal. There were no tribal utopias where people shared everything, and nobody ever went hungry again. In fact, our preference for altruism was really quite muted. It simply became gradually more common. Much as it is now, altruism was just one of a bigger group of what we call "modern" human behaviors that also includes individualism ("looking out for myself") and mutualism ("I'll work with you because I'll get more from doing this together than alone").

Those caveats noted, the points made in this section not only provide an insight into the origins of organizations but say something very profound about what it means to be human. Firstly, that our ability to cooperate with other people is inextricably connected with our evolution as a species. Second, that whilst greed and selfishness are an ingrained part of what it is to be human, so is altruism. We will look out for ourselves, but we're also willing to cooperate and contribute towards common projects. And we'll cooperate and contribute generously even when we're unlikely to derive proportional benefits. Keep this in mind when you're getting frustrated with your colleagues in your next group project.

1.5 Introducing Part 1: The Big Four

In organizational terms, we have clearly moved a very long way since we first started figuring out the intricacies of how to cooperate with one another and coordinate our activities. By any standard in our history, today's modern organizations are absolutely massive and hugely complicated. How we got to this point is an interesting story, which I'm going to introduce you to in this book.

From the outset though, I want to emphasize that the path we followed to where we are today was not one of continuous uninterrupted progression. At certain points in our history we had incredibly sophisticated organizations that were doing impressive things (like moving letters quickly across vast distances, and building massive pyramids). However, as civilizations died out so their organizations went with them (for the most part). The Qin state in China, and the Roman state in Italy, are obvious examples. Both were remarkably well-organized societies, and their disintegration brought with it significant periods of social and organizational regression.

Something else you'll learn as you read this book is that when it comes to organizations, there is an infinite range of possibilities. There are literally tens of thousands of different types of organization out there—Parker, Fournier, and Reedy (2007) had a crack at listing them all. To make things easier and slightly more manageable, I'm narrowing things down quite a lot in this book. Here, I'm only going to talk about three major categories of organization. These are **formal**, **informal**, and **criminal** organizations.

Of these three categories, formal organizations get slightly more attention. These are organizations that have been "deliberately designed to achieve certain goals and established with a number of explicit (formal) authority structures and roles" (Blau & Scott, 1963, p. 5). Formal organizations get more space because they are widely regarded as a "key phenomenon of modern times" (Perrow, 1991, p. 725). Also, because they are generally regarded as the most productive forms of organization ever created. It is through formal organizations that we got some of our greatest achievements—space flight, vaccines, and the Big Mac.

Accordingly, our study of formal organizations is split into two separate chapters. In the first of these I'm going to talk to you about "public" organizations. That is, about the formal organizations set up and run by governments to either: (1) administer the state (as in the tax office), (2) protect the state (as in the army), or (3) provide services to citizens on behalf of the state (as in public hospitals). I'll talk to you about both the historical origins and contemporary manifestations of public organizations. And, about the thinking that influences how they operate, and how their success is evaluated.

The next chapter on formal organizations looks at private organizations—also known as "for-profit" organizations. Here, again, I've narrowed things down a lot. Rather than looking at all the different types of for-profit organizations that are out there, I focus on corporations. This pushes out some really important types of organization, such as sole traders, partnerships, and cooperatives. However the corporation is widely considered to be *the* dominant form of private, for-profit organization in the world today (Crouch, 2004; Fleming & Spicer, 2007). For this reason, and many others, Chapter 3 is dedicated to corporations.

After the two chapters on formal organizations come chapters on informal, and then criminal organizations. These two chapters are about organizations that variously lack Blau and Scott's (1963) explicitly formal, authoritarian structures and roles. However I've included them in this book because they're really important in the world today. I accept that these aren't the kind of organizations most people think about working in. However, just because you don't want to work in an informal or criminal organization, doesn't mean they're not important. These organizations' impact on the world is massive—far greater than most people think and give them credit for. You'll understand what I mean when you read these chapters.

1.6 Introducing Part 2: How Organizations Work

The second part of this book is all about how organizations work. So, where Part 1 is all about the dominant forms of organization that define the world, Part 2 is all about the mechanics of organizing. It's about our practical and theoretical understanding of how people are brought together in organizations and their efforts channeled, motivated, and managed.

Before we get stuck into the theories we have about how organizations work, one thing I want to be clear about is that my account of organization theory is slightly different to what you'll read in other textbooks. A growing body of work is showing that many foundational ideas in management and organization studies' textbooks have become distorted and misrepresented over time. You can read more about this in Cummings, Bridgman, Hassard, and Rowlinson (2017).

What this means is that in this book, I'm going to give you a slightly different account of how organizations work, compared to other textbooks. In particular, I'm going to give you a lot more of the history of certain forms of organizational practice. My aim in doing this is to impress the point that organizing is something we humans have been doing for millennia, and that much of what we do today has decidedly ancient origins.

With this in mind, the first chapter in Part 2 of this book (Chapter 6) is all about record-keeping, rules, and the invention of something called bureaucracy. You'll learn about bureaucracy's ancient Middle Eastern, and then Chinese origins, and how it has come to underpin modern organizations the world over. You'll learn about where you can find bureaucracy, and what it means to work in a bureaucratic organization. You'll also learn about why the world loves a good bureaucracy, and also about why they don't.

The next chapter pushes our discussion of bureaucracy a step further. It explores more broadly the concept of "rationalized" organizations. So, I'll talk to you about our enduring habit of trying to set up and run quantifiably efficient organizations. And, about how our ability to do this was turbocharged during the European Age of Enlightenment. I'll explain how human labor was rationalized in the world of industrial manufacturing, and about the rationalization of the contemporary services economy. You'll finish this chapter wondering if there is anything we do in life that isn't rationalized in one way or another.

In Chapter 8, I focus on the vexing problem of motivation. This chapter is all about the question of how to get people in an organization into line and happily working as hard as they possibly can. You'll learn that this is not a new problem, but one that has come to preoccupy people greatly, particularly since the demise of slavery. You'll also see that motivating a workforce is a fiendishly difficult thing to do. I'll tell you a bit about the different tactics people use to motivate others in organizations, and about why there are no easy answers to this complex problem. This chapter then is all about the "big sticks" and "juicy carrots" we use to keep people in organizations chipper and working hard. Or, at the very least, begrudgingly doing what we want them to do.

Chapter 9 is the last chapter in the book. It builds on what you learnt in Chapter 8, by talking a bit more about the concept of power in organizations. From there it moves on to the concept of resistance, and the idea that efforts to control and regulate the workers might not always be all that popular or successful. From this introduction to the theory and practice of resistance, you'll come to see organizations as what Fleming and Spicer (2007) call "contested" space. So, not cutesy places stuffed full of docile workers diligently working towards the same centrally prescribed goal, but gritty, argumentative places characterized by struggle, strife, and disagreement.

References

Barker, J. R. (2001). Concertive control in self, managing teams. *Organizational Studies: Modes of Management* 1(3), 262.

Blau, P. M. & W. R. Scott. (1963). *Formal Organizations: A Comparative Approach*. London: Routledge & Kegan Paul.

Bowles, S. & H. Gintis. (2013). *A Cooperative Species: Human Reciprocity and its Evolution*. Princeton: Princeton University Press.

Briant, P. (2002). *From Cyrus to Alexander: A History of the Persian Empire*. Michigan: Eisenbrauns.

Crouch, C. (2004). *Post-Democracy*. Cambridge: Polity.

Cummings, S., T. Bridgman, J. Hassard, & M. Rowlinson. (2017). *A New History of Management*. Cambridge: Cambridge University Press.

Fleming, P. & A. Spicer. (2007). *Contesting the Corporation: Struggle, Power and Resistance in Organizations*. Cambridge: Cambridge University Press.

Graeber, D. & D. Wengrow. (2021). *The Dawn of Everything: A New History of Humanity*. UK: Penguin.

Kappeler, P. M. & C. P. Van Schaik. (2006). *Cooperation in Primates and Humans*. Springer.

MacGregor, N. (2011). *A History of the World in 100 Objects*. UK: Penguin.

McBrearty, S. & A. S. Brooks. (2000). The revolution that wasn't: A new interpretation of the origin of modern human behavior. *Journal of Human Evolution* 39(5), 453–563.

Mech, L. D. & L. Boitani. (2010). *Wolves: Behavior, Ecology, and Conservation*. Chicago: University of Chicago Press.

Parker, M., V. Fournier, & P. Reedy. (2007). *The Dictionary of Alternatives: Utopianism and Organization*. London: Zed Books.

Perrow, C. (1991). A society of organizations. *Theory and Society* 20(6), 725–762.

Pitman, R. L., V. B. Deecke, C. M. Gabriele, M. Srinivasan, N. Black, J. Denkinger, et al. (2017). Humpback whales interfering when mammal-eating killer whales attack other species: Mobbing behavior and interspecific altruism? *Marine Mammal Science* 33(1), 7–58.

Rand, D. G. & M. A. Nowak. (2013). Human cooperation. *Trends in Cognitive Sciences* 17(8), 413–425.

Seabright, P. (2010). *The Company of Strangers: A Natural History of Economic Life-Revised Edition*. Princeton: Princeton University Press.

Singer, R. & J. Wymer. (1982). *The Middle Stone Age at Klasies River Mouth in South Africa*. Chicago: University of Chicago Press.

Spence, K. (2000). Ancient Egyptian chronology and the astronomical orientation of pyramids. *Nature* 408(6810), 320–324.

Waldron, A. (1990). *The Great Wall of China: From History to Myth*. Cambridge: Cambridge University Press.

PART 1
THE BIG FOUR

2
Public Organizations

> **Keywords**
>
> public organizations; Tell Sabi Abyad; Qin China; bureaucracy; neoliberalism; Edu-factories

> **Consider**
>
> What are public organizations?
> Why do we have them and how do they work?

2.1 Introduction

What do school teachers, police officers, tax collectors, fighter pilots, nurses, and James Bond all have in common? The answer is that in pretty much every country in the world, they work for the government. These people are all employees of *public organizations*, which are the focus of this chapter.

In the pages that follow, I'm going to talk to you about what public organizations are and why I think you should learn about them. I'm also going to tell you about the very earliest public organizations in history, and what we know about how they worked. The basics established, I'll then go over some of the big challenges associated with public organizations today, and the competing visions that exist about how they should run.

What you're ultimately going to get from this chapter is an understanding of what we mean when we talk about public organizations, and why they matter in the world we live in. You'll get a sense of how public organizations work, and why they work in the way they do. You'll also get a sense of the political complexities of public organizations. So, an understanding of why some people can't get enough public organizations, and why others want the smallest, fewest number of public organizations it is possible to have.

2.2 What are public organizations?

Public organizations comprise the part of the economy that is controlled by the state. The state being what Max Weber defines as whoever has "the monopoly on the legitimate use of physical force within a given territory" (Weber, in Gerth & Mills, 2014, p. 48). Weber's point being that if you have all the guns, you're the one in charge. In practice, state government is a bit more complicated than this. For now though, it's enough just to know that the state is simply the government (elected, or otherwise) that runs the country you live in.

Conceptually, public organizations are relatively straightforward things to get your head around. They're organizations "formally established" (Blau & Scott, 1963, p. 5) to either: (1) administer the state (as in the tax office), (2) protect the state (as in the army), or (3) provide services to citizens on behalf of the state (as in public hospitals). One way of thinking about public organizations is as the organizational equivalent of a kind of benevolent parent, older sister, or big brother. They're a unique type of organization that is there to regulate society and look out for its citizens.

Exactly what public organizations do varies enormously. It really depends on where you live in the world. For example in Norway, Denmark, and Sweden, the public sector is quite large and does a lot of different things. In contrast the public sector in Japan and South Korea is quite small and does correspondingly less. In very, very general terms, it can be said the Scandinavians pursue what's called "collectivist" solutions to social problems, while the Japanese and South Koreans are more "individualistic" societies where people are left to sort themselves out.

2.3 Why learn about public organizations?

There are three main reasons why I think you should learn about public organizations. The **first** is actually three reasons in one. You should learn about public organizations because: (1) there are loads of them, (2) they're often massive, and (3) they employ a huge number of people.

My point here is that while private corporate-type organizations, like Walmart, are really big, no matter where you go nobody employs more people than the government does. Literally nobody, anywhere. In every single country that exists, government-funded public organizations are invariably the single biggest employers in town—usually by a considerable margin.

In the US, for example, the Department of Defense employs a whopping 2.91 million people—about the same number as those living in Toronto (Canada) or Haikou (China). It is the biggest organization in the world. The next biggest public organization in the world is the Chinese People's Liberation Army (PLA). The PLA employs about 2.3 million people. After that, it's China Railway which employs about 2 million people. 1.4 million people work for the Indian Armed Forces and 1.4 million people work for Indian Railways.

These examples aren't just weird anomalies. If you look up the biggest organization in the country you live in, I'll bet money it's a public one. In the UK, the state-run National Health Service (NHS) is by far the biggest organization in the country. A staggering 1.4 million people work for the NHS. That is a huge number when you consider that there are only 32.5 million working aged people in the entire country. For context, if there was an equivalent of the NHS in China, it would employ 48 million people. That's 16 times more people than work for the American Department of Defense, or about the same number of people as live in Spain, Kenya, or Argentina.

The **second** reason why I think you should learn about public organizations is because they are absolutely fundamental to the societies we all live in. It doesn't matter whether you live in Cuba (where about 72% work for the state) or Japan (where roughly 18% work for the state) very, very little happens without public organizations in one form or another.

If you're not too convinced by this, think carefully about the public organizations around you. Think about what they do in the community you live in. Now imagine life without them. Imagine life without public hospitals, district police stations, fire departments, and all the rest. They're pillars of the community. Without them our world would be a chaotic, disorganized place and a lot of really important work would not get done. This is the second reason you should study public organizations.

The **third** reason I think you should study public organizations is because they're ideologically complex places. In every country in the world there rage bitter debates about what public organizations should be funded, how much they should get, and how they should use their funds. We're also endlessly debating whether public organizations are, in fact, doing what society needs them to do, and in ways that represent value for money.

These fraught battlegrounds are important to understand. Even if you don't want to weigh into the debate, simply having an idea of what they're about is helpful. It'll mean you know a bit about why public organizations operate differently in different countries, and why politicians on either side of the political divide are constantly pulling them in different directions. This is the third reason why I think you should study public organizations.

2.4 The first public organizations in history

In this section, I'll tell you about the very first public organizations in history. I'm going to do so in two parts. In the first part, I'm going to tell you about what we think is the very first public organization that ever existed. In the second, I'm going to tell you about what we think is the very first public organization to operate in a distinctly modern way. Both are fascinating and important cases, but for quite different reasons.

2.4.1 The very, very first public organization

For the story of the very, very first public organization in history we have to defer to our archeological colleagues. The story they tell is an intriguing one. We're not talking about some genius queen in a grand old ancient city coming up with a great new type of organization. Instead, we're talking about a small neolithic community and what seems to have been a very basic shared storage facility in a place called Tell Sabi Abyad, which is in the Balikh River Valley in modern day Syria.

Archeological studies of this facility suggest it was built and run by an early, egalitarian, agro-pastoralist society. So, by a community in which everyone was equal, where some people farmed crops and others reared animals or made things. From the evidence we have, it seems that the facility was built to enable pastoralists (people who farm animals) to store their belongings when they left the village (Akkermans et al., 1996).

The facility seems to have worked a bit like this. Before leaving the village, pastoralists would seal their belongings inside special containers. These containers were marked using a stamp embossed with pastoralists' own unique designs. These sealed, stamped containers were then deposited in the store, where they were kept safe until the pastoralist got back from the fields. To withdraw their belongings pastoralists simply stamped a new fresh piece of clay. This stamp was then matched with the right container and kept by the facility manager as proof the transaction had taken place. Simples.

At the time the storage facility burnt down, at least 65 different people were regularly using it, and that was just in Tell Sabi Abyad. Many more of these facilities have been discovered all over northern Syria. So, in a quirky twist of fate, it looks like the very, very first public organization in history was basically a chain of left-luggage offices. It was an organization that worked a bit like the ones you'll find in any modern airport, train station, or bus station anywhere in the world. It was also extremely popular.

At this point, you might be questioning what a neolithic left luggage office has got to do with anything. The answer is found in thinking about what this ancient storage facility tells us about Tell Sabi Abyad and the sort of society that existed there. Think about why people in Tell Sabi Abyad went to all the effort of building an organization like this and the sort of benefits they would have got from it.

I'll explain. The storage facility in Tell Sabi Abyad is important because it marks a point in our history when people shifted from just looking after themselves and their families, to supporting vulnerable members of their society in systematic and coordinated ways. It marks a time when some people began to set up organizations specifically to address a particular social need in their community. In this case, people needed somewhere safe to store their things when they went out to work. This need was addressed by everyone working together to build an unusually large storeroom and concocting an unusually elaborate system of administration to operate it.

Note that the system of administration used to manage the storeroom in Tell Sabi Abyad was very innovative for the time. Sealed containers, stamps, and clay receipts might seem pretty basic stuff, but at this point in our history it was a highly advanced way of doing things. Remember: nobody was reading and writing at this point in our history, so setting up something like this was really quite new and clever.

It's also worth noting that the day-to-day operation of the storage facility would have been a community endeavor. Trusted members of the community would have been recruited specifically to manage the storeroom. These storeroom managers would have looked after the facility instead of doing things like weaving baskets, farming animals, or growing crops. Thus the people who managed the storeroom were probably the first civil servants in history. They were the first people to be paid to work for the community they lived in.

The storage facility in Tell Sabi Abyad is also important because of the massive effect it had on everyday life. From the evidence we have it's clear that the storage facility wasn't just some monumental structure that made the village look grand. It transformed peoples' lives—particularly pastoralists. Think about it. How would your life change if you didn't have to risk losing everything you owned every time you went to work?

The storage facility in Tell Sabi Abyad was also not just life changing for pastoralists. It changed society as a whole. The entire community benefited for the simple reason that pastoralists could spend longer out in the fields, roam further, and generally do a better job of raising animals. This was a big deal. Better pastoralism meant more, better-fed animals for everyone to eat or trade. Good pastoralism was good for everyone.

As well as supporting food security and trade, the storage facility also seems to have had other quite complex effects. One of these was, we think, supporting Tell Sabi Abyad's egalitarian social structure and the idea that everyone was equal (Frangipane, 2007). The basic argument here is that social equality in Tell Sabi Abyad was maintained because giving pastoralists somewhere safe to store their things significantly reduced the chance of them falling into poverty. Saving pastoralists from poverty made it less likely they would become dependent, second-class citizens, which was a big risk if they lost everything they owned.

Relatedly, the storage facility also helped to preserve the population. Destitute pastoralists would probably die, making Tell Sabi Abyad smaller and less resilient than it would otherwise have been. So again, good pastoralism mattered, but in ways that were not necessarily immediately obvious. It mattered because of what it ultimately prevented (destitution, starvation, and death) as well as what it directly enabled (safe storage).

Clearly, much of the previous information is conjecture. It's impossible to know exactly what effect the storage facility had in Tell Sabi Abyad. However, the general consensus is that it would have been a very useful thing. After all, why build it if nothing good came from it? Consequently, what we get from the case of Tell Sabi Abyad is a beautiful illustration of why we have public organizations—because they can be immensely beneficial to society.

2.4.2 The first distinctly modern public organization

It is from Qin China that we get the first distinctly modern public organization in history—think state bureaucracies, such as the tax office. The story is another fascinating one.

Very briefly: the Qin empire was seven centuries in the making, but once established (in 221 BCE), lasted for just 15 years (until 206 BCE). Despite the rapidity of the Qin's demise, organizations established by the Qin endured in one form or another for millennia (Finer, 1997; Kiser & Cai, 2003). Moreover, the ideas upon which they were based spread widely throughout the world, apparently informing the design and organization of modern European states and their institutions (Jacobsen, 2013, p. 629).

Precisely how Chinese organizational innovations traveled to Europe is unclear and hotly debated—though it may possibly have had something to do with the 12th century Sicilian King Roger II. Some reject the possibility entirely (e.g., Harvey, 2012), others are more convinced. For example, Graeber and Wengrow (2021, p. 29) argue that from the very moment Europeans came into contact with Chinese ideas they started building "almost exactly the [same] system that had existed for centuries in China" (also see Ertman, 1997).

Either way what is undeniable is that centuries before the European Enlightenment the Qin had established massive public organizations that civil servants today would have felt quite at home in. They were relatively rationalized, hierarchical places that had emerged out of an absolutely epic period of "precocious bureaucratization" (Kiser & Cai, 2003, p. 512). It would take until 1450 AD—or as late as the 18th and 19th centuries in some countries—for Europeans to establish organizations that were anywhere near as advanced (Brewer, 2002, pp. 52–72; see also Ertman, 1997; Mann, 2012).

The Qin's contribution to our organized world centered on techniques of administration. Specifically, on the efficient, large-scale operation of a system of organization that we today call "**bureaucracy**." I'll talk a lot more about bureaucracy in Chapter 6. For now though, it's enough to know that bureaucracy is a hierarchical, authoritarian, office-based system in which people are allocated defined jobs based on their individual competencies. For a classic, instructive account of bureaucratic systems of administration in mid-20th century American government organizations read Blau (1963)—or flick to Chapter 6.

If you do flick to Chapter 6, it's worth highlighting that the Qin weren't in fact the inventors of bureaucracy. The Mesopotamians were. However, unlike the Qin, the Mesopotamians only ever used bureaucracy on a small scale and in a very limited way. They used bureaucracies to administer taxation in quite small city-states (Charvát, 2013, p. 116), and beer production in temple breweries (Nissen, Damerow, Englund, & Englund, 1993, p. 36). The Qin's use of bureaucracy was in an altogether different league.

In Qin China single all powerful rulers and patrimonial relationships were ultimately supplanted by dispassionate bureaucratic systems of rule. At its zenith in 206 BCE, Chinese public organizations were places where people were "(1) appointed and promoted on the basis of merit, (2) organized and monitored in a centralized hierarchy based on written regulations, (3) [did not] own their positions, and who were (4) paid fixed salaries in money" (Kiser & Cai, 2003, p. 511). This way of running organizations might not sound especially radical but it is a distinctly modern way of operating. Two millennia ago, it was revolutionary.

The story is made even more intriguing when you consider that the Qin's super-sized public organizations were not actually established and run by a similarly super-sized, bureaucratic state. At least to begin with, quite the opposite is believed to have been true; super-sized public organizations came first, and it is these that provided the template upon which the Qin state and its key institutions was later established (Downing, 2020).

So, what do you think was the very first distinctly modern public organization in China? What was the organizational ancestor of today's big, state-run public organizations? Was it the ancient Qin's civil service, which reportedly employed some 100,000 people? Or was it some kind of mega-bureaucracy that administered the taxation of some 18 million people?

In truth, there is substance to both of these answers. The Qin did set up an extremely large civil service complete with defined jobs, human resource (HR) departments, and an entrance exam (Ebrey, 1996). In fact, the whole concept of using written exams to make merit-based assessments apparently originated in the Qin civil service (Han, 1946). The Qin also built an extraordinarily efficient organization to collect taxes and manage state finances. However, the actual answer is that the very first, truly super-sized public organization in history was the Qin army.

At its peak in 206 BCE, the Qin army had as many as 600,000 soldiers (Lewis, 2009, p. 31) and was an organizational masterpiece. It had its own centralized command structure, sophisticated communication system, and salaried soldiers divided into hierarchical units and systematically trained to use standardized weapons. The army was also supported by vast numbers of people that we today call "bureaucrats." These were people whose sole job was administration. They were there to keep track of resources, make sure everyone got fed, equipped, and paid on time. That sort of thing.

All this means the Qin army has a unique place in our history. This is not just because of what it achieved at the time, but because the innovations that underpinned it ultimately spread widely across the whole world. Today's public organizations owe much to the ancient Chinese Qin army—as do you, for your end-of-term exams. Good luck!

2.4.3 One more thing...

Hopefully by now, you'll have got the basic point of public organizations—that they're a particular invention we humans have come up with to get socially important stuff done. Whether that be fighting wars, looking after luggage, or providing social services for vulnerable people, public organizations are there to serve and contribute to the greater good of society. That's the point of them.

Before we move on its worth saying one more thing about how public organizations work. This is that one of their crucial functions is to **share risk** between people in society. Consider this example. One thing I am lucky enough to benefit from in the UK is a state-run health service that's free at the point of use. Remember those 1.4 million NHS workers? The UK is one of the very, very few countries in the world with this kind of system. What it means is that if I get ill or have an accident, I don't have to wave my credit card or flash some insurance papers to get medical help. I can just call a doctor or turn up at any Emergency Department.

So, in the UK, the risk—by which I mean the cost—of healthcare is transferred from me as an individual to society as a whole. The cost of an individual's healthcare is shared across (paid for by) everyone in the country. Precisely how this happens is quite complex, but the end result is that it doesn't matter whether you're rich or poor. Employed or not. Everyone gets the care they need, when they need it. Nobody needs to stash cash under the mattress for an emergency colonoscopy or lay awake stressing about the cost of a hip replacement.

Having an organization like the NHS means that when I was knocked off my bike, I didn't have to re-mortgage my house to pay for the helicopter that airlifted me to hospital. Nor did I have to cover the week I spent in intensive care, or the month I spent on a mega-expensive trauma ward. I also didn't have to beg my family for money to pay for the 10+ operations I've had in the years that followed, or the medicines I'll be taking for the rest of my life. The cost of all this is covered by the state. That is, by everyone in society through a massive, centrally funded public healthcare organization.

2.5 Why not everyone thinks public organizations are the best thing since sliced bread

None of what I've said so far is especially controversial. I've just talked about organizations that administer and protect the state and provide services to citizens: tax offices, police departments, schools, and hospitals. Reasonable, simple everyday stuff, right?

The truth is that while the basic idea of a public organization is simple enough, that's about all that is. The world is defined by sharply contrasting beliefs about virtually every other aspect of public organizations. From the sort of things they should be doing, to how best to run them. Nothing is settled. There are no definitive answers and little agreement about anything.

Yet despite the immense diversity of opinion there are distinct sets of ideas—ideologies—pertaining to what people think is the best way to conceive of and run public organizations. In this last section, I'm going to talk you through one of these ideologies. It's called neoliberalism. It's not the only ideology out there but it is widely regarded as one of the most important and influential. As McChesney puts it: "neoliberalism is the defining political economic paradigm of our time" (Chomsky, 2011, p. 7).

In the sections that follow, I'll explain what neoliberalism is and then talk you through the implications it has for public organizations. As you read this section note that this chapter's Research Insight and Case Study also connect with this topic. As does the article by Peter Fleming that I've recommended in the "Things to Watch, Things to Read" section. Also keep in mind that the space I have to articulate this complex and difficult concept is quite limited. What follows is therefore a bit of a caricature (at best). You should supplement this material with further reading to broaden and deepen your understanding.

2.5.1 The basic concept of neoliberalism

The concept of neoliberalism is a slippery one to get your head around. Annoyingly, there's no handy pamphlet-sized manifesto detailing its central precepts. It has also evolved considerably since its inception, and it has been interpreted quite differently by different people at different times. There's also the issue of leading neoliberals receiving the Nobel Prize for Economics (e.g., Friedrich Hayek in 1974 and Milton Friedman in 1976) along with its biggest critics (e.g., Joseph Stiglitz in 2001). Remember what I said about there being little consensus?

The first thing to know about neoliberalism is that it's not an especially "neo" [meaning new] concept. It's actually a reworked version of the far older concept of classic liberalism which emerged during the early stages of the European Enlightenment (for more detailed insight into neoliberalism see Barry, 1987; Brennan & Tomasi, 2012; Butler, 2015). Think 14th century.

Originating in Europe just before the start of the Second World War (c1938), neoliberalism was a response to growing concern amongst liberals that their way of thinking (classic liberalism) was in demise. People like Ludwig von Mises and Friedrich Hayek were especially concerned about what they saw as a global lurch toward collectivism. They were concerned about Nazism (in Germany), Communism (in Russia), but also Franklin Roosevelt's New Deal (in the USA), and Britain's shiny new welfare state. They regarded these global events as different manifestations of the same problem: governments becoming overbearing and crushing individual freedoms on their way to achieving totalitarian control. It was scary stuff, in scary times.

For our pioneering neoliberals the solution to this problem was the aggressive rejection of all forms of collectivism. In its place they advocated unfettered free-market capitalism and its concomitant ideals. Things like liberal economic policy, privatization, deregulation, globalization, free trade, and austerity. The steadfast belief was that we humans would only ever be well served by governments "liberating individual entrepreneurial freedoms and skills within an institutional framework characterized by strong private property rights, free markets, and free trade" (Harvey, 2007, p. 2).

The near total abandonment of, in Hayek's words, "government planning" sat at the heart of neoliberal thinking (see Hayek, 1944, 1976). The basic thesis being that big governments encroach on peoples' lives and take away their civil liberties. So rather than controlling governments what we need are individualized societies. That is, places where people have all the freedom and independence to choose exactly how they want to live their lives. Nothing should be centrally provisioned.

This is heavy stuff. To learn more about it watch Milton Friedman's 10-part documentary "Free to Choose." It's a truly incredible crash course in neoliberal thinking. It'll give you a sharp insight into why Friedman and his colleagues believe that governments should remain small, and people (and businesses) left to their own devices.

2.5.2 Bring in the private sector

For-profit organizations unconstrained by government regulation sit at the heart of neoliberal ideology. Their position is sacrosanct. It is based on an understanding that while governments can theoretically get involved in running things like public services, they really shouldn't. The reason for this is because neoliberals think public organizations lack a crucial driving force that you only find in private organizations—the ever-compelling desire to make a profit.

The profit motive matters because it is uniquely good at getting people in organizations to obsess about eliminating waste and inefficiency without dropping quality. In public organizations this drive simply doesn't exist in quite the same way. Sure, civil servants may feel an obligation to spend taxpayers' money wisely, but they'll never have the urgency of profit-hungry shareholders breathing down their necks. Nor will civil servants go bankrupt if they screw things up. On the other hand, they won't experience the allure of profit-linked bonuses. So compared to private organizations, public ones will always be cumbersome and inefficient. That's the neoliberal logic.

Within the neoliberal school of thought the solution to the problem of public organizations' natural inefficiency is obvious—don't have any at all. Alternatively, if you're going to have public organizations, they should be very small in both number and size. Moreover, if public services are going to be delivered (which they really shouldn't), the best way to do it is to subcontract the work out to private organizations. Public services should literally be auctioned off to whoever can do them best, for the lowest possible price.

2.5.3 Marketizing government institutions

Another corner stone of neoliberal thinking is the idea of marketization, specifically, the idea that the provision of things, like public services, should never be monopolized by a single provider, private or otherwise. Instead, a market should exist in which different service providers compete with one another. People should have choice.

They should be conceptualized as customers, allowed to shop around, and decide who they want to buy their public services from.

Think about this example: courtesy of my bike accident, I am someone who needs a hip replacement. In all probability, I'll need a couple, because hip replacements don't last that long. Luckily for me, the NHS will cover the cost. As an added bonus, I get to choose who does the operation. The reason I get this choice is because the NHS has been reformed along neoliberal lines. This means that the NHS conceives of me as a customer, and every NHS hospital in the country is in competition for my business. Whoever I choose to replace my hip will get paid by the government for doing so.

The thinking here is that while government-run public services might fulfil an important social need, they also deprive people of choice. This is the point that Friedman hammers home in the docuseries "Free to Choose" (on which more will follow). The implication is that if you're going to provide a public service, then public service users must be able to decide who they get that service from.

Under the old NHS system, my hip replacement would have been done by my local hospital. I wouldn't have had a choice in the matter. In the new neoliberal NHS I can get the operation done wherever I like. I can go out and spend time searching for the cleanest hospital and safest clinical team. When I'm happy with the service provider I can commission them to do my operation. This is what marketized public services look like in practice.

The principle of marketized public services also doesn't just apply to the NHS. In many countries, things like railways are considered public services. In India and China, for example, railways are publicly owned and operated. In the UK, the government owns the railway tracks, but not any of the trains that run on them. The tracks are actually leased to private companies who bid for contracts every few years to provide the service element of railway transportation.

It's a similar story in the energy sector. In some countries the government owns both the distribution network (e.g., the power lines) and the facilities that generate the power. In the UK, the government owns the power lines, and private companies generate the power and sell it to customers like me. As it stands, I currently have the choice to buy electricity from any one of 24 different companies. I can buy everything from classic coal-generated dirty power to ultra-green, vegan-friendly power. It's a consumer choice paradise, and another example of what marketized public services look like.

Thinking critically about neoliberalism

Despite neoliberalism's unabashed confidence in the private sector, no privately run public service utopia has ever really materialized. Capitalists may abound, but there is little evidence to suggest that private organizations do a fundamentally better job of providing public services than ones that are run by the government. As a crude indicator take healthcare spending: the UK's publicly run NHS cost the British government a whopping £277 billion in 2021. That's about 12% of the UK's gross domestic product (GDP). However, that cost is dwarfed by the US's largely privatized healthcare sector that costs nearly double the amount—almost 25% of US GDP.

Consider also that NHS experiments with neoliberal inspired subcontracting arrangements have produced distinctly unimpressive results. For example, today more than 33% of UK NHS-funded hip replacements are performed in the private sector (Kirkwood & Pollock, 2022). In some cases, good outcomes are achieved. Some patients treated in private hospitals get better operations and are less likely to be readmitted with post-operative complications. That's impressive.

However, the reality is that in the same way that some NHS hospitals achieve better clinical outcomes than others, some private healthcare providers achieve better clinical outcomes than others. Studies show that overall private hospitals do not do better than NHS ones (Kirkwood & Pollock, 2022). This is true even when they're paid up to 40% more than their NHS competitors. Indeed, private hospitals actually often achieve *worse* outcomes when treating patients with complex needs. In these cases in particular, clinical outcomes are poorer, and costs are far higher than in the NHS.

Research also shows that NHS work subcontracted to private hospitals actually exacerbates care inequality. So when healthcare is subcontracted to private providers, rich people benefit more than poor people from that type of arrangement (Cookson et al., 2016; Moscelli, Gravelle, & Siciliani, 2021). Furthermore, one recent study showed that hip replacements done in private hospitals actually have a higher mortality rate than those done in NHS hospitals (Street, 2022). In England between 2013 and 2020, there were an estimated 557 additional deaths amongst hip replacement patients treated by private providers than would have been expected had they been treated in the NHS (Goodair & Reeves, 2022).

Ironically, neoliberalism's increasing popularity in the British NHS means that I can choose not to have my hip replaced by a private organization. Remember, the NHS is a marketized public service, so I get to choose where I have my operation done. On this occasion, when I get the choice, I'm going to elect to be treated by a public hospital. It's the rational thing to do because in an NHS hospital I'm statistically less likely to die.

2.6 Summary

In this chapter, I've explained the basic concept of a public organization. Using examples from history I've explained what public organizations are, what they do, and how they work. In using the examples I have, I've highlighted humanity's willingness to set up collectively funded organizations whose job it is to support the greater good of society. I've also described something of the political complexities of public sector organizations. I've described why some people can't get enough of public organizations and why others want the smallest, fewest number of public organizations it is possible to have.

Things to Watch, Things to Read

In the following table are suggestions for things you can watch and things you can read to learn more about this topic. I've also included a very short commentary, so you know why I've recommended a particular source and what to look for.

| **Read in two to three hours** | Fleming, P. (2023). "Never Let a Good Crisis Go to Waste": How Consulting Firms are Using COVID-19 as a Pretext to Transform Universities and Business School Education. *Academy of Management Learning & Education* 22(3): 425–438. |

This article looks at how extreme versions of neoliberalism are being driven into universities around the world by management consultancy firms and the problem associated with this. It also describes how those concerned with the loss of university's traditional civic orientation and role within society might resist this change. You should read this article in conjunction with this chapter's Research Insight, Case Study, and the documentary "Free to Choose" that I've recommended. Together these four sources will deepen your knowledge and understanding of neoliberalism's different dimensions, and its wider significance. If you want to know more about neoliberalism in higher education, read Fleming (2021).

| **Read in a day or two** | Wang, H., Xiong, W., Wu, G., & Zhu, D. (2018). Public–private partnership in Public Administration discipline: A literature review. *Public Management Review* 20(2): 293–316. |

This article reviews what we know about the centuries-old practice of governments partnering with private organizations to deliver large-scale infrastructure projects, but also all manner of other public services. The article delivers four main insights into the phenomenon of public-private partnerships (PPP). It gives an overview of the concept of PPPs and explains what they are. It describes how PPPs are structured to share risks between private enterprises and state government. It explains what drives PPP adoption, and it describes what we know about how well PPPs work.

| **Read in a week or three** | Blau, P. M. (1963). *The Dynamics of Bureaucracy: Study of Interpersonal Relations in Two Government Agencies* (rev. edn). Chicago: University of Chicago Press. |

This book is a classic in the field of organization studies. It gives a fascinating insight into the nature of working life in an American governmental organization in the late 1940s. While clearly dated, its significance extends beyond its tremendous historical value. What Blau illustrates beautifully is a near-perfect example of Weberian bureaucracy, facets of which still surround us today.

Watch in an evening	Nanau, A. (Director). (2019). *Collective* (Originally *Colectiv*) [Documentary]. Magnolia Pictures. https://www.collectivemovie.com

This multi-award winning documentary centers on the 2016 public health scandal following the Colectiv nightclub fire in Romania that killed 27 people and injured another 180. The documentary focuses on the 37 people injured in the fire who went on to die because of healthcare failings in the public hospitals they were being treated in. The film follows investigative journalists at the Romanian newspaper *Gazeta Sporturilor* as they work to uncover corruption and maladministration that underscored this healthcare crisis. What you get from this documentary is a chilling insight into the devastating consequences of mismanagement in public hospitals.

Watch in a week	Massey, G. (Director). (1980). *Free to choose* [Docuseries]. Public Broadcasting Service (PBS). Based on the writings of Milton Friedman.

In this staggeringly biased documentary, you'll get a crash course in neoliberalism. Across 10 episodes (in the 1980 version), or 5 episodes (in the 1990 version) you'll hear one of neoliberalism's key proponents—Milton Friedman—articulating their Nobel Prize winning theories of laissez-faire economics. Far from dull and boring, this documentary offers an extreme, uncompromising vision of how society, governments, and their institutions should work. The astute amongst you will notice how, in certain areas of the world, Friedman's thinking has been implemented—sometimes tentatively, sometimes cautiously, and with a variety of effects.

Research Insight: Bearing the burden of austerity

Source: Walsh, D., R. Dundas, G. McCartney, M. Gibson, & R. Seaman. (2022). Bearing the burden of austerity: How do changing mortality rates in the UK compare between men and women? *Journal of Epidemiology Community Health* 76(12): 1027–1033.

> **Edited abstract:** this study presents evidence from the UK showing that improvements in mortality rates slowed down around 2010 and then began to get worse. The study shows that the poorest 20% of people in the UK were more likely to die after 2010, than before. These increased mortality rates are attributed to the aggressive removal of billions of pounds from social security and other vital public services that supported the very poorest people in British society. The study shows that the government's defunding of the public sector resulted in approximately 335,000 excess deaths.

Case Study: The Edu-factory

Based on Fleming, P. (2021). *Dark Academia: How Universities Die*. Pluto Press.

Introduction

Universities are a very particular kind of public organization. Some are private companies. Most are socially oriented charities. Particularly in Europe, universities are historically civic institutions (Whyte, 2015). They are "places for the dissemination of universal learning" (Rothblatt, 1997, p. 53). Their mission in life is to push the boundaries of human knowledge and provide higher levels of education in mainly non-vocational subjects. Via subject experts they "create meaning and search for truth" (Sack, 1997, p. 69) and enable people to go out and do great things in the world.

That all seems quite nice and straightforward. But what exactly are these subject experts researching? What are they teaching their students? Is their teaching and research any good? Who's benefiting from it? What good will knowledge created and taught in universities do in the world? Who's paying for it all? How much are they paying? Is it really worth it?

In this case study, you're going to get an insight into how neoliberalism has framed debates about issues such as these. What you'll see is how it's led to primarily financially orientated evaluations of universities and created what Peter Fleming (2021) calls the **Edu-factory**. This case study is all about the concept of the Edu-factory, what it means for students like you and academics like me. It can be read in conjunction with other books, such as Kirp (2003); Thornton (2014); Hill (2012); and Kezar, DePaola, & Scott (2019).

Neoliberalism, revisited

Just in case you've forgotten, neoliberalism is an economic and political ideology that has evolved from classical liberalism. It's opposed to the idea of collectivism. That is, to things like government-run health, education, and social services. Collectivist solutions to social problems are the literal opposite of what neoliberals advocate.

Instead of collectivism, neoliberals advocate individualism. They severely limit the role of governments in society. The guiding logic is that governments should not intervene in, regulate, or control peoples' lives. For neoliberals, individual freedom, independence, and self-reliance are what life is all about. We're all responsible for our own lives, and everyone must be free to live in whatever way they want.

Under neoliberalism, the government's role is restricted to law enforcement and protecting the borders. Rather than governments, free market capitalism rules supreme. Society is defined by strong private property rights, free trade, and a cornucopia of choice for the individual. Instead of individuals having to take what they're given by the state, they buy everything they want from private providers. Prices are low and efficiency and value for money are guaranteed because every organization is in competition with one another. May the best one win.

The capacity to lead the neoliberal good life is dependent on wealth. This is achieved by those who knuckle down and earn their own living. These people don't rely on the benevolence of others. They build their own place in the world and take what's rightfully theirs. Similarly, society's losers only have themselves to blame. Destitution is a personal choice. There are always going to be people who can't be arsed. If only they made the effort, benefits would surely accrue. Things like structural inequalities are myths. We're all free and equal, and that's all that matters.

Into the Edu-factory

Since the 1970s, neoliberal ideas have increasingly permeated universities, particularly in North America, Australia, New Zealand, and the UK.

In these places, you'll find the best examples of Edu-factories. Perhaps you'll recognize them, they look a bit like this:

(1) In the Edu-factory, education is *conceived as big business*. Universities may have civic roots and socially oriented missions, but the real aim of the game is to make money and expand. Global domination is achieved through the sale of products and services to monied customers (mainly career-oriented students).

(2) If you're a student in the Edu-factory, *you're responsible* for your own learning. You'll get lectures and probably some tutorials. They might even be quite entertaining; however, it's up to you to learn and makes sense of most of the material. You're a free, independent, and self-reliant individual after all. No spoon-feeding here.

(3) Education is a *private commodity*. It's most definitely not a public good. It's something you buy. It's an investment in yourself. You buy an education to build your social and intellectual capital. Getting an education is how you make yourself valuable in the job market. You buy an education to improve your life chances. Specifically, to enhance your earning potential and ability to gain access to high-status professions.

(4) Relatedly, it's great if you're actually interested in what you're learning about at university, but ultimately it doesn't matter. Remember education is about *making yourself more economically valuable*. You don't go to university to satiate your quaint curiosity about Greek mythology or learn about the mythical pixies of Europe's Middle Ages. Be serious.

(5) The person who wants an education pays for it. As Fleming puts it "why should anyone else pay for your fancy science degree?" (Fleming, 2021, p. 132). So instead of the cost of your education being borne by society and recouped via future taxation—which is what would happen if education was conceived as a public good—*you pay* for it yourself. You also pay for it upfront and in full, usually through some kind of interest-bearing student loan. No IOUs here. Your degree. Your debt.

(6) The cost of your education is determined by the market. An education that grants you the right to demand a large compensation package is priced accordingly. The university has enhanced your value, so it's only fair they take their cut, whatever it may be.

(7) *You buy an education that will yield the best return on investment.* What's the point in studying something that doesn't improve your employability? Degrees that don't enable you to earn more are a waste of time. What's the point of them?

Learning in the Edu-factory

In Edu-factories, learning happens in its very own unique way. The dominant strategy draws inspiration from the modernist paradigm. Forget collegial small-groups seminars, we're talking standardization, low-cost, and high volume. Think Ryanair and McDonalds. That sort of thing. What results is an academic life that looks a bit like this:

(1) *Teaching is depersonalized* and mainly happens during big-group lectures. We're talking hundred-, even thousand-person affairs that take place in concert-sized theatres. Most lectures are filmed, so you don't even have to show up. The kind of interactive pedagogy you got at school that teased out and hammered home complicated concepts is nowhere to be seen. Certainly don't expect your lecturer to know your name. No chance of that.

(2) If you're lucky, you'll get a few small group tutorials to help your learning along. These will probably be taught by an adjunct. That is, *by someone who is paid by the hour (or a fixed fee)* to teach a course. They might have a doctorate. They might not. Either way they make up 70% of teaching staff in universities today (Kezar et al., 2019). Most make less money than I did teaching swimming to toddlers in the early 2000s. They get no pension or sick pay. You'll be able to spot them. They're the bookish types sleeping in their cars and showering in the gym (as in Kilganon, 2014).

(3) If you're really lucky, the lectures you go to will be quite entertaining. Probably not though. Most academics aren't especially funny. They might crack the odd joke, but a decade spent in the library

isn't much help when it comes to producing entertaining lectures on Foucauldian thinking. It also doesn't help that the typical academics workload allocation model only allows about three hours to prepare a two-hour lecture. You might be paying top-dollar, but it doesn't mean the university is passing those resources on to the person providing you with your education.

(4) The chances are that even if the lecturer was able to figure out how to perform pedagogical magic in the three hours they had to prepare your lecture, you won't be there to see it. If the lecture isn't going to be on the exam, you probably don't need to bother going. All you need is a grade at the end of the day, and *there are other more important things you could be doing*. Like trying to figure out how to deal with that chronic cash shortage. Food, accommodation, and that steadily ballooning student debt won't pay for itself.

(5) As it happens, you could probably get away with skipping a few lectures, or even all of them. Research shows that it's increasingly easy to get a decent grade at university. This is because as valued, fee-paying customers, your student satisfaction rules supreme. Measured through mid- and end-of-term evaluations, your satisfaction affects your lecturer's pay and career prospects. Cue grade inflation and easy content. Students with bad grades don't score their lecturers well, particularly if that lecturer isn't an aging white male professor (Heffernan, 2022, 2023; Heffernan & Harpur, 2023). Consequently, standards drop, and grades go up. Students are happy because they get good grades, and academics are happy because they get to keep their jobs. Who cares if the really difficult stuff gets cut from the module?

As bad as all that?

Clearly, the Edu-factory I've described above is a caricature. It's a provocative, radical characterization of higher education under neoliberalism. Or is it?

Some institutions fit Fleming's Edu-factory model more or less perfectly. Others don't at all. Some academics get fired if their teaching evaluation scores drop below 75%. Some don't. Some academics ward off student discontent by dumbing down content and giving out higher grades. Some don't. Some academics get paid by the hour. Some don't. Some students work in Starbucks to pay for the classes they don't have time to attend. Some don't.

You'll find the more extreme examples in places like North America, Australia, New Zealand, and the United Kingdom. That is, in places where neoliberalism has been enthusiastically embraced. In these places, the Edu-factory's raison d'être "grates with the basic values of academe" (Fleming, 2020, p. 136). However, it proliferates nonetheless. In these places, students pay more, but often get less from their time at university than ever before.

It's not all bad though. An education from the Edu-factory may be limited pedagogically, but the facilities are great. The lecture theatres are plush, and the tutorial rooms are state of the art. The student union is brand new and has more coffee shops and juice bars than you could possibly need. Student accommodation is also pretty sweet. It's often better than most hotels. No shared bathrooms in the Edu-factory.

Universities are also increasingly easy places to get into. As long as you can pay the bill you're on the course (mostly). Sure, you might have slightly less choice about what you can study, but at least you know you're going to be employable in the end. With student debt in America hitting the $2 trillion mark, and £200bn in the UK, that's a very, very good thing indeed.

Questions

1. Do you think universities should be organized and run in the same way as corporations?
2. What would you rather: lectures that are superficial but entertaining or ones that are rigorous but uncomfortable?
3. How do you know if you've got a good education?
4. Is there a better way to evaluate learning than anonymously rating courses and instructors on a scale of 1 to 10?
5. In the 1970s, academics outnumbered university administrators by quite some margin. Today, it's the other way round. Does that matter?

References

Akkermans, P. M., K. Duistermaat., R. Bernbeck, S. Cleuziou, E. M. Frangipan, A. Le Brun, et al. (1996). Of storage and nomads. The sealings from late Neolithic Sabi Abyad, Syria [with comments]. *Paléorient* 22(2), 17–44.

Barry, N. (1987). *On Classical Liberalism and Libertarianism*. New York: Springer.

Blau, P. M. (1963). The dynamics of bureaucracy: Study of interpersonal relations in two government agencies (rev. edn). Chicago: University of Chicago Press.

Blau, P. M. & W. R. Scott. (1963). *Formal Organizations: A Comparative Approach*. London: Routledge & Kegan Paul.

Brennan, J. & J. Tomasi. (2012). *Classical Liberalism*. Oxford: Oxford University Press.

Brewer, J. (2002). *The Sinews of Power: War, Money and the English State 1688–1783*. London: Routledge.

Butler, E. (2015). *Classical Liberalism–A Primer*. London: London Publishing Partnership.

Charvát, P. (2013). *The Birth of the State: Ancient Egypt, Mesopotamia, India and China*. Chicago: Karolinum Press.

Chomsky, N. (2011). *Profit over People: Neoliberalism and Global Order*. New York; Toronto; London: Seven Stories Press.

Cookson, R., M. Asaria, S. Ali, B. Ferguson, R. Fleetcroft, M. Goddard, et al. (2016). Health equity indicators for the English NHS: A longitudinal whole-population study at the small-area level. *Health Services and Delivery Research* 4(26). Retrieved from https://ueaeprints.uea.ac.uk/id/eprint/61185/1/FullReport_hsdr04260.pdf.

Downing, B. (2020). *The Military Revolution and Political Change: Origins of Democracy and Autocracy in Early Modern Europe*. New Jersey: Princeton University Press.

Ebrey, P. B. (1996). *The Cambridge Illustrated History of China* (Vol. 1). Cambridge: Cambridge University Press.

Ertman, T. (1997). *Birth of the Leviathan: Building States and Regimes in Medieval and Early Modern Europe*. Cambridge: Cambridge University Press.

Finer, S. E. (1997). *The History of Government from the Earliest Times: Ancient Monarchies and Empires* (Vol. 1). USA: Oxford University Press.

Fleming, P. (2020). Dark academia: Despair in the Neoliberal Business School. *Journal of Management Studies* 57(6), 1305–1311. doi: https://doi.org/10.1111/joms.12521

Fleming, P. (2021). *Dark Academia: How Universities Die*. London: Pluto Press.

Fleming, P. (Forthcoming). "Never let a good crisis go to waste:" How consulting firms are using COVID-19 as a pretext to transform universities and business school education. *Academy of Management Learning & Education* 22(3), 425–438.

Frangipane, M. (2007). Different types of egalitarian societies and the development of inequality in early Mesopotamia. *World Archaeology* 39(2), 151–176.

Gerth, H. H. & C. W. Mills. (2014). *From Max Weber: Essays in Sociology*. London and New York: Routledge.

Goodair, B. & A. Reeves. (2022). Outsourcing health-care services to the private sector and treatable mortality rates in England, 2013–20: An observational study of NHS privatisation. *The Lancet Public Health* 7(7), e638–e646.

Graeber, D. & D. Wengrow. (2021). *The Dawn Of Everything: A New History of Humanity*. UK: Penguin.

Han, Y.-S. (1946). The Chinese civil service: Yesterday and today. *Pacific Historical Review* 15(2), 158–170.

Harvey, D. (2007). *A Brief History of Neoliberalism*. USA: Oxford University Press.

Harvey, D. (2012). *The French Enlightenment and its Others: The Mandarin, the Savage, and the Invention of the Human Sciences*. New York: Springer.

Hayek, F. A. (1944/1976). *The Road to Serfdom*. London: Routledge.

Heffernan, T. (2022). Sexism, racism, prejudice, and bias: A literature review and synthesis of research surrounding student evaluations of courses and teaching. *Assessment & Evaluation in Higher Education* 47(1), 144–154.

Heffernan, T. (2023). Abusive comments in student evaluations of courses and teaching: The attacks women and marginalised academics endure. *Higher Education* 85(1), 225–239.

Heffernan, T. & P. Harpur. (2023). Discrimination against academics and career implications of student evaluations: University policy versus legal compliance. *Assessment & Evaluation in Higher Education* 1–12.

Hill, R. (2012). *Whackademia: An Insider's Account of the Troubled University*. New South Wales: New South.

Jacobsen, S. G. (2013). Chinese influences or images? Fluctuating histories of how enlightenment Europe read China. *Journal of World History* 24(3), 623–660.

Kezar, A., T. DePaola, & D. T. Scott. (2019). *The Gig Academy: Mapping Labor in the Neoliberal University*. Maryland, Baltimore: Johns Hopkins University Press.

Kilganon, C. (2014). Without tenure or a home. *New York Times, 2014*. Retrieved from https://www.nytimes.com/2014/03/30/nyregion/without-tenure-or-a-home.html.

Kirkwood, G. & A. M. Pollock. (2022). The return of inverse care: Case study of elective hip surgery. *The Lancet Regional Health–Europe* 21.

Kirp, D. L. (2003). *Shakespeare, Einstein, and the Bottom Line: The Marketing of Higher Education*. Boston: Harvard University Press.

Kiser, E. & Y. Cai. (2003). War and bureaucratization in Qin China: Exploring an anomalous case. *American Sociological Review* 68(4), 511–539.

Lewis, M. E. (2009). *The Early Chinese Empires* (Vol. 1). Boston: Harvard University Press.

Mann, M. (2012). *The Sources of Social Power: Volume 2, The Rise of Classes and Nation-States, 1760–1914* (Vol. 2). New York: Cambridge University Press.

Moscelli, G., H. Gravelle, & L. Siciliani. (2021). Hospital competition and quality for non-emergency patients in the English NHS. *The RAND Journal of Economics* 52(2), 382–414.

Nissen, H. J., P. Damerow, & R. K. Englund. (1993). *Archaic Bookkeeping: Early Writing and Techniques of Economic Administration in the Ancient Near East.* Chicago and London: University of Chicago Press.

Rothblatt, S. (1997). *The Modern University and its Discontents: The Fate of Newman's Legacies in Britain and America.* Cambridge: Cambridge University Press.

Sack, R. D. (1997). Homo geographicus: a framework for action, awareness, and moral concern. Baltimore: John Hopkins University Press.

Street, A. (2022). For-profit health care might be damaging population health. *The Lancet Public Health* 7(7), e576–e577.

Thornton, M. (2014). *Through a Glass Darkly: The Social Sciences Look at the Neoliberal University.* Canberra: ANU Press.

Whyte, W. H. (2015). *Redbrick: A Social and Architectural History of Britain's Civic Universities.* USA: Oxford University Press.

3
Private Organizations

> **Keywords**
>
> private sector; corporations; shareholder ownership; immortality; limited liability; *publicani*; Marxism; the East India Company

> **Consider**
>
> What are private organizations?
> Where did they come from?
> How do they work?

3.1 Introduction

In the last chapter, I talked to you about organizations formally set up by state governments to serve the public good. I talked to you about ***public*** organizations. In this chapter I'm going to talk to you about another major type of formal organization—***private*** ones. This chapter then, is all about organizations purposefully set up to serve individual private self-interests.

One of the things you'll see as you read through this chapter is that private organizations come in all sorts of different shapes and sizes. I'm not going to cover them all. Instead, I'm going to focus on the type of private organization that dominates the world today—the corporation. Think sharp suits, shareholders, and profit and loss accounts. Also, as it happens, togas, aqueducts, and Carthaginian mines.

This chapter begins with me explaining, in fairly general terms, what private organizations are and why I think you should learn about them. After that, I'll talk you through the concept of a corporation. I'll tell you about the simple, transformative ideas that underpin corporations, and why they're so important today. The basics established, I'll then go over some of the big challenges associated with corporations, and the competing visions that exist about how they should operate.

What you're ultimately going to get from this chapter is an understanding of what we mean when we talk about private organizations, particularly about corporations. You'll get a sense of how they work and why they work in the way they do. You'll also get a sense of the practical and moral complexities of corporations. You'll understand a bit about why some people think humanity's cause is best served by huge numbers of loosely regulated corporations and why others think the exact opposite.

3.2 What are private organizations?

Perhaps the very simplest way to think about private organizations is as the binary opposite of public organizations. So, where public organizations are set up and run to serve public interests, private organizations are set up and run to serve private self-interests.

As with public organizations, there are lots of different types of private organizations. Some of the most common types are shown in Table 3.1. Very briefly, first in the table you'll see **sole traders**, which are a kind of micro-enterprise. Essentially, those individuals who've officially set themselves up in business on their own; people like the plumber who fixed my bathroom toilet and the florist who did the flowers for my brother's wedding.

After sole traders you'll see enterprises like the mother and daughter removal firm I hired to help me move house. They were a **partnership**, which is another type of (usually quite small) private organization. Then there are people like my buddy George and his parents. Their dairy farm is set up as a partnership. As it happens George and his dad

Table 3.1 Types of private organization

Name	Description
Sole trader	A person who is the exclusive owner of a business, entitled to keep all profits after tax has been paid, but liable for all losses.
Partnership	An association of two or more people as partners for the running of a business, with shared expenses, profit, and loss.
Cooperative	An association or society, esp. one concerned with the production or distribution of goods or provision of services, which is owned and run jointly by its members, and shares its benefits among them.
Corporation	An incorporated entity with the capacity to act as a legal person, having an identity in law distinct from those of the individual or collection of individuals of which it is comprised at any point in time ... [created] under an act of the legislature, having its own powers, duties, and liabilities in perpetual succession.

also own a share in a ***cooperative*** that processes their milk, before selling it on to big supermarkets. Cooperatives are usually medium-large enterprises that are owned by their members. That is, by the people who use it and/or who benefit directly from the profits it generates.

Last in the table comes the ***corporation***. This type of private organization actually encompasses quite a lot—from relatively small-scale enterprises (like the company that converted my loft), to trillion-dollar multinationals like Alphabet, Apple, and Amazon. There's a brief description of the corporation in Table 3.1, but most of the rest of this chapter is given over to this particular form of private organization.

3.3 Why learn about private organizations?

There are three reasons why I think you should learn about private organizations, and about corporations in particular. The **first** is really two reasons in one. You should learn about private organizations because there are absolutely loads of them, and they employ a whole ton of people. In fact, if you have a contract of employment in a "formal" organization, the chances are that it's with a private one. The public organizations we discussed in the last chapter may be the biggest organizations in the world, but private organizations employ more people overall.

Some data to illustrate this point. The UK's Office for National Statistics reports that 82% of Brits in formal employment work in the private sector. In France, 79% of formally employed people work in the private sector. In Chile, close to 90% of formally employed people work in the private sector. In South Africa, it's 75%. Note: the "formally" employed categorization is important, for reasons that will become clear in Chapter 4.

These are some big numbers. They're also remarkably consistent. They mean that while all countries have a sizeable public sector, pretty much wherever you go most formally employed people work in the private sector. They're employed as for-profit sole traders, within partnerships, cooperatives, and corporations of one size or another.

The **second** reason you should study private organizations is because of their defining influence of the world. It was corporations that enriched, but also built (and then helped destroy) the ancient Roman Empire (Magnuson, 2022). It was also corporations that conquered India, killed millions, and channeled the country's great wealth to Europe (Dalrymple, 2019; Robins, 2012). Today's corporations fight in wars, build planes, and spaceships. They build smart phones, self-driving cars, and give us the ability to read emails anywhere in the world. Ours is a world defined by the corporation.

The **third** reason you should study private organizations—and corporations in particular—is because they're ideologically complex places. Or at least, the debate about them is. In much the same way that some people think that the world will be better off with the smallest state and the fewest number of public organizations possible, so these same arguments apply to private organizations.

The ideological battlegrounds are fraught and center on the corrosive effects of private organizations on society. The corporate form in particular is (in)famous for its capacity to enrich the few, at the expense of the vast majority. If nothing else, it's important to understand the arguments—you don't have to weigh into the debate, but it is helpful to have an idea of what's being discussed. It'll mean you know a bit about why private organizations operate more or less freely in different countries, and why politicians on either side of the political divide are constantly pushing for greater or less regulation of them.

Creatures of statue

Some theoretical foundations. If you look up the word "corporation" in the Oxford English Dictionary (OED), you'll see a simple, Latin derived entry. It means "the legal action of incorporating or of being constituted as a corporate body." Gripping stuff, no?

Actually, yes. When we talk about corporations we're talking about the particular organizational form created by a very clever piece of legal jiggery-pokery. Specifically, about an administrative process that gives birth to a legal entity "that can act, and be acted upon" in its own right (Magnuson, 2022, p. 10). So, we're talking about an organization with its own distinct legal identity and characteristics. These being:

(1) **Shareholder ownership.** Corporations are defined by something called the shareholder model of ownership. Very briefly, where sole traders and partnerships are owned by their operators, and cooperatives by their members, corporations are owned by people called shareholders. Also known as capitalists, shareholders are people who invest money in a company but don't actually run the company themselves.

Under the shareholder model of ownership, company shares can be traded freely at prices that reflect a general understanding of what the organization is worth. So, when you buy company shares, you're literally buying a proportion of that company and a right to a share in all its future profits.

For example, on the 30 September 2022 I bought a single share in a tech company called Apple. I now own one of the 16.3 billion shares Apple has sold in the company. The share price on that day was $138.20 USD making Apple worth about $2.2 trillion. Of

Apple's 16.3 billion shares, an investment fund with the world's dullest name [the Vanguard Group] owns about 1.2 billion of them. That's around 7.6% of the entire company. Every quarter Apple pays me, the Vanguard Group, and all its other shareholders a proportion of its profits. It's usually about 23 cents per share. This is the shareholder model of ownership.

(2) **Immortality**. One of the really clever things about corporations is that they can cheat death. What I mean by this is that they have no end date. The legal process of incorporation creates an ever-lasting legal entity. So whereas organizations like sole traders and partnerships die with their owners, corporations don't. If I die, my single share in the Apple corporation goes to my wife. When Apple's chief executive officer (CEO) Steve Jobs died on the 5 October 2011, they just recruited a new one—Tim Cook.

The point here is that for as long as the sun keeps shining and the world keeps turning, corporations like Apple will continue to exist. The only way to really kill Apple—or any other corporation—is to reverse the legal process through which it was formed in the first place. Nothing else will do it. Even then, it's not that easy. The investment bank Lehman Brothers went bankrupt at the start of the 2008 financial crisis. Seventeen years later it's still going. Technically, it's not trading anymore—it's being "wound up." Meaning, essentially, that its administrators are knee-deep in paperwork trying to figure out how to shut everything down.

(3) **Limited liability**. Perhaps the quirkiest characteristic of corporations is the concept of limited liability. This is the idea that company shareholders can enjoy unlimited rights to company profits, but have strictly limited liabilities for things like company debts and other responsibilities. What this means is that all liabilities associated with a company are the sole responsibility of the company. Nobody else—no actual people—can ever be held liable for them.

More generally, in the context of private organizations this is an extremely unusual arrangement. Think about it. If a company goes bankrupt, out-of-pocket creditors can only make claims against the company's assets. They cannot make claims against the people who own the company. Company shareholders are legally protected from all the liabilities a company might rack up.

The idea of limited liability is also not restricted to the issue of debt responsibility. If laws are broken by company employees, then it's the company that goes to court. There are some exceptions to this rule, but the basic point is that neither the people who work for the corporation, nor its shareholders, are liable for corporate wrongdoing. To get a sense of why this is a big deal, watch the documentary "Downfall: The case against Boeing." You'll see I've recommended it in the following "Things to Watch, Things to Read" section.

3.4 The first corporations

It is generally held that the first corporations in history were set up in ancient Rome (Avi-Yonah, 2005, p. 772). Assuming this is true—which not everyone does (e.g., Poitras & Willeboordse, 2021)—then the first evidence we have of corporations comes from the 5th century BCE. It's not much. Just a piece of work written by Dionysius of Halicarnassus containing a reference to a group of people called the *publicani*—public contractors. Or, in their organized form, *societas publicanorum*. The society of publicans.

Magnuson (2022) gives an excellent account of the *societas publicanorum*—see pages 22–48 in particular. These being, basically: societies formed to do contract work on behalf of the Roman senate. They were groups of people who pooled resources and shared expertise to take on large-scale government projects, like building roads, aqueducts, and city sewage systems, but also collecting taxes, running state mines, and supplying equipment to the Roman army.

Romans' use of the *societas publicanorum* was prodigious. Across the empire, nothing got done on any serious scale without them. That the *societas publicanorum* were able to achieve all they did was precisely because of Rome's pioneering invention of the corporate form and the sort of benefits it delivered. Then, as corporations have now, the *societas publicanorum* had special powers in law. As Malmendier (2009, pp. 1088–1090) describes, they were allowed to operate as distinct legal entities and to cheat death through a system centered on the idea of nominated succession. It also seems that the *societas publicanorum* could raise capital by issuing tradeable shares—called "*partes.*" These *partes*, like the shares issued by companies today, could be bought by anyone and went up and down in value according to the fortunes of the company. Moreover, also like shareholders today, the owners of *partes* were not directly involved in the management of the company. Nor were they held responsible for its liabilities.

Through the *societas publicanorum*, Rome mobilized the "money, manpower and expertise" of private capitalists on a massive scale and with incredible results (Magnuson, 2022, p. 45). Yet for all their achievements the *publicanis* were perhaps best well-known for their exploitative, fraudulent, and corrupt business practices. In this ultra-deregulated, corporate wild-west, the Romans had few mechanisms to control the *publicanis*. The *publicanis*' tendency to revert to greedy, exploitative practices is well documented. For many members of the *publicani*, the allure of profits was simply too much; thus, the *societas publicanorum*'s place in history is celebrated but also reviled. Indeed, some go as far as to suggest that the *societas publicanorum* bear at least partial responsibility for Rome's ultimate demise.

Either way, as far as the history books go, the concept of the corporation is unmistakably Roman. Thankfully it has also been much revised since the age of Dionysius. From the mid-14th century, European monarchies started taking steps to exert control over corporations, alert to corporations' propensity to be enticed by big profits. For the most part, these European monarchies struggled to actually regulate the day-to-day practices of corporations. However, a degree of control was achieved by heavily restricting the ability of people to form corporations in the first place.

Beginning in the 14th century, those with an entrepreneurial spirit in places like the UK could only establish a corporation if they first obtained consent form the ruling Monarch. For example, in the UK, wannabe corporate-types had to petition the monarchy for what was known as a "Royal Charter." The only way to get one of these, and the special rights, powers, and privileges that came with it, was by convincing everyone that the corporation was going to do great things for the country. If this couldn't be done, the corporation wouldn't get a charter. And, because charters were generally only issued for set periods of time, if a company failed to live up to its promises, they'd have their charter revoked.

Accordingly, in early modern Europe most of the chartered corporations in existence were civic-orientated. Organizations such as universities, trading guilds, schools, and hospitals. In the UK, the very first corporation formed by Royal Charter was the University of Cambridge, which received its charter in 1231. The second was the University of Oxford, which received its Royal Charter in 1248. The third was the Worshipful Company of Saddlers, which received its charter in 1272. Staggeringly, all three are still in existence, albeit not in quite the same forms as originally envisioned.

A crucial feature of the system of Royal Chartership was that the special rights, powers, and privileges granted in the charter varied on a case-by-case basis. For example, Cambridge University's Royal Charter was limited to the right to discipline members and an exemption from some taxes. Oxford University's was broadly similar. The award of limited liability was severely restricted. In the UK at least, only a few limited liability corporations were allowed to be set up (initially). The most famous amongst these were the Muscovy Company (in 1555) and the UK's first major trading company; the Eastland Company (in 1579) to foster trade links between Scandinavia and the Baltic States; and the East India Company (in 1600) which is the focus of this chapter's Case Study.

The first country to abolish state approval of corporations was the newly independent United States of America. Following the American revolution, every state in the country was allowed to issue its own corporate charters. The result was an explosion in the number of corporations and a profound shift in the role of the corporation in society (Avi-Yonah, 2005, pp. 785–786). The reasons for this shift are complex, but initially reflected the corruption of the process through which charters were being issued.

By the 1830s, the process was so crooked that proposals were put forward to strip US states of their right to grant corporate charters entirely. In the end, these proposals weren't passed. The right to set up a corporation was democratized instead. Laws were passed that enabled anyone to set up a corporation, enjoying all the rights and privileges this entails. From this point onwards, all that was required was some paperwork, a small fee, and hey presto!, a company was born. This is the dominant system in the world today.

3.5 Why we love corporations

We love corporations because they are a uniquely powerful instrument for getting things done. Few other organizational forms are in anything like the same league as corporations when it comes to mobilizing resources, bringing people together, and controlling and channeling their collective effort.

To get a sense of what I mean by this, think about the kind of benefits you get from organizations with the sort of characteristics I've outlined previously. Think about what the shareholder model of ownership delivers, as well as the concepts of corporate immortality and limited liability. Organizationally, each has quite major implications, which include the following.

(1) **Shareholder ownership = rapid access to boat loads of cash.** Short of robbing a bank, there aren't many better ways for CEOs to raise a ton of cash than by selling company shares. In 1980, Apple's initial public offering (IPO) shifted an impressive 4.6 million shares. At $22 USD per share, it raised about $101 million USD. That was a pretty big deal at the time, but that amount of money is peanuts today. The oil and gas company Saudi Aramco debuted on the stock market in 2019 and raised a colossal $25.6 billion USD.

What these numbers demonstrate is the capacity of the shareholder model of ownership to tap the vast resources of the private sector quickly and easily. So while we may be in the midst of a climate crisis, Saudi Aramco was still able to raise an absolutely mind-blowing amount of money that it could use to invest and do other things.

(2) **Transcending the CEO.** In business, death is a problem. Perhaps less so now that people live on average into their 70s, but historically, this has not always been the case. At the turn of the 19th and 20th centuries, average global life expectancy was just 32 years (Riley, 2005). This wasn't great for anyone—including businesses. If you were in business with someone who died, their business would die with them. End of story.

The good thing about a corporation is that their CEO can take a dive down the plug hole whenever they want. From an organizational point of view, it really doesn't matter. Sure, shareholders might get jittery, and it'll take a while to find a replacement, but CEOs are replaceable. With or without them, the corporation keeps on going.

The point here is that immortality makes corporations an entirely different type of organization to transact with. One can work with a corporation in a way that simply isn't possible with an organization set up as a sole trader or partnership.

(3) **Risky business.** Perhaps the thing we (capitalists) love most about corporations is that they're a really great instrument for doing fundamentally risky business. Remember what I said before about the concept of limited liability? One of the implications of limited liability is that corporations can take massive risks without too much fear of the consequences.

The limited liability model means that nobody is ever going to be held personally liable for any of the debts or legal liabilities that a corporation might rack up—remember the Boeing 737 MAX? Clearly, if a CEO makes bad decisions then company shareholders are going to be angry. Harsh words will be flung about, maybe they'll get fired, but nobody is going to come after their Ferrari, superyacht, or Mumbai mansion.

The point is that limited liability enables people to make high risk investments safe in the knowledge that if it goes well, they'll earn a lot of money; and, that if it all goes wrong, they'll never lose more than they invested. The end result is that you can invest in something like oil and gas exploration knowing two important things: (1) If all goes well, you'll make big bucks. And (2) if everything goes wrong, nobody is going to be chasing you for the clean-up costs.

3.6 Why not everyone thinks corporations are the best thing since sliced bread

Not everyone is a fan of corporations. You might possibly have already got a sense of this from the previous chapter on public organizations, particularly from the section on neoliberalism. We're going to explore the critique of corporations in more detail by drawing on a second big system of ideas. That system is called Marxism.

In the following sections, I'll explain what Marxism is and what it means for our understanding of corporations. As you read through this section, keep in mind that the Research Insight, Case Study, and Things to Watch, Things to Read all connect with the Marxist critique of corporations. Also keep in mind that my account is just a brief summary of a very complicated set of ideas. As with my account of neoliberalism, what follows is a caricature of Marxism. You can learn more from Singer (2018). Or if you're feeling energetic from Harvey (2018). If you're feeling really energetic you could have a go at reading Marx's original work (e.g., Marx, 1986, 2000).

3.7 Introducing the concept of Marxism

Like neoliberalism, Marxism is another slippery concept to get your head around. Also like neoliberalism, one of the big challenges with Marxism is that there are lots of different versions of it. Marxism means different things to different people, and can be translated into scenarios as radically different as totalitarian communist rule and anti-authoritarian libertarianism. It's confusing stuff, even for ardent devotees.

One way to demystify Marxism is to think about it as the ideological opponent of neoliberalism. So where neoliberals believe in the sanctity of capitalist markets and an individualized human existence, Marxism is all about the utility of collectivism and necessity of government monopolies. One gives you small governments, a deregulated economy, and vegan electricity, the other gives you big governments and no capitalist system at all (or at the very least, a highly regulated one).

As far as corporations go, two really big ideas sit at the heart of Marxism—both are critiques of the corporate form and of capitalism in general. The first idea pertains to corporations' huge capacity to create great wealth, but also to unevenly distribute that wealth in society. The second idea pertains to corporations' tendency to alienate the people they employ in a startling variety of different ways. I'll explain these critiques in more detail in the next two sections. First though, some historical context.

3.7.1 Marxism's historical context

Historically, Marxism is attributed to a man called Karl Marx and his close intellectual partner Friedrich Engels. You've probably heard of Marx. For nearly half the world he's a messianic-type figure as recognizable as Jesus Christ, Justin Bieber, and Coca-Cola (Singer, 2018, p. 1). Engels is less well known but no less important. Engels contributed much to his prophetic sidekick's thinking, and indeed bankrolled him for much of his life. Without Engels, we probably wouldn't have Marxism in the way we do today.

Marx and Engels lived in 19th century Europe. This was a time when the **Age of Reason** was in full swing and Europe was industrializing rapidly. People were migrating in massive numbers from the countryside into towns and cities and switching from an agricultural subsistence-type existence to one based around industrial work and hourly wage labor.

As we'll explore in more detail in Chapter 7, the factories of 19th century Europe worked by concentrating people and machinery together on a massive scale and organizing them in highly rationalized ways. Factories were also organized in a way that extended the working day to ensure the maximal use of the machinery, intensifying, simplifying, and standardizing the labor process (Braverman, 1998). Factories were dark, dank, dirty, dangerous places, but they were also highly productive organizations. They were the engines of the new industrial age.

Not everyone was impressed though. Industrialization may have been driving unprecedented economic diversification and growth, but poverty was rife. Indeed, life expectancy had changed little since the middle ages (Riley, 2005). As Marx himself noted in *Capital* (volume 1)—If you were rich, you'd probably make it to 35. If you were poor, you'd be lucky to see your 17th birthday (see Marx, 2018).

Marx and Engels were amongst a great number of people that were concerned with the direction the world was going in. They formed part of a growing crowd that were attempting to make empirical and theoretical sense of how the world was changing, and experiment with alternatives to the capitalist system. Their aims were hugely ambitious and impressively optimistic. They wanted nothing less than the complete restructuring of society. They wanted wealth to be redistributed fairly and for suffering to be eliminated.

3.7.2 Marxism and wealth inequality

The problem of wealth inequality and its elimination greatly preoccupied Marx. The European industrial revolution enriched society, but much of this wealth was channeled into the pockets of a relatively small number of people. Societies were improving, but they were improving unequally. Some people were doing a lot better than others.

For Marx, the entire capitalist system was the problem. As aggressive forms of capitalist enterprise, corporations were particular offenders. Marx was specifically concerned with factories, which he found appalling. He was also appalled by the atrocities committed by a new breed of globalized corporation—the multinational—exemplified at the time by the East India Company (EIC). Discussed in the following Case Study, the EIC's atrocities were being laid bare at precisely the moment Marx was at his most productive. As the EIC crawled towards its final demise, Marx found himself with a wealth of examples to draw on to illustrate his theories.

Marx's problem with corporations—and with capitalism—was the way they worked. In his theory of surplus value, Marx described how profit was ultimately achieved by business owners systematically exploiting their workforce to the greatest extent possible. By withholding a proportion of the surplus value laborers created, capitalists (business owners) could make huge profits. Marx found this deeply problematic.

Marx saw this arrangement as fundamentally contradictory. Capitalists (e.g., business owners) and laborers (e.g., workers) were locked in a never-ending, unresolvable conflict with one another. Motivated by the ever-compelling desire for more profit, capitalists needed to ensure employees were never paid their true worth. The aim was (and would always be) to secure the work of laborers at the lowest possible price. The lower the cost of labor could be pushed, the higher the amount of the profits that could be accumulated. The ultimate goal being to fix the price of labor at a level that enabled workers to survive (to live) but nothing more. For a graphic illustration of what this looks like in practice, read *The Grapes of Wrath* by John Steinbeck.

Clearly, this wasn't a state of affairs any sane laborer would want to play out. Laborers thus needed to recognize their exploitation and attempt to redress the imbalance in whatever way possible, but particularly through strategies of collective bargaining (e.g., unionizing). Capitalists' desire for retained profits had to be constantly resisted by the labor force, the latter compelled by the desire not to be pushed into a subsistence mode of being.

3.7.3 Marxism and alienation

The second big idea at the heart of Marx's thinking pertains to the capacity of corporations to create acute, overwhelming feelings of alienation. That is, to trigger in a person a deep sense of estrangement from themselves and their sense of humanity. Again, Marx leveled this critique not just at corporations, but at the entire capitalist system, which he cast as fundamentally dehumanizing. For Marx, workers within the capitalist system experienced four distinct types of alienation:

(1) Marx believed that *the capitalist system alienated workers from their productive activities*. It alienated them from their labor. Whereas previously workers identified with the work they did—they produced goods according to their own ideas and to satisfy their own needs—under capitalism they simply sold their time to others (to capitalists). Capitalists then put them to work in places like factories where they slotted in amongst the machines and did mundane, boring, repetitive jobs devoid of any creativity. The labor process was simply a matter of time and energy—of how long someone should work for and how hard they would do that work.

(2) Marx's second form of alienation centered on the idea that not only are workers alienated from the process of production—from their labor—but they are *also alienated from the object of their labor*. That is, from the products or services they are producing. Disconnection occurs here because the products made in, for example, factories are experienced by the workforce as depersonalized and meaningless. The individuals' contribution to the finished product is minimal. There is nothing of themselves in what they make. They don't think about, design, or make anything personally—they just make elements of the product, components that are combined together by something or someone else. Thus their part in the production process is small, and they never own the thing they make. If they want the product of their labor, they have to buy it like everyone else.

(3) Marx's third form of alienation centered on the idea that *in a capitalist system workers are alienated from one another*. In relation to this form of alienation, Marx's starting point was the assumption that people need to cooperate with one another in order to appropriate from nature what they need to survive; however, in the capitalist system people work in order to *buy* what they need. Capitalist systems were therefore inherently antisocial, and actually pitted workers against one another by putting them into competition to see who could produce the most in the shortest amount of time. What was lost was the classic, romantic notion of human collaboration and cooperation. This was replaced by individuals working independently and alone to service their own wants and needs.

(4) Lastly, Marx argued that workers in a capitalist system are alienated from their own potential. Instead of work transforming the individual and facilitating their emancipation—the full expression of their human nature—Marx argued that work in industrial society oppressed the individual. For Marx, the human spirit and individual identity was pushed to the peripheries of the working day. His point was that it was only after the working day had ended that the individual could set about being themselves. Thus when humans are at work, Marxism says humans are least connected to who they are and the humanity in them. In the industrial complex of the 19th century, it's not difficult to see how people were reduced to mere cogs in a massive machine.

3.7.4 Corporations are bad, right?

Seen through the lens of Marxism, there is little to celebrate about corporations. The Marxist critique renders them little more than exploitative, alienating instruments of domination that should be highly regulated, if not abolished completely. Marxist notions are attractive because they place the proponent on "the right side of history" (Claeys, 2018, p. 261). Afterall, Marxism is an ideology explicitly geared to the emancipation of humanity, the end of poverty and suffering. Where neoliberalism accepts and even presumes a certain amount of destitution and human suffering, Marxism does not. It entirely rejects that notion arguing instead that humanity should be working to achieve something altogether more ambitious—a caring and just society. In this more humane Marxist world, there is little room for the corporation, at least in the way it was conceived and operated within the capitalist system.

Yet for all Marxism's appeal as an ideology grounded in explicitly high(er) ethical precepts, the kind of utopia it advocates has never materialized—despite considerable attempts to create one. Indeed, some of the most famous Marxist-inspired experiments in history have resulted in quite dystopic outcomes. Things like totalitarian rule and a general worsening of conditions. Rather than enriching everyone, entire societies have been brought down to the lowest common economic denominator and subject to unprecedented levels of control and subjugation. The idea that people might collectively and spontaneously start believing that we all belong to one human family, can live in a society where nobody will be exploited, and where we'll forgive, love, and live as equals has yet to become a reality. The corporation, it seems, is here to stay.

3.8 Summary

In this chapter, I've explained the concept of a private organization, and why I think you should learn about them. After that I talked you through the concept of a corporation. I've outlined the simple, transformative ideas that underpin corporations, and why they're so important today. I've then described some of the big challenges associated with corporations, and the competing visions that exist about how they should operate. From reading this chapter, you've got a sense of how the private sector works and why it works in the way it does. Hopefully, you've also got a sense of the practical and moral complexities of this type of organization, and now understand a bit about why some people think humanity's cause is best served by huge numbers of loosely regulated corporations, and why others think the exact opposite.

Things to Watch, Things to Read

In this table are suggestions for things you can watch and things you can read to learn more about this topic. I've also included a very short commentary, so you know why I've recommended a particular source and what to look out for.

Read in two to three hours	Pandeli, J., M. Marinetto, & J. Jenkins (2019). Captive in cycles of invisibility? Prisoners' work for the private sector. *Work, Employment and Society* 33(4), 596–612.
This article looks at prisoners' attitudes towards the work they undertake while incarcerated. It is based on data collected in a privatized (for-profit) male prison in the UK, which the authors give the pseudonym "Bridgeville." Bridgeville contracts with private sector firms to provide market-focused prison work—so-called "real work" experiences—for inmates in some of its workshops. What the study reveals is how this work is mainly mundane and low-skilled. Rather than upskilling prisoners and preparing them for a successful life in society, prisoners learn little and leave pessimistic about opportunities for employment post-release.	
Read in a day or two	Wood, A. J., M. Graham, V. Lehdonvirta, & I. Hjorth. (2019). Good Gig, Bad Gig: Autonomy and Algorithmic Control in the Global Gig Economy. *Work, Employment and Society* 33(1), 53–75.
This article evaluates "job quality" in a specific subsection of the gig economy—the remote provision of digital services mediated by online labor platforms. If focuses on workers in southeast Asia and Sub-Saharan Africa (semi-structured interviews with 107 people across six different countries and a cross-regional survey involving 679 people). The study shows that, despite varying country contexts and types of work, algorithmic control is central to the operation of online labor platforms. It shows that algorithmic management techniques tend to offer workers high levels of flexibility, autonomy, and task variety and complexity. However it also shows that these mechanisms of control can also result in low pay, social isolation, working unsocial and irregular hours, overwork, sleep deprivation and exhaustion.	

Read in a week or three	Drucker, P. (1946/1993). *Concept of the Corporation*. London: Routledge. [2017]).

Published in 1946, and re-published in 1993, this classic book claims to be the first ever study of the constitution, structure, and internal dynamics of a corporation. The book's focus is the American company General Motors, and it is based on analysis that took over two years to complete. Working during the closing years of the Second World War, Drucker tries to understand what makes the company work so effectively. He focuses on what he calls the "core principles" of General Motors and how he believed these contributed to its successes.

Watch in an evening	*Downfall: The case against Boeing*. Directed by Rory Kennedy in 2022. Imagine Documentaries and Moxie Films, 89 minutes.

This award-winning documentary reports on the investigation into the two Boeing 737 MAX crashes that killed 346 people in 2018 and 2019. It explores the root causes of the crashes and their human cost. A central theme in the documentary is how the traditional "safety first" culture at Boeing changed when it merged with another company, McDonnell Douglas in 1997. It shows how, over time, the old emphasis on safety was replaced by an emphasis on profit maximization. In the new amalgamated company, profits and the company's stock price were the key measure of success. This documentary describes the catastrophic consequences this ultimately had, and continues to have.

Watch in a week	Dirty Money, season 1 (2018) and season 2 (2020). Produced by Adam Del Deo Yon Motskin, Lisa Nishimura, Stacey Offman, Jason Spingarn-Koff, Alex Gibney, Pierre Subeh. Jigsaw Productions, 50–77 minutes.

This docuseries tells the stories of some of the highest profile corporate scandals of recent times across two seasons. It illustrates the lengths corporations will go to achieve dominance and their willingness to flex, push, and break both moral and legal boundaries. It hammers home the point that corporate greed is rife in the contemporary globalized economy even within corporations historically known for their trustworthiness. As well as showing what can happen when corporations think nobody is looking, the series offers a primer for some of the topics that will be discussed in more detail in Part 2 of this book.

> **Research Insight:** ExxonMobil and the great climate cover-up
>
> **Source:** Supran, G., S. Rahmstorf, & N. Oreskes. (2023). Assessing ExxonMobil's 2019 global warming projections. *Science* 379(6628).
>
> **Edited abstract:** This study quantitatively evaluates all available global warming projections documented by—and in many cases modeled by—Exxon and ExxonMobil Corp scientists between 1977 and 2003. It finds that most of their projections accurately forecast warming that is consistent with subsequent observations. Their projections were also consistent with, and at least as skilful as, those of independent academic and government models. Exxon and ExxonMobil Corp also correctly rejected the prospect of a coming ice age, accurately predicted when human-caused global warming would first be detected, and reasonably estimated the "carbon budget" for holding warming below 2°C. On each of these points, however, the company's public statements about climate science contradicted its own scientific data. In short, ExxonMobil knew and understood the catastrophic consequence of fossil fuels on the Earth's climate as long ago as 1970. However, to preserve their business model, they launched a decades long campaign of denial to slow down the world's response.

Case Study: The corporation that ruled a country

Based on: Dalrymple, W. (2019). *The Anarchy: The Relentless Rise of the East India Company*. London: Bloomsbury Publishing; and
Robins, N. (2012). *The Corporation that Changed the World: How the East India Company Shaped the Modern Multinational*. London: Pluto Press.

Introduction

In a wet, windy corner of the UK is a place called Powis Castle. Built in the 12th century for the Welsh Prince Gruffydd ap Gwenwynwyn, Powis Castle is famous for its ornate gardens. Also for quietly housing one of the most significant collections of south Asian artefacts anywhere in the UK. As the historian William Dalrymple puts it "Powis is simply awash with loot from India" (Dalrymple, 2019, p. xxix).

Some of Powis' loot was bought or given. The rest was acquired via the conquest and plunder of Mughal India by a man called Robert Clive. Clive was an employee of arguably the most powerful corporation that has ever existed: the EIC. At the EIC Clive held the position of British Governor of Bengal (Watney, 1974). He was a company man, but also a "violent, utterly ruthless and intermittently mentally unstable corporate predator" (Dalrymple, 2019, p. 70).

Courtesy of Robert Clive Britain enjoyed what Dalrymple calls "one of the oddest events in world history: a trading company based in one small building in the city of London defeating, usurping and seizing power from the once mighty Mughal Empire" (ibid.). At its peak the EIC would control more than two thirds of modern-day India—nearly 200 million people. It did this with a well-equipped army of 260,000 soldiers, and a navy that included some of the best ships in the world.

When the IEC finally quit India it left behind millions dead, and much of the country's great wealth had been transferred to Britian—possibly the modern equivalent of as much as $45 tn (Hickel, 2018). Today the EIC serves as a cautionary tale about the dangers of unchecked corporate power. It is a gruesome reminder of why we have powerful regulatory mechanisms to keep corporations under control.

Background

The EIC was established in 1600 as a simple import-export business. Until it wound up in 1874 it was officially nothing more than a bunch of adventurous merchants out to make a buck or two. As they put it at the time, it was men come together [sic] "to venter in the pretended voiage to ye Est Indies and other Ilands and Cuntries thereabouts there to make trade" (Stevens, 1886, p. 5).

Like multinationals today, the EIC was set up as a limited liability company. It was also what's called a "state chartered" enterprise. The EIC's charter was granted by Britain's Queen Elizabeth I, who gifted the company with an absurdly generous 20-year monopoly on trade with nearly two thirds of the world—everything from the Horn of Africa (the tip of South Africa) to the straights of Magellan (the sea between Chile and Antarctica). She also granted the EIC permission to mint coin, establish settlements, make laws, exercise justice, raise an army, and wage war. The EIC could do pretty much whatever they wanted, as long as they were well away from Britain.

The EIC's inaugural voyages were broadly successful—though as much because of their privateering (piracy) as their business acumen (Keay, 1991, p. 23). In truth, the EIC were late to the game. By the time their ships were rolling into Asian waters the Dutch East India Company (VOC) had been trading there for years, and was well ensconced in the Spice Islands (modern day Indonesia, and the EIC's original target). By literal force of VOC cannon the EIC was encouraged to trade elsewhere.

Landing in India for the first time in 1608, the EIC found the resident Mughal emperor apathetic, but ultimately receptive to their mercantile overtures. After a great deal of toadying and gift giving—partly by a royal envoy sent on the company's behalf (Brown, 2014; see also Roe, 1860)—a trade deal was signed. So, in 1618 the EIC formally set up shop in India. They did this with little fanfare, just slotting in alongside their already resident French, Dutch, and Portuguese rivals.

The opportunity to trade with India was a big deal for the EIC. At the start of the 17th century India was the richest kingdom on earth and home to more than 142 million people (Broadberry, Custodis, & Gupta, 2015). It produced about a quarter of the world's manufactured goods (Eaton, 2019, p. 373) and had a standing army with possibly as many as 4 million soldiers (Parker, 1996, p. 135). Britain was a tiny nation by comparison. With a population of just 5 million people, it was among the poorest in Europe and produced little more than 3% of the world's manufactured goods (Maddison, 2007, pp. 116–120, 309–111, 379; Tharoor, 2018, pp. 2–3).

For much of the next 130 years the EIC largely operated according to the terms of their treaty (Bayly & Bayly, 1987, p. 16; Bowen, 2005, p. 2). They built factories and established their first fortified trading base in Armagon (in 1626). Ultimately indefensible, the base was abandoned six years later and replaced in 1634 by another—Fort St. George in Madraspatnam (now Chennai). The village of Madras (as it was known) grew into the company's first major colonial town, with its own civil administration, currency and population of some 40,000 people (Stern, 2011, pp. 35–36).

Until 1686 the EIC largely behaved. However this changed when the colossally arrogant and greedy then-governor of the EIC, Josiah Child, decided to wage war with the Mughal Emperor. He did this at quite possibly the very worst moment in history (Letwin, 2013, p. 37). At a time when, as Dalrymple points out, "the Mughals had just completed their conquest of the two great Deccani Sultanates of Bijapur and Golconda" (2019, p. 24), Child decided to [sic] "seize what we can & draw the English sword" (Wilson, 2016, p. 49).

Child's attempt to flex the EIC's military muscle was comprehensively defeated, and the brief war ended with a contrite petition for peace. This was granted by the Mughal Emperor, who fined the company a whopping £150,000 (£160m today) and cast them into mercantile purgatory. After several years of quiet contemplation, all was forgiven. In 1670 the company was allowed to rebuild its factories and forts and start trading again.

Turning points

Although the EIC had been defeated in 1686, the Mughal Empire was in decline. Stretching from Kabul in the northwest (modern day Afghanistan) to the Carnatic in the far Southeast, the Mughal empire was too big to govern. Its armies were overstretched, and its treasury depleted. Armed rebellions were springing up all over the country and the aging Emperor Aurangzeb was struggling to quash them all (see Bhargava, 2014, p. 43).

The real turning point came in 1707 when the ruling Emperor Aurangzeb died. His empire held together for a short time after his death but then descended into bitter, violent disputes about succession. As civil unrest grew the empire fractured. Regional governors declared their independence from Delhi and ceased to pay tribute.

In the midst of the chaos the EIC's directors gave orders to build up their private army and the company started to become precocious. The similarly resident French "Compagnie des Indes" did much the same. Alongside the EIC they took to hiring out their soldiers to the highest bidder. In exchange for land and/or money, the different warring factions of the Mughal Empire bought the services of one company army or another and fought each other.

In the end the ensuing battles achieved little, except to prove unequivocally that new European tactics and military hardware were staggeringly effective against Indian adversaries. With this creeping realization came an understanding within the EIC that India was precarious. With the country in the midst of a bloodbath, it wouldn't have taken much to overrun the entire country.

Imperial ambitions, realized

Things properly kicked off in the mid-1750s when the specter of war between Britain and France loomed large, and then began (in 1754). Conscious of the risk bands of marauding Frenchman posed to business, and unsure of the Mughal's ability to protect them, EIC Governors were instructed to recruit yet more soldiers and further build up their defences. This they did, much to the anger and frustration of their local rulers who attempted to intervene.

Over the next three years there was a series of bloody battles in which the EIC's local hosts sought to contain the company's militarization in the country. They may well have succeeded, but for the arrival (in 1756) of EICs favorite military commander, Robert Clive, on a squadron of Royal Navy warships.

Robert Clive was a militaristic company commander who had retired from the EIC a few years earlier. He was now back in India with a small army and orders from London to protect the company's interests from the French. Thus it was that Robert Clive, his army, and the British Navy were not actually in India to defend the EIC from aggrieved local rulers. However it didn't take much to spur them into action against the Mughals. Moving quickly, Clive retook the lost city of Calcutta and formally declared war on the Mughals in the name of the company. Admiral Watson of the British Navy did the same in the name of the British government.

Together they then captured the port of Hughli Bandar, and launched a surprise night attack on the army of the Nawab of Bengal, Siraj ud-Daula. Despite Clive believing the attack to have been a failure, Siraj ud-Daula withdrew and sued for peace. On the 9 February 1757 Siraj ud-Daula signed the Treaty of Alinagar, restoring EIC privileges and allowing the company to keep their (upgraded) forts.

Siraj ud-Daula's defeat had catastrophic consequences for his regime. The air of indomitability that previously surrounded it disappeared and old allies started plotting his downfall. Chief amongst these was a man called Mir Jafar. Backed by powerful Indian financiers, Mir Jafar quietly approached Robert Clive for help with desposing Siraj ud-Daula.

After a great deal of haggling Clive agreed to back Mir Jafar's coup in return for a fixed payment to the EIC of £3m (£315m today); Rs110,000 a month to pay for the loan of EIC troops (£1,430,000 today); land holding rights for the EIC in Calcutta; duty free trade and a further £1m in compensation for the destruction of Calcutta (£105m today). Under the terms of the agreement, the European inhabitants of Calcutta would also get £0.5m in compensation (£60m today). Clive personally stood to win a cash bonus of £234,000 (£25m today), and landed estate in India worth £27,000 annually (£3m today).

Once the agreement was ratified and signed Clive was quick to act. On the 13 June 1757 he sent an ultimatum to Siraj ud-Daula falsely accusing him of breaking the terms of their treaty. Without waiting for a response, Clive moved directly to attack Siraj ud-Daula. This was a tense moment for Clive. He was now militarily exposed and operating well beyond his original remit. The danger was also seemingly felt by Clive's co-conspirators. As Clive went all-in, Mir Jafar and his financiers got cold feet. Communications between them became sparse and noncommittal. Clive's army was grossly outnumbered and even in his own camp few believed he could actually win.

The Battle of Plassey began on the morning of the 23rd June 1757. Against all the odds, Clive emerged victorious. Mir Jafa followed through on his promises and the defeated army of Siraj ud-Daula beat a hasty retreat.

Consolidating governmental powers

After the Battle of Plassey Clive installed Mir Jafar on the Bengal throne, and in doing so triggered payment of the astronomical sums that had been agreed. This was an absolutely ground breaking moment. Not just because Clive had secured possibly the biggest corporate windfall payment in history, but because the EIC had used its private army to acquire real, serious political power for the first time.

In the years that followed the Battle of Plassey Clive returned home and the EIC worked to consolidate its military and political power in the region. Initially, through the largely ceremonial leadership of Mir Jafar, and then through a series of other puppet emperors. During this time the EIC wasn't entirely unopposed. Two further battles were fought and won by the EIC (albeit marginally). On the 3 May 1764 (at Patna), and again on the 22 October 1764 (at Buxar), the remnants of the Mughal Empire combined their forces in last ditched attempts to overthrow the EIC and kick them out of India.

Spooked by this continued resistance, the EIC dispatched Robert Clive back to India for a third time to sort things out. Arriving just after the Battle of Buxar, Clive discovered the Mughals now totally defeated. With no battles left to fight, he set about placing the region on a more stable footing. As he had with Mir Jaffar, he bought off the new claimants to the emperor's throne with large cash bribes and purely symbolic roles. The otherwise ousted, powerless rulers took the cash and agreed to formally cede control of India's three richest provinces—Bengal, Bihar, and Orissa—to the EIC.

Thus it was that on the 12 August 1765 the EIC formally made the transition from mercantile trader to state corporation. In Robert Clive's campaign tent, on a make-shift throne made up of a silk-draped armchair balanced on top of a dining room table, the now nominal Mughal Emperor, Shah Alam, officially signed the Treaty of Allahabad. The central component of this treaty was the granting of Diwani rights to the EIC. In return for £260,000 a year, the new Mughal Emperor consented to the EIC taking full economic and administrative control of the whole of north east India.

By any measure this was another truly seismic moment. With the signing of the treaty, independent government for the estimated 20 million people of north east India ended. The Mughal Empire now existed only in name, with the emperor little more than a powerless, ceremonial figurehead. In every way that mattered, the region was under the control of a for-profit trading company based thousands of miles away in Britain.

For the EIC the Treaty of Allahabad granted them the unprecedented right to generate revenues in Bengal, Bihar, and Orissa however they wanted. This the company did. For over 100 years the wealth of India was systematically, aggressively, and mercilessly extracted by the EIC on an absolutely unprecedented scale. This wealth went on to fund the EIC's conquest of more than two thirds of modern-day India. The great deal that was left was then transferred back to Britain where it propped up the cash-hungry British government, lined the pockets of EIC directors and funded the company shareholders' annual dividend.

Conclusion

The EIC was eventually crippled by the colossal weight of its imperial and mercantile ambitions. Going bankrupt in the early 1800s, the company was twice bailed out by the British government, nationalized and then eventually dissolved in the latter part of the 19th century. At this point the administration of India was taken over by the British government. It wasn't until nearly 200 years after the signing of the Treaty of Allahabad that Indians were finally able to reclaim their country and form their own independent government.

The extraordinary story of the EIC provides a stark warning of the potential consequences of allowing for-profit corporations entirely unchecked freedom. In this case, attempts were made throughout the company's history to control and regulate it. However, these ultimately proved ineffective. The greed of company officials was impossible to control. Moreover, the way the company was set up freed directors, investors, and company officials from any and all liabilities associated with their activities. Crucially, it enabled them to ignore the great human and financial cost of their brutal trading practices on India. Their duty first and foremost was to turn a profit—to enrich themselves and the company—in whatever way possible.

In Britain there were those who reviled the activities of the EIC, and the company itself did take some steps to curb the very worst excesses its officials inflicted on the people of India. However, for all the directors' well-documented aversion to risk, and to costly wars in particular, there was little obvious will within the company to reform their practices. While extolling the virtues of moderation, restraint, and stability both executives and investors were grateful for the cash brought back by their governors' military conquests.

Robert Clive's name will forever be attached to the events that gave rise to the corporate state; however he was in fact just one of a great number of company officials who liberally interpreted the boundaries of what was legally and morally permissible in India. The Dutch, French, Portuguese, and Swedes all played much the same game, but it was the British EIC who ultimately conquered all.

Questions

1. Should companies be allowed to run countries?
2. What do you think the chances are of a modern corporation doing what the EIC did in India?
3. Do you think for-profit companies can be relied upon to regulate themselves?
4. How would you regulate a corporation like the East India Company?
5. How important do you think the concept of limited liability was to the success of the East India Company?

References

Avi-Yonah, R. S. (2005). The cyclical transformations of the corporate form: A historical perspective on corporate social responsibility. *The Delaware Journal of Corporate Law* 30, 767.

Bayly, C. A. & C. A. Bayly. (1987). *Indian Society and the Making of the British Empire* (Vol. 1). Cambridge: Cambridge University Press.

Bhargava, M. (2014). *The Decline of the Mughal Empire*. Oxford: Oxford University Press.

Bowen, H. V. (2005). *The Business of Empire: The East India Company and Imperial Britain, 1756–1833*. Cambridge: Cambridge University Press.

Braverman, H. (1998). *Labor and Monopoly Capital: The Degradation of Work in the Twentieth Century*. New York: New York University Press.

Broadberry, S., J. Custodis, & B. Gupta. (2015). India and the great divergence: An Anglo-Indian comparison of GDP per capita, 1600–1871. *Explorations in Economic History* 55, 58–75.

Brown, M. J. (2014). *Itinerant Ambassador: The Life of Sir Thomas Roe*. Lexington: University Press of Kentucky.

Claeys, G. (2018). *Marx and Marxism*. UK: Hachette.

Dalrymple, W. (2019). *The Anarchy: The Relentless Rise of the East India Company*. London: Bloomsbury Publishing.

Drucker, P. (2017). *Concept of the Corporation*. London: Routledge.

Eaton, R. M. (2019). *India in the Persianate Age: 1000–1765*. UK: Penguin.

Harvey, D. (2018). *A Companion to Marx's Capital: The Complete Edition*. London: Verso Books.

Hickel, J. (2018). How Britain stole $45 trillion from India (and lied about it). *Aljazeera* Retrieved from https://www.aljazeera.com/opinions/2018/12/19/how-britain-stole-45-trillion-from-india.

Keay, J. (1991). *The Honourable Company: A History of the English East India Company*. London: HarperCollins.

Letwin, W. (2013). *The Origins of Scientific Economics*. London: Routledge.

Maddison, A. (2007). *Contours of the World Economy 1–2030 AD: Essays in Macro-Economic History*. Oxford: Oxford University Press.

Magnuson, W. (2022). For profit: A history of corporations. New York: Basic Books.

Malmendier, U. (2009). Law and finance at the origin. *Journal of Economic Literature* 47(4), 1076–1108.

Marx, K. (1986). *Karl Marx: A Reader*. Cambridge: Cambridge University Press.

Marx, K. (2000). *Karl Marx: Selected Writings*. USA: Oxford University Press.

Marx, K. (2018). *Capital Volume 1*. Lulu. com. Delhi: Fingerprint! Publishing.

Pandeli, J., Marinetto, M., & Jenkins, J. (2019). Captive in cycles of invisibility? Prisoners' work for the private sector. *Work, Employment and Society* 33(4), 596–612.

Parker, G. (1996). *The Military Revolution: Military Innovation and the Rise of the West, 1500–1800*. Cambridge: Cambridge University Press.

Poitras, G. & F. Willeboordse. (2021). The societas publicanorum and corporate personality in roman private law. *Business History* 63(7), 1055–1078.

Riley, J. C. (2005). Estimates of regional and global life expectancy, 1800–2001. *Population and Development Review* 31(3), 537–543.

Robins, N. (2012). *The Corporation that Changed the World: How the East India Company Shaped the Modern Multinational*. London: Pluto Press.

Roe, T. (1860). *Letters from George Lord Carew to Sir Thomas Roe: Ambassador to the Court of the Great Mogul. 1615–1617*. London: Camden Society.

Singer, P. (2018). *Marx: A Very Short Introduction*. Oxford: Oxford University Press.

Stern, P. J. (2011). *The Company-State: Corporate Sovereignty and the Early Modern Foundations of the British Empire in India*. Oxford: Oxford University Press.

Stevens, H. (1886). *The Dawn of British Trade to the East Indies: As Recorded in the Court Minutes of the East India Company, 1599–1603; Containing an Account of the Formation of the Company, the First Adventure, and Waymouth's Voyage in Search of the North-west Passage*. London: H. Stevens.

Tharoor, S. (2018). *Inglorious Empire: What the British Did to India*. UK: Penguin.

Watney, J. (1974). *Clive of India*. Farnborough, Hants: Saxon House.

Wilson, J. (2016). *India Conquered: Britain's Raj and the Chaos of Empire*. New York: Simon and Schuster.

4
Informal Organizations

> **Keywords**
>
> informality; street vending; trust; microfinance; exploitation; control

> **Question**
>
> What are informal organizations?
> Why do they matter?

4.1 Introduction

In the last two chapters, I talked to you about formally established public and private organizations. In this chapter I'm going to talk to you about their chaotic cousins—*informal* organizations. We're talking here about organizations that provide legitimate goods and services, but in ways that are purposefully hidden from authorities for monetary, regulatory, and institutional reasons (ILO, 2012; see also Medina & Schneider, 2018, p. 4).

The point of this chapter is to connect with the organizations that operate in backstreets and basements around the world, in what's called the informal economy. As you read this chapter, keep in mind that while the focus of this chapter is commercially orientated informal organizations, there are informal organizations out there doing anything and everything imaginable—from organizing community book exchanges and chess competitions to bird watching and sex parties. The concept of an informal organization is a broad one.

4.2 What are informal organizations?

The sort of informal organizations we're concerned with in this chapter are the ones that provide legitimate goods and services, but in ways that are purposefully hidden from authorities for monetary, regulatory, and institutional reasons (Medina & Schneider, 2018, p. 4; ILO, 2012). We're talking here about informal street vendors and illegal shadow factories, that kind of thing.

In the context of organizations, it's important to understand that formality isn't a binary thing. Economists distinguish between the "formal" and "informal" economies, but when it comes to organizations, it can be hard to make clear distinctions (Breman, 1976). This is because most formal organizations have a degree of informality, and most informal organizations have a degree of formality (De Castro et al., 2014, p. 90). It's rare for an organization to be entirely formal or entirely informal. Normally, they're a bit of both.

Informal organizations also vary in the extent to which they are "isolated" from the formal economy or "integrated" into it. Highly integrated informal organizations essentially feed the formal economy. They feed the formal economy because all the goods and services they produce are consumed in the formal sector. A good example is the groups of *Garimperos* ("cowboy" prospectors) mining gold around the Inambari River in Peru. Garimperos mine gold on an entirely informal basis, that they then sell to formal, tax-paying organizations operating in the mainstream economy (Martinez et al., 2018). You might think this is pretty niche, but as you can see in Photo 4.1, it actually happens on an absolutely enormous scale.

In contrast, *isolated* informal organizations are ones that only service the shadow economy. These organizations have relatively little to do with the formal sector. Consider Brazil's Favellas, South Africa's Townships and the slums of Dhaka, Mumbai, Nairobi, Caracas, and Cairo (and many other places). Think about the organizations you'll

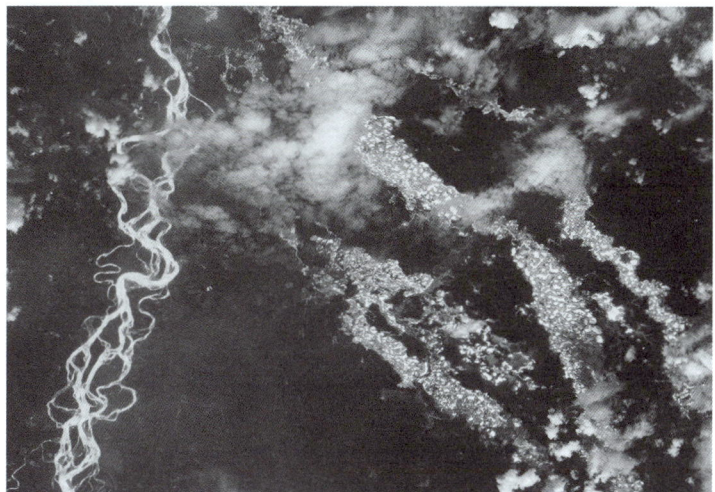

Photo 4.1 Gold Rush in the Peruvian Amazon
Source: https://eoimages.gsfc.nasa.gov/images/imagerecords/147000/147891/iss064e016203_lrg.jpg.

find in these places. There's no Walmart, Carrefour, Tesco, or 7-Eleven. Instead, people buy everything from pop-up vendors and makeshift stores. So, from informal organizations that only operate within their community (as in Alcock, 2018).

A helpful way of thinking about informal organizations is to use Figure 4.1: "Key dimensions of informal organizations" (adapted from Biles, 2009, p. 217). This figure maps organizations against two main axes. First, the horizontal axis maps the organization's characteristics from "extremely informal" (left) to "extremely formal" (right). The vertical axis maps the nature of the organization's relationship with its employees from "extremely informal" (bottom) to "extremely formal" (top).

In this diagram, Quadrant 1 represents organizations that are highly formal. Examples are banks and government departments like the UK's *Department for Work and Pensions* and Germany's *Federal Bundes Finanz Ministerium* (BZSt). So, highly bureaucratic organizations where workers have tight contracts, unambiguous jobs, and clearly defined ways of working. That sort of thing.

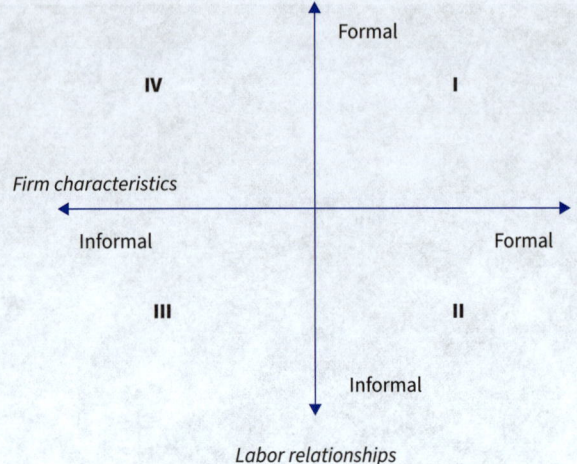

Figure 4.1 Key dimensions of informality
Source: © 2008 James J. Biles. Journal Compilation © 2008 Blackwell Publishing Ltd. NASA vis visible Earth.

Quadrant 3 represents highly informal organizations. Essentially, simple organizations like groups of informal construction workers (Wells, 2001), street hawkers (Henderson, 2010), and backstreet manufacturers. These are the most informal organizations in the world. They are low technology, low revenue, low capital organizations that aren't registered with state authorities, don't pay taxes, or fulfil any legal obligations to their workforce (Potts, 2008).

Quadrant 2 represents organizations that comply with some or all regulations, but to varying degrees enter into unregulated relationships with workers. Some farms, in places like Europe and North America, fall into this category when they hire "off the books" seasonal workers (Barrientos, 2013; Hartman, 2008). These organizations have an entirely legitimate workforce but also an entirely informal one. The former gets a salary and sick pay. The latter gets paid cash and have to hide if police show up (Barrick et al., 2014; Zhang et al., 2014).

Quadrant 4 represents organizations that are generally unregistered and unregulated, but have a relatively formal relationship with the workforce. Examples include online businesses that employ people, provide legitimate goods and services, but aren't actually legally registered with any government authority.

Figure 4.1 is therefore an illustration of how incredibly different informal organizations can be. It also shows that organizations can also be both formal *and* informal at the same time. In the sections that follow, we'll work through the different Quadrants in more detail. We'll skip Quadrant 1, because it refers to tight, formalized organizations that are covered in Chapters 2 and 3.

4.3 Why learn about informal organizations?

For some of you it might seem weird that I'm asking you to think about informal organizations. Why should you care? The answer is simply that you should think about informal organizations because they are absolutely everywhere. Their impact on the world is massive. For sure, you might get a job in a formal organization like a bank, supermarket, or shipping company but that doesn't mean you won't come across informal organizations.

To give you some context, from the most recent data that we have available, between 1991–2015 an estimated 31.9% of global gross domestic product (GDP) came from the informal shadow economy (Medina & Schneider, 2018). Think about that for a second. 31.9% of the monetary value of all finished goods and services in the entire world was generated by people working informally in organizations that didn't legally exist (see also Williams & Schneider, 2016). That's a lot of yen, euros, and dollars.

In some countries, the informal shadow economy is actually bigger than the formal economy. For example, in Bolivia and Zimbabwe the informal shadow economy represents 66.1% and 61.8% of GPD respectively (Williams & Schneider, 2016, p. 64). In Austria and Switzerland—paragons of formal organization—the figure is much lower but is still significant at 9.8% and 8.5% respectively (Medina & Schneider, 2018). In the UK and Norway that number is closer to 13% (Williams, 2019).

Now think about those numbers in terms of living, breathing people. The International Labour Organization (ILO) estimates that globally

2 billion people work informally (Bonnet et al., 2019). That's about 61% of the global working population. In some areas of the world, such as Africa, 85.8% of employment is informal. In Asia and the Pacific, it's 68.2%. In the Arab nations, it's 68.6%. Across the Americas (North and South combined), it's 40%, and in Europe and Central Asia, it's 25.1%. Within these regions, there are huge variations. In northern Europe, just over 10% of people work in the shadow economy. In southern Europe, as much as 40% of people work in the shadow economy.

The point is that if you have a contract of employment in a tax-paying organization, you are in the minority. Most people in the world don't earn a living this way and never will (Perry et al., 2007). Instead they'll earn their living through working informally, and in doing so generate over one third of the world's economic output. This is a really good reason to study informal organizations.

4.4 Extremely informal organizations in focus

This section looks at extremely informal organizations in more detail. It's all about the organizations you'll find in Quadrant 3 in Figure 4.1. It looks at where you find them, how they work, and their role in the world.

4.4.1 Identifying extremely informal organizations

Extremely informal organizations all involve relatively simple, labor-intensive activities that generate just enough money for the individual (and usually their family) to survive. Street vendors are perhaps the easiest example to work with. Every country has them, and they often form an incredibly important, vibrant part of communities and their economies (Duneier & Carter, 1999).

This might feel like a bit of an exaggeration, particularly if you live in a country with an extremely formalized economy, like Austria, Germany, Switzerland, Norway, or the USA. In places like these, street vendors are certainly less common. However, think about this: in Los

Angeles (LA) there are an estimated 647,500 informal workers, of which around 10,000 are street vendors (Flaming et al., 2005, p. 16; Muñoz, 2008, p. 3).

Considered in a global context, LA's 10,000 street vendors are actually quite unusual. Not because there are so many, but because there are so few. In India there are more than 10 million entirely informal vendors working on the streets. In fact, estimates suggest that around 2% of all Indian urbanites earn their living as street vendors (Bhowmik, 2010). Two in every 100 people is a huge number of people. If 2% of LA's population were selling goods on the streets, that would be about 79,340 people, just in LA's main metropolitan area. That number balloons if you include the suburbs as well.

Street vendors aren't organized in a formal sense. In many ways, it's a real stretch to call them organizations, at all. They don't look or work anything like Walmart or 7-Eleven. However, if you tone down your expectations you'll see that they are in fact extremely well organized—it's just that they're not organized along classic Weberian lines.

Street vendors are organized in the sense that you will often see them working in the same place every day, selling the same things often to the same people (Llewellyn & Burrow, 2008). Sure, some will be haphazard, chaotic enterprises—there one day, gone the next. But think about the rest. Think about the vendors who are there all the time. People like the unlicenced trader selling fish from a van in the car park down the road from me. He doesn't have a licence or pay taxes (I asked him), but he's there every Saturday with the freshest fish in town and a massive line of customers. This kind of consistency doesn't happen by chance. There is planning, complexity, and continuity to what he's doing. He's organized, just not in the same way Walmart is.

Think I'm wrong? Watch the "City Rising" documentary I've recommended in "Things to Watch, Things to Read" section. Now think about the street vendors you see in the towns and cities you live in. Have you ever wondered how a vendor's stall makes it onto the street? Where does the stock come from? Who supplies it? Where does it all go at night? How is it decided which vendors can sell where? How does one vendor stake a claim on a particular piece of pavement, and keep it?

If you make the effort to find answers to these questions, you'll see that extremely informal organizations are in fact extremely well organized—albeit possibly in not quite the way you might expect.

4.4.2 How extremely informal organizations work

To understand how extremely informal organizations work, consider Burbidge's (2013) study of an illegal marketplace in Mwanza, Tanzania. Specifically, consider his description of what happens when the police show up to close things down. It goes a bit like this: the cops show up, and a very particular group of people—the people who sell disposable plastic bags for people's shopping—fight them back. While they do this all the other vendors pack up and bolt for the exit.

This might not seem like much, but bag sellers' brawling betrays a kind of secret, unwritten system of organization. It's not a complex system of organization. It's simply: bag sellers make trouble, everyone else makes for the exit. It's that simple. That's what extremely informal organization looks like in real life. It might not seem like much, but being organized in this kind of way matters enormously. Think about it: if you're an impoverished vendor in an illegal marketplace, having a plan that helps everyone to stay in business (and out of prison) can be, quite literally, life-saving.

Here's a question for you: why would a bag seller want to risk being arrested by brawling with the cops? Would you do it? Would you cause trouble with the police so someone else can run away? Probably not—unless you were going to get something really good back in return.

What do you think Mwanzan bag sellers got for brawling with the police? According to Burbidge the answer is trust and money. How so? Well, what Burbidge saw was more than simple altruism. Remember that from Chapter 1? He saw bag sellers brawling with the cops because it was a good way to show other vendors they were personally invested in the marketplace. That is: by helping people to escape, the bag sellers could show they were good and trustworthy people within that community.

This makes sense if you understand that our Mwanzan bag sellers depend on other vendors (such as tomato sellers) for business. When a tomato seller sells someone tomatoes, they call over a bag seller, who then sells the customer a bag to carry the tomatoes home in. Ultimately, the marketplace was full of people selling bags—any one of which a tomato seller could call over. So a bag seller could make sure they were the one who got called over by befriending and helping out the other vendors. Brawling with the cops, so the other vendors could escape, was one way of doing this.

In Burbidge's (2013) study, fighting off the cops was a really good way for bag sellers to build what's called a "**trust anchor**" between them and the other vendors in the marketplace. A trust anchor is a reason to trust and cooperate with someone. This matters because extremely informal organization like the Mwanzan marketplace are built on trust. Trust facilitates cooperation by helping to bind people together. This is important in organizations of all shapes and sizes, because if people don't have a reason to work together, they don't.

So what we get from Burbidge's (2013) study is two things: we get a perfect example of an extremely informal organization. And we also get an insight into the inner workings of this kind of organization. We see its structures and how the organization is defined by degree planning, complexity, and continuity over time.

These points are reinforced by Varcin's (2000) study of market traders in Turkey. In his study Varcin (2000) shows how market traders coordinated and worked together via an intricate system of well-established, well-coordinated, and well-enforced norms and practices. Through this system traders collectively exerted considerable control over commerce on the streets (see also Anderson et al., 2009). They erected barriers to entry that protected their marketplace from new entrants, but also collaborated with one another to create considerable economies of scale. For example, traders combined and shared resources in a way that enabled businesses to grow by providing social support to each other and fixed prices to ensure everyone's profit margins remained high.

Crucially, perception of the illegal marketplace as a chaotic, disorganized space comprising of multiple, transient, independent, self-interested traders is wrong. These are highly organized spaces where individuals cooperate and work together on the basis of entirely informal, open-ended agreements. Nothing is written down, no contracts are signed, yet organization happens none-the-less. What is achieved through this type of informal organization is both economic and social security for the people involved. Indeed, an important aspect of what Varcin (2000) found was that within the marketplace, vendors actually moderated (limited) competition. Rather than each vendor trying to make as much money as possible, vendors prioritized building and maintaining relationships (Varcin, 2000). Theoretically, all the vendors were competitors, but the informal way they organized themselves limited this competition to ensure individual and collective welfare.

To an extent, what Varcin (2000) reports, Burbidge (2013) saw as well. He saw bag sellers risking their livelihood to help another trader. You get a sense of the sheer significance of this, and thus the lengths these individuals will go to encourage and support cooperation, especially when you consider that Mwanza's bag sellers comprise part of a broader population of approximately 28 million people in Tanzania who rarely earn more than $1.90 USD per day (World Bank, 2020). For these people, sacrificing their own income and welfare has serious, immediate, and very real consequences. Yet they do it anyway.

4.5 Semi-formal organizations in focus

This section looks at semi-formal organizations (organizations from Quadrants 2 and 4 in Figure 4.2). It looks at where you find them, how they work and their role in the world.

4.5.1 Identifying semi-formal organizations

To be classified as "formal," an organization has to pay taxes and social security contributions, participate in government bureaucracies, observe all relevant regulatory frameworks, and the rule of law (ILO, 2012). Semi-formal organizations do some of these things, but not all.

They participate in some elements of government bureaucracy, but not others. They observe some regulations, but not others. They obey some laws, but not others.

Weirdly, and unhelpfully, most organizations in the world—even the really big ones—can actually be considered semi-formal organizations (Williams, 2008). This is quite a big claim, but it reflects the reality that few organizations are either entirely formal or function without input(s) from the informal sector. There are two important points to note here.

The first point to note is that it is fair to say that large organizations are typically more formal than small- and medium-sized organizations. As you'll have seen in Chapters 2 and 3, it is actually quite hard to run a large organization on an informal basis. Informal practices really aren't great in large organizational contexts—they're surprisingly inefficient and are just not very good at motivating, directing, and controlling the efforts of large numbers of people (Kistruck et al., 2015; Assenova & Sorenson, 2017; Williams & Schneider, 2016).

The second point to note is that although large organizations typically operate in formal ways, informality creeps in via their interactions with smaller, less formalized organizations. The most obvious way this happens is when organizations outsource activities to other organizations. Think about this: organizations like the GAP, Apple, and Nike (and many others) do not actually make the products they design and sell (LeBaron, 2014). Manufacturing is subcontracted out to other organizations. This is all great, except what sometimes happens is that while so-called "first tier" subcontractors do some of the work, they sometimes subcontract part of the work to another organization. That organization sometimes does the same again. And so on. This happens to such an extent that manufacturing supply chains can have up to five, and even six layers of subcontracting (Jenkins, 2020). In certain areas of the world, it is estimated that 99% of organizations with a formal outsourcing contract are directly supported by an informal "shadow factory" (LeBaron, 2014).

All this matters because the further down the supply chain you go, the more informal the organizations involved usually are. First-tier subcontractors might operate in a very formalized way, but there is a good chance that much of the work will actually be done by people working in far less formal settings (Phung, 2018; see also Wilson, 2010, p. 342; Stringer & Michailova, 2018).

4.5.2 How semi-formal organizations work

How semi-formal organizations work varies enormously, but is broadly understood to be contingent on calculations about the cost of formalization verses the benefits it delivers (see De Castro et al., 2014). The basic guiding assumption is that organizations will operate in a formal way when there are specific (e.g., economic) benefits associated with doing so. Organizations formalize their operations when they are likely to benefit from things like a functioning legal system, government support programs, and access to markets (Besley & Persson, 2014). If the benefits associated with formalization are limited, an organization is less likely to formalize its operations.

Whilst technically illegal, organizing on an informal basis can make economic sense. As Williams (2019) describes, participating in the formal economy can be very, very expensive. Taxes and social security payments need to be made, complex bureaucracies must be navigated, and legal frameworks have to be observed. Doing these things massively increases the costs of business. Therefore opting out of some or all of these—even if doing so is illegal—can deliver a very low cost base.

Adopting informal practices also enables organizations to be extremely flexible compared to more formal competitors (Portes & Sassen-Koob, 1987). This has positive—if unethical—implications for the organization's ability to compete with others and the costs associated with doing so. Specifically, informal and semi-formal organizations are relatively unconstrained by legislation and bureaucracy and can therefore respond rapidly to change. We're talking hours and days, rather than the months and years that formal organizations can take to change.

Informal organizations can also respond to change very cheaply. If the business environment changes, they can instantly fire workers and not bother with expensive redundancy payments. They can relocate their operations without worrying about tenancy agreements and expensive break-clauses. They can also change their product ranges without having to pay off suppliers for the inconvenience. This obviously isn't great if you work for an informal organization, rent it real estate, or sell it stock (Assenova & Sorenson, 2017); however, what it means is that informal organizations can be incredibly flexible.

An informal or semi-formal organization can theoretically do the same work as a formal organization, but for a much lower price. This is one reason why you get informal and semi-formal organizations that are highly integrated into the formal economy. If an organization can operate an informal business model, but still access the formal marketplace, a lot of money can be made.

4.6 Why informal organizations matter

For the poorest people in the world, informal organizations are vehicles for survival and the alleviation of extreme poverty. For governments, policy makers, and competitors in the formal sector they distort markets and facilitate the exploitation of extremely vulnerable people. These issues are the focus of this section.

4.6.1 Poverty, survival, and the value of informality

Extremely informal organizations, like the illegal marketplace in Mwanza, are incredibly important. They provide goods and services to people not well served by the formal sector, and employment to people who live in circumstances where other means of making a living are not available (Ketchen Jr, et al., 2014).

These positive effects aren't restricted to developing nations. In highly developed nations the informal organizations that comprise the shadow economy support marginalized communities and people in conditions of extreme poverty. For example, it is well documented that migrants (particularly illegal immigrants) in developed nations face significant barriers to entry into the legitimate job market. These include low levels of education, weak language skills, limited country- and industry-specific work experience, and ethnic or racial discrimination (Piperopoulos, 2010).

In this context, informal organizations play two important roles. First, they enable people to support themselves and their families. Second, they provide opportunities to acquire important skills via informal apprenticeships and training (Darbi et al., 2018, p. 306). In effect, the informal sector functions as a kind of platform from which workers can transition into formal organizations, where they will get better pay, benefits, and working conditions (Assenova & Sorenson, 2017).

Reflecting their significance, extremely informal organizations have historically been encouraged in developing nations. As you'll see in the following microfinancing Case Study, governments, NGOs, and major banks have tried to support the poorest in society to set up and run extremely informal and semi-formal organizations. The rationale being that support for these organizations stimulates economic activity and creates jobs that enable people to survive and work their way out of poverty (Autio & Fu, 2015; Bruton et al., 2011; Bruton et al., 2013; Tebaldi & Mohan, 2010).

The informal sector is also increasingly well recognized as a kind of business incubator (Williams & Martinez, 2014a; Musara & Nieuwenhuizen, 2020). The general perception is that the shadow economy gives new businesses the opportunity to test their products and services in a flexible and low-cost way. If everything works out, they can then scale up their operations and (re)organize along more formal lines (Sutter et al., 2017).

In the UK, where I live, it is estimated that one-fifth of all new formal enterprises began life in this way (Williams & Martinez, 2014b). Autio and Fu (2015) suggest that globally, the figure is much higher. They estimate that up to two-thirds of new businesses begin life in the shadow economy (see also Williams & Schneider, 2016, p. 13).

If you think this is an exaggeration, have a read of Steve Job's autobiography. Apple Inc. began life in a small garage in a quiet suburb in Los Altos, USA. Hewlett-Packard (HP) was also founded in a garage (in Palo Alto, USA). Microsoft began life in a garage in Albuquerque. The point is that to begin with all these now massive multinationals were extremely informal enterprises.

4.6.2 Distorted markets and the race to the bottom

For many scholars (e.g., Williams & Schneider, 2016), the positive benefits of the informal economy (e.g., poverty reduction, new business incubation, and the creation of job pathways into the formal economy) do not outweigh its negative effects. For the wider economy and society in general, these negative effects can be significant.

In particular, societies are harmed because informal organizations operate outside of the state. While money earned in the informal economy usually finds its way into the formal economy in the end, informal organizations don't pay taxes or observe important regulatory frameworks. This limits government resources and ultimately their ability to function effectively.

Informal organizations also harm the formal economy because whilst they are fundamentally inefficient (see Assenova & Sorenson, 2017, p. 806), informal organizations' low-cost base often enables them to undercut legitimate, formal organizations. In markets dominated by informal organizations, it is extremely difficult for formal organizations to survive.

To an extent, formal organizations are able to mitigate the lower cost-base of informal organizations by leveraging the benefits of formalization. They can operate on a larger scale and in more efficient ways. They can also access credit, decent real estate, mainstream markets, and the legal system. These are all things informal organizations can't do. However, often this isn't enough, and some formal organizations maintain their profit margins by informalizing their own operations. This happens in two main ways. First, a formal organization might adopt informal practices themselves. For example, by hiring informal laborers instead of legitimate, salaried workers (Jones et al., 2006; Kar & Marjit, 2009). Second, a formal organization may simply give up trying to compete with less formal competitors, and just ask them to do the work for them instead (Wilson, 2010, p. 343).

This second strategy is how work shifts from highly formalized organizations to informal organizations. The same work gets done, but for a much lower cost (Chen, 2005; Holt & Littlewood, 2014). While unethical, and illegal, this strategy enables organizations to achieve a kind of hybrid model and enjoy the benefits of both worlds. That is, the benefits of (apparent) legitimacy (such as unrestricted access to mainstream markets) but without the associated costs and constraints (Karlinger, 2014; Phillips, 2011; Williams & Kosta, 2020).

4.6.3 The human cost of informality

The consequences of informality go far beyond reduced government tax receipts and distorted markets. The cost of informality is highest of all for the people who work in the informal sector (see Slavnic, 2010; Phillips, 2011; Mayer & Phillips, 2017). We're talking about people who are among the poorest, most desperate, and vulnerable in the world.

Ultimately, the low-cost base informal organizations enjoy is achieved through exploitation. Informal workers have little/no job security, and their wages are invariably too low to live on. They also work in what can often be extremely dangerous environments.

In areas where there is high unemployment, informal sector workers' pay and benefits can be too low to live on (Kara, 2014). Indeed, the most recent data available (from 2012) estimates there are 18.7 million people in the world who are paid so little, they are effectively working as slaves in informal organizations. Collectively, their efforts are believed to generate profits in excess of $44 billion USD annually (de Cock & Woode, 2014: 16). For an illustration, see Kara's account of modern slavery in the shrimp and tea farming industries in Bangladesh (Kara, 2017, pp. 103–131). See also Chantavanich et al's. (2016) account of the Thai fishing industry, and LeBaron's (2014) discussion of clothing manufacturing.

Because informal organizations can be hard to see, the risk of extreme forms of exploitation—such as slavery—in global supply chains is believed to be significant (LeBaron, 2014, p. 237). Indeed, it is reported that a key characteristic of slavery in global supply chains is that it occurs primarily in "organizations that are distanced from lead firms through multiple layers of subcontracting" (Phung & Crane, 2018, p. 12; see also Allain et al., 2013, p. 43). In these hidden, unregistered shadow factories, exploitative practices are not an anomaly, but a core part of the business model (Jenkins, 2020, p. 239).

4.7 Summary

This chapter develops the point that organizations are simply collaborations between people who have a degree of planning, complexity, and continuity over time. What it enables you to see is that organizations don't have to have a board of directors, complex bureaucracies, or rigid structure to function. It shows that organizations can (and very often do) function really quite well through fairly loose collaborations based on trust and reciprocity between generally small numbers of people.

This chapter also shows you what informal organizations can look like and how they work. It distinguishes between "extremely informal organizations" and "semi-formal organizations." The former being microenterprises—very, very simple social structures that involve a very small number of people working together. Excellent examples being the loose to extremely loose, but collaborative networks you find organizing and controlling life in things like illegal marketplaces all around the world.

The latter—semi-formal organizations—are presented as an unhelpfully massive group of organizations (potentially most organizations in the world) that to varying degrees incorporate elements of informality into their business model. The important thing to note here is not the pointlessness of the category of "semi-formal organizations," but the sheer extent to which informality permeates and underpins our modern world. The point is that while we distinguish between formal and informal organizations, the reality of the world we live in is much, much messier.

Lastly, what this chapter also shows you is that while informal organizations are everywhere and play a massive role in our world, they are not always the best expression of what humanity is capable of. Informal organizations support livelihoods and enable people to live, but they can also be a vehicle for exploitation. While exploitation can happen in any organization, in informal organizations it can be extreme.

Things to Watch, Things to Read

In this table are suggestions for things you can watch and things you can read to learn more about this topic. I've also included a very short commentary, so that you know why I've recommended a particular source and what to look out for.

Read in two to three hours	Burbidge, D. 2013. Trust creation in the informal economy: The case of plastic bag sellers of Mwanza, Tanzania. *African Sociological Review/Revue Africaine de Sociologie* 17(1), 79–103.
This very interesting article is discussed in more detail in the section of this chapter that looks at extremely informal organizations. The article is an in-depth account of life in an illegal marketplace (called Soko Kuu) in Mwanza, Tanzania. It looks at how the market place works, specifically elaborating on how people build trust between themselves, and in doing so establish a basis for cooperation. It's a fantastic account of how things work in classically informal contexts.	
Read in a day or two	Williams, C. C. 2019. *The Informal Economy*. London: Agenda Publishing.
This is a "key ideas" text written by one of the leading experts in the world on the informal economy. It explains what the informal economy is, what it isn't, and the best way to measure it. It is a good introduction to the topic of informality because it talks you through the informal economy in the context of developed, developing, and transitional economies. The result is that no matter where you are from in the world, you will be able to see the impact the informal economy has on the world around you.	
Read in a week or three	Alcock, G. G. 2015. *Kasinomics: African Informal Economies and the People who Inhabit Them*. Jonathan Ball Publishers.
This is not an academic book. It's written by someone with direct experience of the South African informal economy, the people and organizations that operate within it. It does a fantastic job of bringing to life their stories, and can be read alongside Burbidge (2013).	
Watch in an evening	"*City Rising: The Informal Economy.*" (2018). Retrieved from https://www.imdb.com/title/tt9398244/.

This documentary explores the informal economy in California, USA. It is another great introduction to what the informal economy is. Much like Alcock (2018), it explains why people work in the informal economy and shows you what sort of work they do. A big focus of this episode is street vendors—the informal entrepreneurs we discuss in detail in the section on "extremely informal organizations." However it also focuses on the organizations we discuss in the section on "semi-formal organizations." So, formal, legitimate organizations that incorporate informal practices (such as employing people "off the books") into their business model. As well as being revelatory of what these different types of organizations look like and how they operate in practice, this documentary addresses important critical issues. For example, the legislators who criminalize and persecute vulnerable groups working informally (e.g., street vendors), but fail to act against the corporations exploiting cheap, immigrant laborers working for them informally.

Research Insight: An underground business

Source: Fletcher, A., F. Jamal, N. Fitzgerald-Yau, & C. Bonell. (2014). "We've got some underground business selling junk food:" Qualitative evidence of the unintended effects of English school food policies. *Sociology* 48(3), 500–517.

Edited abstract: the focus of this article is students at six different English secondary schools, and the informal "junk" food markets that exists within them. Most obviously, it provides a very accessible example of the omnipresence of informal markets and the informal organizations that operate within. As such, it reveals how students' formed underground businesses in response to increased state regulation of school food and drink provision. It shows that, as schools clamped down on the vast quantities of sugary, fatty, salty foods students were eating, informal entrepreneurs stepped in to fill the gap. However the study also shows that these informal student entrepreneurs weren't just helping their peers satiate their desire for junk food. The study shows that they were also helping their peers to navigate the challenges of sometimes unruly secondary school life. By selling junk food in school playgrounds and common rooms, these informal student entrepreneurs helped their peers avoid school canteens which they experienced as unsafe and antisocial.

Case Study: Poverty, microfinance, and extremely informal organizations

Based on: Banerjee S. B. & L. Jackson (2017). Microfinance and the business of poverty reduction: Critical perspectives from rural Bangladesh. *Human Relations* 70(1), 63–91.

Introducing microfinance

With origins in 19th century credit cooperatives (Banerjee et al., 1994), rotating saving and credit institutions (Rutherford, 2000; Collins et al., 2009), microfinance (initially called microcredit) is a market-based economic tool designed to help combat poverty by providing small-scale loans to low-income households (Hulme & Arun, 2009; Yunus, 2009).

In the context of microfinance, "small-scale" means loans of between US$25 and US$500. "Low income" means people living on less than US$1.25 to US$2.00 per day. This is the level at which the World Bank defines you as being "extremely poor" and "poor" respectively (Banerjee & Duflo, 2007).

Providers of microfinance specifically target women. The guiding logic is that women are better at repaying loans than men, and that giving them loans is a good way of empowering them to open new businesses or expand existing ones. Microfinance helps the poor by stimulating economic activity, creating jobs, and enabling them to work their way out of poverty (Autio & Fu, 2015; Bruton et al., 2011; Bruton et al., 2013; Tebaldi & Mohan, 2010).

At the heart of the microfinance concept is a so-called "win-win" scenario. Borrowers win because they gain access to credit, and through it the opportunity to improve their social and economic circumstances. Governments, NGOs, and banks win because in giving people the opportunity to help themselves, the cost of poverty to the state is reduced or eliminated. In fact, the whole program is self-sustaining. Interest paid by borrowers covers the cost of providing the loan, and any profits made are then lent to new customers. The result is a virtuous, self-perpetuating cycle of growth-driven poverty alleviation (Yunus, 2009).

The growth of a movement

From its inception in the 1970s, the concept of microfinance has grown from a localized social development strategy in rural Bangladesh, to a global movement involving millions of people around the world (Bateman, 2010; Yunus, 2009). The movement has benefited from immense support, fervor, and celebration. This has come from all areas. From celebrities and monarchs to current and former presidents and prime ministers of countries from around the world. It has also come from major organizations such as the International Monetary Fund (IMF), the World Bank, and United Nations.

In 2006, the founder of the microfinance movement, Dr. Muhammad Yunus, won the Nobel Peace Prize. He got this for showing it is possible to "provide reliable financial services in poor communities, to create workable business models, to reach women especially, and to do so relatively cheaply and at wide scale" (Cull & Morduch, 2017, p. 34). In his acceptance speech, Dr. Yunus proclaimed that within a generation, children would have to go to a "'poverty museum' to find out what all the fuss was about" (Bateman & Chang, 2012, 14).

The last time data was collected and reported in 2010 there were a total of 3,652 microfinance institutions worldwide. Collectively they had 205,314,502 clients. Of these clients, 137,547,441 were among the poorest people in the world. Of these poorest clients, 82.3 %, or 113,138,652, were women. In total, it was estimated that microfinancing had lifted 687.7 million people out of poverty (see Reed et al., 2011). This included 10–15% of the populations of Bangladesh, Mongolia, and Peru (Cull et al., 2014).

The impossible sustainability challenge

Despite global enrapture with the concept of microfinance, enthusiasm for it has been significantly eroded in recent years by growing evidence that it does not actually deliver many of the benefits that are often claimed. In fact, quite the opposite has been found to be true (Karim, 2011).

Since at least 1997, research has shown that microfinance can actually *exacerbate* (rather than alleviate) poverty (Bateman, 2010; Bateman & Chang, 2012). Not only this, investigative journalists have linked microfinance with hundreds of suicides amongst borrowers (Taylor, 2011). They have also shown that desperate borrowers unable to repay their loans have even resorted to selling their own organs in the shadow healthcare economy (Banerjee & Jackson, 2017, p. 64).

Central to the failure of microfinance to deliver its promises is a set of assumptions that Morduch (2000, p. 620) argues "torture both logic and evidence." From the outset, the case for microfinance has been grounded in sustainability—the creation of a virtuous, self-perpetuating cycle where revenues generated from lending cover the costs of providing loans and creates surplus cash that can be reinvested (Ghatak & Guinnane, 1999). However, in practice, the vast majority of institutions running microfinancing programs have never reached this magic break-even point. Rather than turning a profit, most microfinance organizations have remained heavily reliant on the "continuous inflow of subsidized capital" (Bateman & Chang, 2012, p. 15).

The economics behind this reliance is really quite simple. Loaning money to the very poorest people in the world is not a profitable enterprise (Cull & Morduch, 2017). This matters not just because it means someone somewhere, has to cover the losses, but because attempts to make microfinance profitable have had extremely negative consequences for already impoverished people. Specifically, lenders try to compensate for the poor profitability of microfinance by making ever-larger loans and increasing the interest they charge (Hermes & Lensink, 2011). For example, in 2007 the Mexican microfinance provider "Compartamos" charged its borrowers annual interest rates of up to 195% (Bateman & Chang, 2012). Others charged even more.

Even when lenders charge incredibly high interest rates, microfinance generally remains unprofitable. Indeed, subsequent analysis has shown that for many providers of microfinance, it is actually impossible for them to break even (Cull & Morduch, 2017). As interest rates rise, demand for borrowing declines along with borrowers' ability to repay (Dehejia et al., 2012; Karlan & Zinman, 2019). Put simply, people in poverty can't afford loans with interest rates of 195% (Morduch, 1999; Buckley, 1997; see also Armendáriz & Morduch, 2010).

Failing to deliver real-world impact

Research also shows that even when people are able to access relatively "cheap" microfinance (e.g., loans with an interest rate of 39.9%) it does not significantly improve their lives (Angelucci et al., 2015). Research in this area shows that microfinance helps people develop self-employment activities that supplement income (Armendáriz & Morduch, 2010; Roodman, 2012; Banerjee et al., 2015b) but does not create entirely new jobs (Morduch, 1999, p. 1610).

One reason microfinance does not have much impact is because microloans are, very often, not used to develop new and existing businesses. Instead, money from microfinance loans is used by people to simply survive. Families take out loans to pay for food, clothes, and healthcare, rather than to start new businesses or develop existing ones (Banerjee & Jackson, 2017).

Moreover, even in cases where microfinance loans are used to create new and develop existing businesses, studies show that the benefits realized are often extremely limited. It's hard for people to make money in impoverished communities, and income generating activities do not always result in the anticipated benefits. This is particularly the case in agricultural businesses which, historically, have attracted high levels of microfinance loans. For example, in the Indian state of Andhra Pradesh just under 82% of all farmers were in debt by the mid-2000s (Taylor, 2011). Many of these agricultural businesses fail as a consequence of farmers' limited knowledge and understanding of farming, the small scale on which they operate and unanticipated climate events such as droughts or floods.

What often results is borrowers' debt spiralling out of control. When the anticipated revenues fail to materialize, households borrow more money to make loan repayments (Bateman & Chang, 2012, 16). They then borrow yet more money to continue to operate their business in the hope that one day it will succeed (Banerjee & Jackson, 2017, p. 73–74). Alternatively, they deprioritize living expenses (e.g., food and healthcare) in order to make the loan repayments (Hammill et al., 2008). In either scenario, what results is an exacerbation of an already torrid situation. Poverty is compounded, rather than alleviated.

It has also been found that while loans are primarily granted to women, they are rarely the actual beneficiaries. In as much as 95% of cases the money borrowed by women is taken from them by their husbands or male family members (Karim, 2008). Yet, when repayments must be made, and in the event of default, it is the women who is held liable for the debt both financially and socially. The indicators are that microfinance does little to empower women.

The future of microfinance

Despite the almost hysterical acclaim heaped on the microfinance movement, particularly during the late 1990s and early 2000s (e.g., Pitt & Khandker, 1998), it is now well recognized that microfinance is not the magic, market-based solution to global poverty that it was initially claimed to be. There are people who benefit from microfinance, but there aren't many of them. Indeed, most of the impressive claims made by proponents of the movement have been shown to be inaccurate, sometimes wildly exaggerating the benefits, and down-playing or ignoring its negative consequences (Duvendack & Palmer-Jones, 2012; Duvendack et al., 2011). The reality is that there are only a very, very limited number of situations in which people benefit from microfinance (Banerjee et al., 2015a).

Yet, providers of microfinance continue to endure despite frequent "sub-prime style microfinance meltdowns taking place around the globe" (Bateman & Chang, 2012, p. 16); examples of this are found in Bolivia in 1999, in Morocco, Pakistan, and Nicaragua in 2008, in Bosnia in 2009, and India in 2010. Organizations such as Compartamos in Mexico still operate, apparently continuing to provide investors with 53% returns on investment by charging borrowers interest on loans that still exceeds 100%.

There have been changes, though. Major organizations have quietly backed away from the microfinance movements and their more extreme claims are beginning to be moderated. For example, the key promise that microfinance will alleviate poverty, relegating it to the history books and dusty corridors of museums seems to have gone. In its place are a new set of claims that microfinance is all about financial inclusiveness: providing poor people with access to credit, not access to *cheap* credit (Morduch, 2000, p. 620).

Questions

1. Why did Dr. Muhammad Yunus win the Nobel Peace Prize?
2. Drawing on what you've learnt in this chapter, explain why people thought microfinancing for extremely informal organizations was a good idea?
3. Why did microfinancing fail to deliver its promised benefits?
4. Do you think microfinancing could be made to work? If so, how? If not, why not?

References

Alcock, G. (2018). *KasiNomic Revolution: The Rise of the African Informal Economy*. South Africa: Jonathan Ball Publishers.

Allain, J., A. Crane, G. LeBaron, et al. (2013). *Forced Labour's Business Models and Supply Chains*. York: Joseph Rowntree Foundation.

Anderson, S., J-M. Baland, & K. O. Moene. (2009). Enforcement in informal saving groups. *Journal of Development Economics* 90(1), 14–23.

Angelucci, M., D. Karlan, & J. Zinman. (2015). Microcredit impacts: Evidence from a randomized microcredit program placement experiment by Compartamos Banco. *American Economic Journal: Applied Economics* 7(1), 151–182.

Armendáriz, B. & J. Morduch. (2010). *The Economics of Microfinance*. Cambridge: MIT Press.

Assenova, V. A. & O. Sorenson. (2017). Legitimacy and the benefits of firm formalization. *Organization Science* 28(5), 804–818.

Autio, E. & K. Fu. (2015). Economic and political institutions and entry into formal and informal entrepreneurship. *Asia Pacific Journal of Management* 32(1), 67–94.

Banerjee, A., E. Duflo, R. Glennerster, et al. (2015a). The miracle of microfinance? Evidence from a randomized evaluation. *American Economic Journal: Applied Economics* 7(1), 22–53.

Banerjee, A., D. Karlan, & J. Zinman. (2015b). Six randomized evaluations of microcredit: Introduction and further steps. *American Economic Journal: Applied Economics* 7(1), 1–21.

Banerjee, A. V., T. Besley, & T. W. Guinnane. (1994). Thy neighbor's keeper: The design of a credit cooperative with theory and a test. *The Quarterly Journal of Economics* 109(2), 491–515.

Banerjee, A. V. & E. Duflo. (2007). The economic lives of the poor. *Journal of Economic Perspectives* 21(1), 141–168.

Banerjee, S. B. & L. Jackson. (2017). Microfinance and the business of poverty reduction: Critical perspectives from rural Bangladesh. *Human Relations* 70(1), 63–91.

Barrick, K., P. K. Lattimore, W. J. Pitts, et al. (2014). Labor trafficking victimization among farmworkers in North Carolina: Role of demographic characteristics and acculturation. *International Journal of Rural Criminology* 2(2), 225–243.

Barrientos, S. W. (2013). "Labour chains": Analysing the role of labour contractors in global production networks. *The Journal of Development Studies* 49(8), 1058–1071.

Bateman, M. (2010). *Why Doesn't Microfinance Work?: The Destructive Rise of Local Neoliberalism*. London: Zed Books Ltd.

Bateman, M. & H-J. Chang. (2012). Microfinance and the illusion of development: From hubris to nemesis in thirty years. *World Economic Review* 1, 13–26.

Besley, T. & T. Persson. (2014). Why do developing countries tax so little? *Journal of Economic Perspectives* 28(4), 99–120.

Bhowmik, S. K. (2010). *Street vendors in Asia: Survey of research. Street Vendors in the Global Urban Economy*. London: Routledge.

Biles, J. J. (2009). Informal work in Latin America: Competing perspectives and recent debates. *Geography Compass* 3(1), 214–236.

Bonnet, F., J. Vanek, & M. Chen. (2019). Women and men in the informal economy: A statistical brief. Geneva: International Labour Office. Retrieved from http://www.wiego.org/sites/default/files/publications/files/Women% 20and% 20Men% 20in% 20the% 20Informal 20.

Breman, J. (1976). A dualistic labour system? A critique of the "informal sector" concept: I: The informal sector. *Economic and Political Weekly* 11(48), 1870–1876.

Bruton, G. D., D. J. Ketchen Jr, & R. D. Ireland. (2013). Entrepreneurship as a solution to poverty. *Journal of Business Venturing* 28(6), 683–689.

Bruton, G. D., S. Khavul, & H. Chavez. (2011). Microlending in emerging economies: Building a new line of inquiry from the ground up. *Journal of International Business Studies* 42(5), 718–739.

Buckley, G. (1997). Microfinance in Africa: Is it either the problem or the solution? *World Development* 25(7), 1081–1093.

Burbidge, D. (2013). Trust creation in the informal economy: The case of plastic bag sellers of Mwanza, Tanzania. *African Sociological Review/Revue Africaine de Sociologie* 17(1), 79–103.

Chantavanich, S., S. Laodumrongchai, & C. Stringer. (2016). Under the shadow: Forced labour among sea fishers in Thailand. *Marine Policy* 68, 1–7.

Chen, M. (2005). *Rethinking the Informal Economy: Linkages with the Formal Economy and the Formal Regulatory Environment*. Harvard: WIDER Research Paper.

Collins, D., J. Morduch, S. Rutherford, et al. (2009). *Portfolios of the Poor: How the World's Poor Live on $2 a Day*. Princeton: Princeton University Press.

Cull, R., A. Demirgüç-Kunt, & J. Morduch. (2014). Banks and microbanks. *Journal of Financial Services Research* 46(1), 1–53.

Cull, R. and J. Morduch. (2017). *Microfinance and Economic Development*. The World Bank. Retrieved from https://openknowledge.worldbank.org/server/api/core/bitstreams/611fc6f2-140b-551e-9371-468eec64c552/content.

Darbi, W. P. K., C. M. Hall, & P. Knott. (2018). The informal sector: A review and agenda for management research. *International Journal of Management Reviews* 20(2), 301–324.

De Castro, J. O., S. Khavul, & G. D. Bruton. (2014). Shades of grey: How do informal firms navigate between macro and meso institutional environments? *Strategic Entrepreneurship Journal* 8(1), 75–94.

de Cock, M. & M. Woode. (2014). Profits and poverty: The economics of forced labour. Report published by the International Labor Organization.

Dehejia, R., H. Montgomery, & J. Morduch. (2012). Do interest rates matter? Credit demand in the Dhaka slums. *Journal of Development Economics* 97(2), 437–449.

Duneier, M. & O. Carter. (1999). *Sidewalk*. New York: Macmillan.

Duvendack, M. & R. Palmer-Jones. (2012). High noon for microfinance impact evaluations: Re-Investigating the evidence from Bangladesh. *The Journal of Development Studies* 48(12), 1864–1880.

Duvendack, M., R. Palmer-Jones, J. G. Copestake, et al. (2011). What is the evidence of the impact of microfinance on the well-being of poor people?: EPPI-Centre, Social Science Research Unit, Institute of Education. Retrieved from https://eppi.ioe.ac.uk/CMS/Portals/0/PDF%20reviews%20and%20summaries/Microfiannce-ST%20-%20IITM2.pdf.

Flaming, D., B. Haydamack, & P. Joassart-Marcelli. (2005). Hopeful workers, marginal jobs: LA's off-the-books labor force.

Fletcher, A., F. Jamal, N. Fitzgerald-Yau, et al. (2014). "We've got some underground business selling junk food": Qualitative evidence of the unintended effects of English school food policies. *Sociology* 48(3), 500–517.

Ghatak, M. & T. W. Guinnane. (1999). The economics of lending with joint liability: Theory and practice. *Journal of Development Economics* 60(1), 195–228.

Hammill, A., R. Matthew, & E. McCarter. (2008). Microfinance and climate change adaptation. *IDS Bulletin* 39(4), 113–122.

Hartman, T. (2008). States, markets, and other unexceptional communities: Informal Romanian labour in a Spanish agricultural zone. *Journal of the Royal Anthropological Institute* 14(3), 496–514.

Henderson, J. C. (2010). Cooked food hawking and its management: The case of Singapore. *Tourism Review International* 14(4), 201–213.

Hermes, N. & R. Lensink. (2011). Microfinance: Its impact, outreach, and sustainability. *World Development* 39(6), 875–881.

Holt, D. and D. Littlewood. (2014). The informal economy as a route to market in sub-Saharan Africa, observations amongst Kenyan informal economy entrepreneurs. In S. Nwanko and K. Ibeh (eds.), *The Routledge Companion to Business in Africa*, 198–217. London: Routledge.

Hulme, D. & T. Arun. (2009). *Microfinance: A Reader*. London: Routledge.

ILO D. (2012). Statistical update on employment in the informal economy.

Imbens, G. W. (2014). International Labor Organization - Department of Statistic Report. Instrumental variables: An econometricians perspective.

Jenkins, J. (2020). Struggle in the garment sector. *Theory & Struggle* 121(1), 68–78.

Jones, T., M. Ram, & P. Edwards. (2006). Shades of grey in the informal economy. *International Journal of Sociology and Social Policy* 26(9/10), 357–373.

Kar, S. & S. Marjit. (2009). Urban informal sector and poverty. *International Review of Economics & Finance* 18(4), 631–642.

Kara, S. (2014). *Bonded Labor: Tackling the System of Slavery in South Asia*. New York: Columbia University Press.

Kara, S. (2017). *Modern Slavery: A Global Perspective*. New York: Columbia University Press.

Karim, L. (2008). Demystifying micro-credit: The Grameen Bank, NGOs, and neoliberalism in Bangladesh. *Cultural Dynamics* 20(1), 5–29.

Karim, L. (2011). *Microfinance and its Discontents: Women in Debt in Bangladesh*. Minneapolis: University of Minnesota Press.

Karlan, D. & J. Zinman. (2019). Long-run price elasticities of demand for credit: Evidence from a countrywide field experiment in Mexico. *The Review of Economic Studies* 86(4), 1704–1746.

Karlinger, L. (2014). The "dark side" of deregulation: How competition affects the size of the shadow economy. *Journal of Public Economic Theory* 16(2), 293–321.

Ketchen, Jr, D. J., R. D. Ireland, & J. W. Webb. (2014). Toward a research agenda for the informal economy: A survey of the Strategic Entrepreneurship Journal's Editorial Board. *Strategic Entrepreneurship Journal* 8(1), 95–100.

Kistruck, G. M., J. W. Webb, C. J. Sutter, et al. (2015). The double-edged sword of legitimacy in base-of-the-pyramid markets. *Journal of Business Venturing* 30(3), 436–451.

LeBaron, G. (2014). Subcontracting is not illegal, but is it unethical? Business ethics, forced labor, and economic success. *The Brown Journal of World Affairs* 20(2), 237–249.

Llewellyn, N. & R. Burrow. (2008). Streetwise sales and the social order of city streets. *The British Journal of Sociology* 59(3), 561–583.

Martinez, G., S. A. McCord, C. T. Driscoll, et al. (2018). Mercury contamination in riverine sediments and fish associated with artisanal and small-scale gold mining in Madre de Dios, Peru. *International Journal of Environmental Research and Public Health* 15(8), 1584.

Mayer, F. W. & N. Phillips. (2017). Outsourcing governance: States and the politics of a "global value chain world." *New Political Economy* 22(2), 134–152.

Medina, L. & F. Schneider. (2018). Shadow economies around the world: What did we learn over the last 20 years? Retrieved from The International Monetary

Fund https://www.imf.org/en/Publications/WP/Issues/2018/01/25/Shadow-Economies-Around-the-World-What-Did-We-Learn-Over-the-Last-20-Years-45583.

Morduch, J. (1999). The microfinance promise. *Journal of Economic Literature* 37(4), 1569–1614.

Morduch, J. (2000). The microfinance schism. *World Development* 28(4), 617–629.

Muñoz, L. (2008). *"Tamales ... elotes ... champurrado ...:" The Production of Latino Vending Landscapes in Los Angeles.* Los Angeles: University of Southern California.

Musara, M. & C. Nieuwenhuizen. (2020). Informal sector entrepreneurship, individual entrepreneurial orientation and the emergence of entrepreneurial leadership. *Africa Journal of Management* 6(3), 194–213.

Perry, G. E., O. Arias, P. Fajnzylber, et al. (2007). *Informality: Exit and Exclusion.* The World Bank.

Phillips, N. (2011). Informality, global production networks and the dynamics of "adverse incorporation." *Global Networks* 11(3), 380–397.

Phung, K. (2018). Slavery and its links to organizations. In Ronald J. Burke and Cary L. Cooper (eds.) *Violence and Abuse in and around Organisations,* 273–291.

Phung, K. & A. Crane (2018). The business of modern slavery: Management and organizational perspectives. In *The SAGE Handbook of Human Trafficking and Modern-Day Slavery,* 177–197. London, UK: Sage.

Piperopoulos, P. (2010). Ethnic minority businesses and immigrant entrepreneurship in Greece. *Journal of Small Business and Enterprise Development* 17(1), 139–158.

Pitt, M. M. & S. R. Khandker. (1998). The impact of group-based credit programs on poor households in Bangladesh: Does the gender of participants matter? *Journal of Political Economy* 106(5), 958–996.

Portes, A. & S. Sassen-Koob.(1987). Making it underground: Comparative material on the informal sector in Western market economies. *American Journal of Sociology* 93(1), 30–61.

Potts, D. (2008). The urban informal sector in Sub-Saharan Africa: From bad to good (and back again?). *Development Southern Africa* 25(2), 151–167.

Reed, L. R., J. Marsden, A. Ortega, et al. (2011). State of the Microcredit Summit Campaign Report 2011. Washington DC: Microcredit Summit Campaign.

Roodman, D. (2012). *Due Diligence: An Impertinent Inquiry into Microfinance.* Washington: Brookings Institution Press, Centre for Global Development.

Rutherford, S. (2000). *The Poor and Their Money.* New Delhi: Oxford University Press.

Slavnic, Z. (2010). Political economy of informalization. *European Societies* 12(1), 3–23.

Stringer, C. & S. Michailova. (2018). Why modern slavery thrives in multinational corporations' global value chains. *Multinational Business Review* 26(3), 194–206.

Sutter, C., J. Webb, G. Kistruck, et al. (2017). Transitioning entrepreneurs from informal to formal markets. *Journal of Business Venturing* 32(4), 420–442.

Taylor, M. (2011). "Freedom from poverty is not for free": Rural development and the microfinance crisis in Andhra Pradesh, India. *Journal of Agrarian Change* 11(4), 484–504.

Tebaldi, E. & R. Mohan. (2010). Institutions and poverty. *The Journal of Development Studies* 46(6), 1047–1066.

Varcin, R. (2000). Competition in the informal sector of the economy: The case of market traders in Turkey. *International Journal of Sociology and Social Policy* 20(3/4), 5–33.

Wells, J. (2001). Construction and capital formation in less developed economies: Unravelling the informal sector in an African city. *Construction Management & Economics* 19(3), 267–274.

Williams, C. & B. Kosta. (2020). Evaluating the impact of informal sector competitors on the performance of formal enterprises: Evidence from Bosnia and Herzegovina. *Journal of Developmental Entrepreneurship* 25(02), 2050014.

Williams, C. & A. Martinez. (2014a). Is the informal economy an incubator for new enterprise creation? A gender perspective. *International Journal of Entrepreneurial Behavior & Research* 20(1), 4–19.

Williams, C. C. (2008). *The Hidden Enterprise Culture: Entrepreneurship in the Underground Economy*. Cheltenham: Edward Elgar Publishing.

Williams, C. C. (2019). *The Informal Economy*. Newcastle upon Tyne: Agenda Publishing.

Williams, C. C. & A. Martinez. (2014b). Do small business start-ups test-trade in the informal economy? Evidence from a UK survey. *International Journal of Entrepreneurship and Small Business* 22(1), 1–16.

Williams, C. C. & F. Schneider. (2016). *Measuring the Global Shadow Economy: The Prevalence of Informal Work and Labour*. Cheltenham: Edward Elgar Publishing.

Wilson, T. D. (2010). An introduction to the study of informal economies. *Urban Anthropology and Studies of Cultural Systems and World Economic Development* 39(4), 341–357.

World Bank Report. (2020). Poverty and Shared Prosperity 2020: Reversals of Fortune. Retrieved from https://openknowledge.worldbank.org/server/api/core/bitstreams/611fc6f2-140b-551e-9371-468eec64c552/content.

Yunus, M. (2009). *Creating a World Without Poverty: Social Business and the Future of Capitalism*. New York: Public Affairs.

Zhang, S. X., M. W. Spiller, B. K. Finch, et al. (2014). Estimating labor trafficking among unauthorized migrant workers in San Diego. *The Annals of the American Academy of Political and Social Science* 653(1), 65–86.

5
Criminal Organizations

> **Keywords**
>
> Bureaucracy; motivation/commitment; secrecy; fraternity; violence; dynamic capabilities; cooperation

> **Consider**
>
> How do criminals organize?

5.1 Introduction

In this chapter, I'm going to talk to you about organizations that operate in illicit markets. It is all about the *criminal* organizations. These are the organizations that provide illegal goods and services that society prohibits but consumes anyway.

The point of this chapter is to give you the organizational story behind things we see on the news all the time. Things like Peruvian cocaine turning up in sleepy Welsh fishing villages; Syrian migrants dying in shipping containers in ports around Europe; illegally logged Ukrainian wood infiltrating the supply chains of "sustainably sourced" Swiss furniture; German-made guns being fired by Da'esh fighters at American soldiers in Iraq, and so on.

These things don't happen by chance. It takes a criminal organization to make and move cocaine around the world; to traffic people from one country to another; to log protected forests and push the wood into the supply chains of legitimate businesses; to procure guns and sell them to terrorists. In the pages that follow, I'll outline how these organizations work. I'll talk about how illicit businesses are structured, interact, and survive in contexts where they are specifically prohibited. I'll also talk about why they matter and where they "fit" in our world.

Don't make the mistake of thinking this chapter is a celebration of criminal organizations. It's not. Sure, they're intriguing from a scientific perspective, but they do the world few favors. Criminal organizations are not romantic, victimless enterprises run by charming, sexy rogues. They are vicious, brutal vehicles for greed and destruction that bring suffering, destitution, and death to countless millions. They are one of the worst examples of what humanity is capable of.

5.2 What are criminal organizations?

When thinking about criminal organizations there are two main things to keep in mind. First, what constitutes a crime varies between countries. As a consequence, what constitutes a criminal organization varies between countries. For example, prostitution is illegal in China. Chinese brothels are criminal organizations. However, in Switzerland prostitution is legal. Swiss brothels are allowed and regulated and have been since 1942. Prostitutes pay taxes, take credit cards as payment, and operate in a free and open way.

The second thing to keep in mind relates to the point at which crime actually becomes organized. When I talk about criminal organizations, I'm referring to organizations that are defined by a degree of planning, complexity, and continuity over time. I'm talking about purposeful collaborations between people with the aim of making money from a particular illicit activity or range of illicit activities. So, organized criminal business, not spontaneous acts of crime.

In very basic terms, a man working on his own as a prostitute in China isn't a criminal organization no matter how good he is. However, a group of women running a brothel in China using men trafficked in from America would be a criminal organization. Acting collectively—that is, in an organized way—is the crucial distinction.

5.3 Why learn about criminal organizations?

As with the chapter on informal organizations, it might seem strange for me to talk to you about criminal organizations. Again, it's unlikely that when you graduate from your degree, you're going to be seeking out work in a criminal organization. However, there are at least three very good reasons why it's important to study criminal organizations:

(1) **Size**. The criminal economy is massive. It's nothing as big as the informal economy, but if there was a country that was home to all the criminal organizations in the world, it would be in the G20. That is, it would be one of the top 20 economies in the world, with an annual gross domestic product (GDP) of $2.1 trillion USD (Dahl, 2012). That's $2,100,000,000,000 or 3.6% of global GDP. What this means is that if you want to understand how things work in the "real world" then you have to think about criminal organizations.
(2) **Integration**. Even in the most sanguine, sanitized societies on this planet most people's lives are regularly touched by the work of criminal organizations. This will be true even if you don't realize it. Before you get too indignant, think about it. Can you honestly tell me you've never had anything to do with a criminal organization? How do you know? You probably haven't traded a kidney on the black market, but I wonder whether you've ever bought something illegal, like drugs? Consider this: in their 2020 World Drug Report, the UN estimates that 269 million people around the world used illegal drugs in 2018 (30% more than in 2009). That's 5.3 people in every 100 globally. If there are 200 people in a lecture theatre (which is a relatively small lecture theatre), have 10 or 11 used drugs recently?

Alternatively, what about bribes? Have you ever paid a bribe—even unwittingly? What about fake goods? Have you ever bought cheap cigarettes smuggled in from low-duty customs areas? What about fake clothes, wallets, watches, or handbags—ever bought any of those? If you're answering "no" to all the previous suggestions, then have you ever bought a smart phone, an impossibly cheap piece of clothing, or perhaps an expensive handmade rug? If you have, then you may potentially have bought something that was either partly or entirely made by a modern slave. By which, I mean someone working in conditions of severe, inescapable exploitation (see Crane, 2013, pp. 50–51).

I'll elaborate; mobile phones contain a rare-earth mineral called cobalt. More than 50% of the global supply of cobalt is mined in the Democratic Republic of the Congo (DRC), central Africa. It is mined by a workforce that includes approximately 40,000 children working as modern-day slaves (Amnesty International, 2016). The cobalt these children mine regularly infiltrates legitimate supply chains and ends up being used in smart phones and other technology by companies such as Apple, Samsung, and LG (Kelly, 2019).

(3) **Impact**. The third reason you should study criminal organizations is because they have a huge, but often overlooked, impact on our day-to-day lives. Every day many things that we do are constrained by systems designed to catch criminal organizations, identify their work or just make their life harder. We can't cross a border without being interrogated by a customs official on the lookout for smugglers. We can't open a bank account without participating in a complex bureaucracy designed to catch money launderers. We can't sit an exam without encountering systems designed to catch people trying to cheat the system. These are just the obvious things, but the point is that criminal organizations are all around us, and they have a big effect on how the world works.

5.4 How criminal organizations work

The uniqueness of how criminal organizations work is rooted in the pressing need for them to operate in near-total secrecy (Abadinsky, 2012; Baccara & Bar-Isaac, 2008). The importance of this incredibly obvious point cannot be overstated. This is because secrecy gives rise to some very specific organizational challenges. Secrecy shapes absolutely every aspect of how criminal organizations work.

Think about it: How do you run an organization when you can't talk openly to anyone about anything? How do you get things done when you don't even know who else is in the team? How do you maintain standards and effectiveness when nothing is ever formalized or written down? How do you keep people committed to the organization and maintain trust between them? How do you enforce contracts when you can't sue someone who reneges on their side of the deal?

The simple truth is that all of these things are incredibly difficult in criminal organizations. People smugglers can't write strategies, set budgets, or produce annual accounts for investors. Mafia middle-managers can't scroll through a process manual on the intranet, nor can they email human resources (HR) for advice about recruitment. Nor can they seek legal advice about how to resolve a contract dispute. Basically, any kind of recourse to or reliance on formality or legal structures is not an option. Criminal organizations operate outside of the frameworks and infrastructure that support and enable legitimate organizations to do business.

Before you feel too much sympathy for our hard-working, stressed-out crime bosses, keep in mind that despite everything, criminal organizations do work. Some of these work really quite well—staggeringly so, in fact. The criminal organization set up by the American George Jung to smuggle Colombian cocaine to the USA in the 1980s made profits in the region of $3 to $5 million USD per day (Porter, 2014). Currently the Calabrian mafia organization, the 'Ndrangheta, is believed to have an annual turnover of €53 billion and profits in the region of €40 billion (Tondo, 2021). If that's true, they're earning the equivalent of 3.5% of Italy's entire GDP, and are one of the country's biggest employers, with around 60,000 people on the books (albeit across 30 different countries). They're bigger than Deutsche Bank and McDonald's combined, and they've been in business since the 15th century. That's pretty impressive for an organization that doesn't legally exist or have any official offices or employees.

These aren't the only organized crime groups doing well either. In fact, it is generally understood that criminal organizations are so effective at what they do globally, we're not actually winning any of the wars on illicit markets. In some cases, we're actually losing so badly that we've given up. There was a reason why America's disastrous early 20th century prohibition on alcohol was reversed 13 years after it was introduced. That reversal had more to do with the estimated $3.25 billion USD it cost the American economy than changing attitudes towards Jack Daniels and other libations (Vitaliano, 2015). More recently, in Canada, the poor success rate and high cost of policing the illicit market in marijuana was one of the major factors driving its decriminalization. The cost-benefit ratio was simply stacked the wrong way. The link between smoking marijuana and diseases such as schizophrenia didn't disappear (Volkow, Baler, Compton, & Weiss, 2014), but the organizations smuggling weed into Canada were simply impossible to beat.

According to the United Nations Office on Drugs and Crimes, the sad and simple reality is that more drugs are being sold and people being smuggled, trafficked, and enslaved by criminal organizations than ever before. The same is true of wildlife, timber, and small arms. There is more poaching, illegal logging, and guns that are being sold now than at any point in our history. So, if organizing crime is so hard, how are these organizations so successful?

5.5 The rule of 21

At the heart of criminal organizations' success is a unique ability to operate in the shadows and respond rapidly to change. They are very good at maintaining secrecy, and when the business environment shifts, they are extremely effective at reconfiguring operations to respond to setbacks and take advantage of new opportunities.

At the heart of this "dynamic capability"—meaning the organization's "ability to integrate, build, and reconfigure internal and external competencies to address rapidly changing environments" (Eisenhardt & Martin, 2000)—is a surprising fact. Most criminal organizations aren't actually that big—and if they are big, they are very, very decentralized.

Analysis by Eck and Gersh (2000) of organized crime in the Washington-Baltimore area of the USA shows that most criminal organizations have fewer than five people in them. Twenty-one is usually the absolute maximum. To put that into context, that's less than a typical university tutorial group. So next time you're in a tutorial, take a look around. The size of your class is about the same size as a typical criminal organization. Criminal organizations are more like cottage enterprises than globalized multinationals.

Why so small? Well, think about the environmental conditions criminals operate in. What are the challenges created by this environment? Can they maintain secrecy? This drives small-scale organizing in two major ways. First, big, all-powerful criminal organizations make great TV, but struggle to survive in illicit business. The reason for this is that they're just not very secret. The less secret a criminal organization is, the more likely it is to be targeted by law enforcement agencies.

When it comes to criminal organizations, keeping things small is a great survival strategy. Fewer people means fewer potential informants. Fewer potential informants mean a smaller chance of being caught. When it comes to crime, big organizations are the exact opposite of what is needed. Big organizations attract a lot of attention, and when that happens, everyone goes to prison. For an illustration of the merits of staying small watch the movie *Layer Cake*, directed by Matthew Vaughn. Pay attention to Daniel Craig's performance as the protagonist and the frustration expressed every time he's forced to do something that draws attention to himself.

A second reason criminal organizations are so small is because large organizations need economies of scale to survive. This is incredibly difficult to achieve in the illicit markets. The competition is (literally) fierce, and criminal organizations simply can't develop markets and cultivate a body of loyal customers. There are no corporate logos or smooth websites sporting confidence-inspiring reviews. There are also no televised celebrity product launches or marketing offensives to drum up sales. You can't compete for customers. All these things are not possible; however, the payoff is the ability to function relatively quietly. The organization will never achieve high levels of market control, but nor will it get unwanted attention.

Small organizations are not just a sensible, risk-management strategy for criminals sensitive to their PR footprint and with an eye on career longevity. It is technically very difficult to run an organization that is truly committed to secrecy. Secrecy requires organizations to be set up and run in very particular ways (Grey, 2012) and creates obstacles to efficient organizing (Baccara & Bar-Isaac, 2008). One of these obstacles is the inability to write anything down. This matters because bureaucracy, as you will see in Chapter 6, is one of the pillars of big, modern organizations. No bureaucracy, and you're back in the stone ages.

The absence of bureaucracy makes it very difficult for a criminal organization to grow past a certain point. This is because it's simply impossible to keep track of everything. Crime bosses and their lackies can't communicate effectively, and they struggle to govern themselves effectively. For example, at one point it took a cryptic conversation about toothache before Sicilian Mafiosi could even be sure they were talking to another member of the same organization (Dickie, 2005; Gambetta, 2011). If it's that hard to check who you're talking to, imagine how hard it is to organize a decent extortion racket.

Similarly, systems of governance might not sound particularly interesting, but you try organizing something without either a record-keeping system or any kind of rules for how to do things. Passing information by word of mouth, storing everything in your brain, and making things up as you go along really limits what you can do. The solution is a small, simple organization that is easy to run.

These multiple effects of secrecy means that criminal organizations running a full-service "end-to-end" operation (e.g., making, moving, and selling all their own drugs) tend to be quite rare. In the illicit markets, there is a tendency for organizations to specialize in particular things (Bichler, Malm, & Cooper, 2017). One organization will make drugs, another will move them. One organization will sell drugs, another will launder the proceeds. And so on.

Paradoxically, this state of relative disorganization (Reuter, 1983) is one of the reasons why illicit markets are so resilient to attempts to disrupt them. The reality is that small, simple organizations can be rebuilt or replaced very, very quickly. So, if one organization gets busted it's easy for a new one to form and step in to fill the gap.

At this point you might be thinking about large-scale criminal organizations, such as the Mafia. These types of criminal organization can form, but really only in very particular kinds of environments. Large-scale criminal organizations need a geopolitical context where state institutions (e.g., the police and judiciary) are weak (or have historically been weak). In these places, criminal organizations can establish secure bases and project their power to other areas of the world.

However, even in places where the environment is right, it is still hard for large scale criminal organizations to exist. Globally large-scale, highly centralized criminal organizations might be the darlings of Hollywood, but they are the exception not the rule. Moreover, studies of these organizations have shown that virtually none of them function as homogenous, highly centralized organizations with a sharp hierarchical pyramid. They might be very good at what they do, but there isn't really a criminal equivalent of Toyota, Hyundai, or Ford (Catino, 2019; Hill, 2003). Criminal organizations are small and hierarchically very flat, and this makes them very hard to see and very, very agile.

This might seem hard to believe because we know there are some big-brand criminal organizations out there—like the 'Ndrangheta I mentioned earlier. However research suggests that most of these are made up of lots of smaller, relatively independent groups (Paoli, 2002; Paoli, Greenfield, & Reuter, 2009; Reuter, 1983). They are actually cartels—networks of quite small organizations working together using the same trademark. You can think about them as a kind of franchise, a bit like McDonald's or Costa Coffee. They're small organizations operating under the same umbrella, paying fees, and following the direction of an overarching boss.

Perhaps the most well-known criminal cartels are those that operate in Colombia (the Medellin and Cali cartels) and Mexico (the Sinaloa, Jalisco New Generation, Gulf, and Los Zetas Cartels). All are dominant players in the North American drugs market and have traditionally been thought of as highly centralized organizations.

This assumption was actually a myth which lasted far longer than it should have, in part because it gave crime agencies a single target to focus on; however, over time it gradually became clear that all these groups were in fact made up of quite vague, flexible collaborations between large numbers of family-based firms. These operated under the same banner, but were in fact quite separate organizations (Thoumi, 1995, p. 142).

Much the same was found to be true of Mafia groups in Europe. The Calabrian 'Ndrangheta and Sicilian Cosa Nostra are not highly centralized organizations, but hierarchically flat criminal holding companies, comprising about 90 separate families, each conducting business independently within a particular geographical area.

5.6 Cooperation in criminal organizations

One of the most intriguing questions about criminal organizations concerns the basis on which members will cooperate with each other. How do you cooperate when you don't trust someone? If you remember the "Introduction," you'll recall that cooperation sits at the very core of what an organization is: organizations are patterns of cooperation linked to a particular purpose that endure over time. So, how do you foster that cooperation in a criminal organization? How do you bind people together and channel their energy in a particular direction?

One obvious answer is money. Time and effort is bought and sold in a criminal organization in much the same way as it is in any other kind of organization (more on this in Chapter 8). Sure, criminals don't get a contract, pension, or payslip, but they also don't work for free. Criminals want payment. Much like I do, and much like you probably do, as well.

However, money isn't the only thing that motivates people. We know this and have known for years—at least since the 1920s—when Elton Mayo started messing around with factory lighting levels as part of the Hawthorne Studies (Hassard, 2012). People will cooperate and work enthusiastically together for a huge number of different reasons.

We'll discuss this more in Chapter 8, but for now it's enough to know that in legitimate organizations, we agree to cooperate with others when we sign a contract of employment. We literally sign up to work for the organization. We'll also work for an organization because we like what it does or stands for, and because our job gives us something interesting to do. If we're lucky we'll get to work with nice people. That helps. If we're *super* lucky the organization might even do things like pay for the office Christmas party or a raucous team away-day to help cement our relationships with colleagues. All these sort of things (and others) have a bearing on our commitment to an organization and how much effort we put into our work.

So how does it work in a criminal organization? Do you see giggling criminal middle-managers in wetsuits building rafts on team-building away-days? Maybe, but as far as the research goes, there are two main things that bind criminal organizations together. The **first** is kinship. Not just the genealogical-kind, but the social kind as well. By this, I mean fraternity centered on quasi-spiritual, lifelong pacts of commitment to the organization. The **second** is violence.

5.7 Ritualized fraternity and cooperation in criminal organization

Ritualized fraternity, by which I mean quasi-spiritual, life-long pacts of commitment, is actually quite a common basis for cooperation between people all over the world (Marshall, 2002). It's not new either. It's been around for centuries (Bell, 1997). In times past, ritualized fraternity in one form or another bound groups as diverse as pious monks, crusading knights, and trade guilds. In modern contexts we see the same basic social mechanisms in action everywhere—from the ritualized investiture of fresh-faced boy scouts, to communities of alcohol-fueled, cocaine-snorting city professionals for whom outrageous antics are a necessary rite of passage in the journey towards social acceptance (Anderson, 2010; Belfort, 2011).

So, when we talk about fraternity what we mean are the rituals people participate in to gain entry into a valued social group. Things like graduation ceremonies, the swearing of Hippocratic oaths, and military "passing out" parades. Also boozy sports clubs or college fraternity initiations where misbehavior and humiliation is a fundamental rite of passage into the group. If you've never had to endure one of these latter types, you'll get an idea of what's involved from Robert De Niro's movie *The Good Shepherd* (2006)—the part where Edward Wilson (played by Matt Damon) is made a "Bonesman" and inducted into Yale University's secretive "Skull and Bones" society. For a less sadistic version of the same thing, watch the 2013 Pixar movie, *Monsters University*—the Oozma Kappa initiation scene.

In the context of organized crime, ritualized fraternity is a hugely important basis for cooperation because it creates a connection between members (Skarbek & Wang, 2015). It is particularly important in the older, larger criminal organizations—Mafias such as the Cosa Nostra, 'Ndrangheta, and Yakuza (Catino, 2019, pp. 59–80). Exact rituals vary between organizations but typically center around the creation of familial-style ties—symbolic father-son, brother-brother type relationships (for a great illustration see Gambetta, 1996). Either way, the end result is broadly the same—membership and fraternal belonging is conferred on an individual that completes the ritual. In doing so, they garner acceptance and belonging by committing themselves totally to the organization and agreeing to follow its written and unwritten rules.

A great example of this is the clans of the Japanese Yakuza, whose ceremonial systems are broadly based on traditional Japanese values and expressive symbols of birth and marriage that formalize a familial-style relationship between individuals (Paoli, 2002). In a way that is not too dissimilar to the kinship rituals used by the Calabrian 'Ndrangheta and Chinese Triads; new Yakuza make a lifelong commitment to the organization through a ceremony in which they agree to commit themselves totally to the organization. As part of this they agree to uphold the organization's interests, obey a particular set of rules, and keep everything a secret.

As well as participating in a formal ceremony, new Yakuza must also demonstrate their commitment by enduring the slow and painful tattooing of their entire torso and thighs—see Photos 5.1 and 5.2

5 | Criminal Organizations 117

Photo 5.1 Full Body Tattoo Suit (Anton Kusters)
Source: courtesy of Anton Kusters, © DACS 2024.

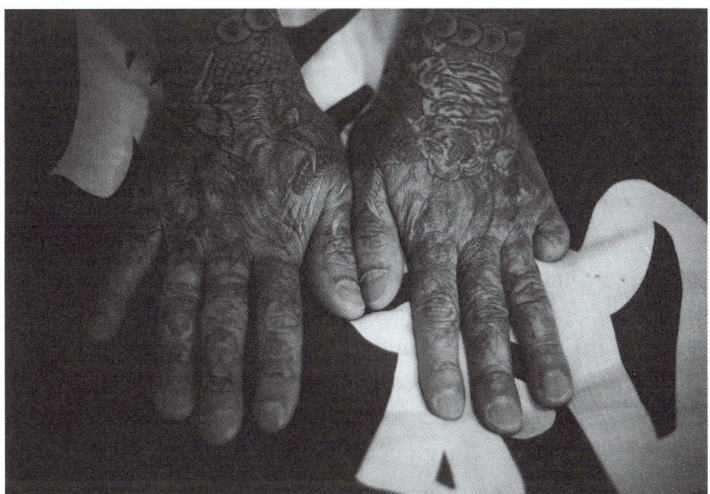

Photo 5.2 Hands (Anton Kusters)
Source: courtesy of Anton Kusters, © DACS 2024.

(Kaplan & Dubro, 2012; Seymour, 1996). Showing that they can endure pain, and suffering is part of the point, but it is also about demonstrative, embodied belonging (see also Burrow, Scott, & Courpasson, 2022). Once tattooed the Yakuza is unmistakably a member. There's no hiding a full-body tattoo. This means there's no leaving the group (Campana & Varese, 2013, p. 268).

The Sicilian Cosa Nostra are slightly more subtle. In this organization, kinship ties are established through a ritual that involves the ceremonial drawing of blood, trials of loyalty, and the swearing of oaths (Paoli, 2002). Equivocal to a kind of a religious conversion, new members commit to a code of conduct and the concepts of brotherhood, generalized reciprocity, and altruism amongst group members.

These ritualized commitments symbolize the passing of a new member into the organized crime family and establish an important framework for cooperation between members. Cooperation becomes possible because fraternalized members share a sense of solidarity and identity (Collins, 2004). In "passing" the ceremony, they become members of the same organization, buy into the same cultural history, and commit to the same values and rules. Crucially, the ceremony provides a basis for people who don't necessarily know each other to work together in criminal enterprise. Through mutual trust some of the constraints of informality can be overcome, and it becomes possible to build large-scale organizations.

Ritualized fraternity also supports criminal organizations in a range of other ways as well. First, ceremonies of initiation reduce the chance of betrayal. This happens because processes of initiation require individuals to commit themselves to maintaining the absolute secrecy of the groups' operations. In Italian Mafia organizations, this is known as "*omertà*" (a code of silence), and this code not only protects the group from exposure but strengthens the homogeneity of the group by reinforcing a sense of acceptance and belonging. In very simple terms, the creation of a secretive "in" group strengthens the ties that bind organizational members.

Second, ritualized fraternity also supports criminal organizations by enabling them to function dynamically and to mobilize people who are able and willing to defend the interests of the group from external threats—sometimes fanatically so. The contracts of employment that you and I sign with legitimate organizations bind us to tightly defined roles and tasks. They have limits. In contrast, the quasi-spiritual contracts made by mafiosi commit them to something bigger—an open-ended and comprehensively non-specific role in the organization that is intricately bound up with their sense of identity. Members can't break their oaths without going against both their commitments to the group *and* their understanding of who they are as a person. As a consequence, a mafiosi can be called on at any time to work for and protect the organization. By dint of their oaths, they are morally obliged to not only obey orders but to do so without question and regardless of the consequences. They can be called on not just for labor but to do work that may require them to sacrifice life or limb at the very least.

In criminal organizations, such as Cosa Nostra, 'Ndrangheta, and Yakuza, which have deep civic roots and a rich cultural history, the strength of what Paoli (2002) calls the "clan formula" is believed to be one of the major cornerstones of their success. The power of ritualized fraternity is reflected in many newer "juvenile" criminal organizations attempting to replicate this formula, either by adopting others' rituals wholesale or by introducing their own imitations. Either way, the aim is to replicate amongst their own affiliates the same level of commitment and internal cohesion (Chin 1996).

Interestingly, there is evidence to suggest that in contemporary criminal organizations the strength of commitments made as part of processes of ritualized fraternity are diminishing—even amongst well-established Mafias (Hill, 2003). People are increasingly less willing to recognize the criminal organizations to which they belong as the principal source of authority, meaning, and identity in their lives. This is particularly true in criminal organizations that are on their way out.

Of course, there is also the issue that the reward that comes from making a quasi-spiritual pact in order to become an "insider" is often not that great. For many, a sense of belonging is often quickly supplanted by feelings of paranoia and betrayal blended with the loneliness of prison time and/or the poverty that comes with abandonment (Adelstein, 2018). This is undermining one of the traditional cornerstones of criminal organizations' cohesiveness, but also exacerbating the challenges criminal organizations face in recruiting new members. Consequently, criminal organizations are increasingly blending fraternalized kinship with a second mechanism that binds and ensures cooperation between members: violence.

5.8 Violence and cooperation in criminal organizations

Violence sits at the heart of criminal organizations and is the second basis upon which commitment and cooperation is orchestrated.

Historically, most major criminal organizations—Mafia in particular—begin life as purveyors of violence—as organized groups of broke musclemen, good at fighting, and keen to sell their services to anyone who'll pay. Glenny (2009) is instructive on this point, particularly in relation to the rise of Eastern European Mafias (see also Varese, 2001). However, the relationship between criminal organizations and violence is far more complex than this. Criminal organizations don't just sell violence, they function through it.

This point might seem very strange given the destructive nature of violence and how criminal organizations need to keep quiet and hidden from view. However, the fear of harm is a very powerful way of suppressing dissent and forcing cooperation amongst dissident actors. Machiavelli (1961/1513) makes this very point in what is perhaps the world's first management "self-help" textbook. For Machiavelli, as for organized criminals, fear is a hugely powerful motivator (see also Gill & Burrow, 2018). Crucially, it is also very easy to manipulate, particularly when hostages are involved (Raub, 2004)—which they often are in criminal contexts. Think about it: what are the chances of someone stepping out of line if they're petrified and/or their family will get hurt?

The practice of using violence to engineer and manipulate fears amongst organizational members is called "fear work." Obviously a very dark concept, the sad reality is that it occurs in different forms, happens quite a lot, and not just in criminal organizations (Gill & Burrow, 2018). For sure, members of criminal organizations experience a very extreme form of "fear works," but it is also very common in mainstream organizations. I'm sure if you think about it, you'll remember the last time someone played on your fears and anxieties to get you to do something? I certainly can.

Violence can also function to foster cooperation between perpetrators. It sounds perverse, but bonds between people can be established through the violence they perpetrate together (Anderson, 2000). Think here about the bonds that tie soldiers together and the horrific experiences through which these ties were made. People in criminal organizations can also experience a heightened sense of belonging as a result of the violence they perpetrate with other members of their organization. This is because violence creates a basis for a kind of shared understanding between group members. Assuming they're not crippled by disgust and guilt, violence can actually strengthen the bonds between individuals as well as their commitment to the organization itself.

The shared experience of violence as a basis for cooperation is often engineered in criminal organizations. For example, Gambetta notes that "members of groups who engage in deviant actions reinforce their internal loyalty to one another by exchanging evidence of their misdeeds, an act which commits them to mutual silence" (Gambetta, 2011, p. 66). So violent gangs are brought together not only by the shared experience of violence, but also by their knowledge of what each other has done (see also Saviano, 2019; Schelling, 1980).

In an organizational context where trust is not assured and the threat of defection is always present (Cook, Hardin, & Levi, 2005), having a huge body of evidence of your co-workers' wrong-doing is a sure-fire way of ensuring they won't disappear into the sunset. You know what they've done, and you have evidence to prove it. They also know what you've done, and they have evidence to prove it. The end result is a kind of cooperation by necessity or mutually assured destruction. Your willingness to contribute to the group is motivated (at least in part) by your own desire for self-preservation.

Knowledge of each-others' violence has been shown to be strong enough to maintain the homogeneity of criminal organizations (Campana & Varese, 2013). Indeed, it has also been shown that even in organizations made up of blood relatives (which some Mafia are), knowledge of each-others' past violence is actually a better predictor of cooperation than genealogy. So, while we are more likely to trust and cooperate with family members in criminal enterprise, familial ties aren't necessarily the most important thing—knowledge of each-others' wrong-doing often is.

Paradoxically, despite there being a kind of symbiotic relationship between criminal organizations and violence, criminal organizations are very often quite violence averse. Violence can give a criminal organization the edge over the competition, but only if it is treated as a key economic asset and used in an organized and tactically astute way. Shoot-outs, assassinations, and violence on the streets get noticed. Getting noticed adds risk. Risk makes it harder to operate. If it's hard to operate, costs go up and profits go down. It doesn't make great TV, but there is a compelling case for using as little violence as possible in a criminal organization (Dell, 2015).

To ensure that violence is used effectively and does not damage the organization, many criminal organizations will set up intricate, complex structures to manage violence both within and outside the organization. For example, certain Nigerian organized crime groups are reportedly going to considerable lengths to avoid violence in any form (Ellis, 2016). For these guys, violence is really a last resort. The Japanese Yakuza are slightly more prone to violence but have structured their organization to minimize violence between members. In fact, violence is specifically prohibited between members of different clans. There are agreed punishments for breaking the rules and even governance mechanisms that ensure they are enforced (Kaplan & Dubro, 2012).

The Sicilian and American Cosa Nostra both have something similar—it's called "the commission" (Critchley, 2008; Dickie, 2005). Today, on both sides of the Atlantic, the commissions for the Sicilian and American branches of the Cosa Nostra function in ways that are not too dissimilar to the executive boards of the modern companies. However, both were set up principally as a way of managing rivalries between different factions and to police the activities of different groups. They're there to moderate and to smooth the process of maintaining internal peace and ensuring cooperation (Dickie, 2005).

5.9 Summary

This chapter has given you an introduction into modern criminal organizations. However, it's important to keep in mind that, much like legitimate organizations, there is great diversity in the criminal underworld. There are many different ways of responding to the challenges of organizing illegitimate business. Yet, at the same time, criminal organizations also grapple with the same basic problems as legitimate organizations. Much like private, public, and charitable organizations, criminal organizations have to grapple with the questions of how to foster commitment to the organization and maintain cooperation between organizational members.

What you have read about in this chapter are just two of the ways through which criminal organizations respond to these challenges—through ritualized fraternity and violence. The practices I've described are specific to criminal organizations, but be aware that the basic social mechanisms they leverage are seen in all forms of organization. The desire to belong in one way or another is a powerful driver of participation in most organizations as is the regulatory, controlling effect of fear. To give you an idea, Gill and Burrow's (2018) concept of "fear work" was developed in relation to practices seen in commercial kitchens. Leaders of criminal organizations are archetypal fear workers, but this does not mean they are the only people in the world to pull that lever in an organizational context to control and regulate people.

Things to Watch, Things to Read

In this table are suggestions for things you can watch and things you can read to learn more about this topic. I've also included a very short commentary, so that you know why I've recommended a particular source and what to look out for.

| **Read in two to three hours** | Guerci, M., R. Sferrazzo, F. Cabras, & G. Radaelli. (2022). Organized crime and employment relations: A personal story of 'Ndrangheta control on employment relations management practices in southern Italy. *Work, Employment and Society* 36(4), 758–768. |

This is a narrative-based article that tells the story of Paolo, an Italian entrepreneur. Paolo worked under the control of an 'Ndrangheta clan for years, but ultimately rebelled against them. Told from his perspective, this article reveals how strongly organized crime can penetrate decision-making processes in organizations and control people's management practices. It is an example of how criminal organizations are "out there" and affecting day-to-day life.

| **Read in a day or two** | Campana, P. & L. Gelsthorpe. (2020). Choosing a smuggler: Decision-making amongst migrants smuggled to Europe. *European Journal on Criminal Policy and Research* 27(5), 1–17. |

This article explores how transactions between smugglers and migrants come about in the context of irregular migration. It offers some theoretical reflections on the challenges that such a context poses to both smugglers and migrants, and points to three main conditions under which smuggling transactions take place: illegality, asymmetrical information, and low trust. Subsequently, it explores the strategies that migrants and smugglers alike employ to overcome these challenges. Three broad sets of strategies are focused on. These relate to information-gathering, information-checking (reputation and the role of physical and virtual communities), and to developing substitutes for trust (guarantees, escrow services, and hostage-taking strategies).

| **Read in a week or three** | Catino, M. (2019). *Mafia Organizations*. Cambridge: Cambridge University Press. |

In this book Catino presents a comparative study of seven different mafias from around the world: three Italian mafias, American Cosa Nostra, Japanese Yakuza, Chinese Triads, and Russian mafia. His concern is with how, in a very practical sense, mafia organizations work—he describes the organizational architecture of these different mafia, the rules they live by, and the main organizational dilemmas mafias face. The book is considered to be one of the greatest accounts of mafia organizations ever written. The level of detail and insight it provides is unparalleled.

Watch in an evening	*Cartel Land* (2015). Directed by Matthew Heineman. Produced by A&E IndieFilms; The Documentary Group; Our Times Projects, 100 minutes long.

This widely acclaimed, award-winning documentary gives a graphic account of the war on organized crime. Its focus is armed vigilantes—self-styled "civilian defense groups" in America and Mexico formed in response to government inaction on organized crime. In Mexico, the film follows a local doctor, José Manuel Mireles Valverde, and explores the horrific circumstances that compelled him (and others) to form an armed vigilante group. It shows him gathering, arming, and organizing groups of concerned citizens and orchestrating a bloody, violent direct-action campaign to drive the criminal cartels from his home state. Initially, popular and successful, the documentary shows the group's subsequent descent into disorganized criminal chaos. It shows armed civilians raiding properties, fighting street battles, detaining and torturing suspects and their extrajudicial killings. In the US, the film follows an American veteran, Tim Foley, similarly forming concerned citizens into a militarized defense group to combat cartels trafficking people and drugs across the Mexican-American border.

Watch in a week	*Vendetta: Truth, Lies and The Mafia* (2021). Directed by Laura Warner, Ruggero Di Maggio, David Gambino, Daniella Volker. Produced by Mon Amour Film; Nutopia, 33–44 minutes per episode.

This docuseries focuses on the simultaneous trials of various members of Sicily's Anti-Mafia coalition—the journalist running a pop-up community television center broadcasting news on mafia wrongdoing, and the high-profile judge responsible for seizing and taking state control of confiscated mafia assets. Both are accused of adopting the very same practices used by the criminal organizations they're trying to bring down. What remains is a messy, complicated state of affairs in which it's unclear who is good and who is bad. You also see the serious challenges associated with first uncovering the operations of organized criminals and proving it in court. Nobody is squeaky clean. Everyone has something to hide, but in the end only one goes to jail.

> **Research Insight: How organized criminals infiltrate mainstream organizations**
>
> **Source:** Radaelli, G., M. Guerci, F. Cabras, & N. Dalla Chiesa. (2019). How are professionals recruited by external agents in misconduct projects? The infiltration of organized crime in a university. *Human Relations* 72(9), 1407–1435.
>
> **Summary:** this article reveals how a mafia organization penetrated a respected Italian university. It explains how professors were recruited, controlled, and used to interfere with the admission, examination, and graduation of medical students. What stands out is how the scheme was largely managed from within the university; that is, orchestrated by corrupt professors who acted as linchpins between external agents and reluctant peers. Thus, the article shows how potentially corruptible professors were identified and targeted and how the reluctant few were coerced into cooperating. Lastly, the article shows how a generalized code of silence enabled the entire scheme to persist for decades. It is a detailed, candid insight into how a respected discipline can come under the control of a shadowy, violent criminal organization.

Case Study: The Japanese Yakuza

Introduction

Japanese mafia organizations and the people involved in them are collectively known as *Yakuza*. To be a Yakuza in Tokyo is like being a mobster in New York or a mafioso in Naples. There are currently 24,000 Yakuza across 30–40 independent clans and four regional divisions. With an estimated $100 billion USD in assets (Hill, 2003) the Yakuza clans are the most wealthy and sophisticated criminal organizations in the world (Reilly Jr, 2014).

A legal criminal organization

Despite their criminal pedigree, the Yakuza clans are actually legal organizations. Their exact legal status is complicated, but they are not outlawed in Japanese law. They have offices (see Photo 5.3), registered

Photo 5.3 Office of the Kobe Yamaguchi-gumi in Awaji, Japan
Source: Kyodo News, Courtesy of Google Earth.

headquarters (see Table 5.1) and even pay tax (Kaplan & Dubro, 2012, p. 153). So, in Japan you'll see buildings clearly marked with the crests of different Yakuza clans. If you go into these buildings, you'll meet people wearing special ornate platinum badges and carrying official business cards (Catino, 2019, p. 187; Kaplan & Dubro, 2012, p. 130). All will be embossed with a Yakuza crest. Most of these people will draw a salary, have health insurance, and even a pension (Economist, 2015). The catch is that while Yakuza organizations are allowed to exist, members must register with the police and their crimes are subject to normal enforcement under the law.

Origins of the Yakuza and their position in society

Most Yakuza clans claim they emerged out of the lawless wilds of middle-ages Japan as a kind of benevolent civil defence group (Reilly Jr, 2014). They protected towns and villages from marauding brigands and bands of unemployed samurai, handed out money to the poor, and upheld civic values (Higgins, 2014, p. 192).

Elements of these claims are true. For example, from the 16th century onwards towns and villages very often did need protection from roaming bands of unemployed samurai. Many places did indeed set up civil defense forces, and these occasionally included members of groups that would

Table 5.1 Major Yakuza crime syndicates, 2001

No.	Name	Address of Main Office	Godfather	Membership
1	Yamaguchi-gumi	4-3-1 Shinoharahon-machi Nada-ku Kobe-shi, Hyogo	Yoshinori Watanabe	17,500
2	Sumiyoshi-kai	6-4-21 Akasaka Minato-ku, Tokyo	Shigeo Nishiguchi	6,200
3	Inagawa-kai	7-8-4 Roppongi Minato-ku, Tokyo	Kakuji Inagawa	5,100
4	Kyokuto-kai	1-29-5 Nishiikebukuro Toshima-ku, Tokyo	Kyu Hwa Cho	1,700
5	Matsuba-kai	2-9-8 Nishiasakusa Taito-ku, Tokyo	Chun Song 1	1,500
6	Aizukotetsu-kai	176-1 Iwataki-cho Agaru Kaminokuti Higashitakasegawusuji Simogyo-ku Kyoto-shi, Kyoto	Toshitsugu Zukoshi	1,100
7	Dojin-kai	6-9 Torihigashi-machi Kurume-shi, Fukuoka	Seijiro Matsuo	530
8	Kokusui-kai	4-3-1 Sezoku Taito-ku, Tokyo	Kazuyoshi Kudo	520
9	Kudo-kai	1-1-12 Kanatake Kokurakita-ku Kitakyushu-shi, Fukuoka	Satoru Nomura	520
10	Soai-kai	5-9-9 Nishi Tatsumidai Ichihara-shi, Chiba	Myong U Sin	460
11	Okinawa Kyokuryu-kai	2-6-19 Tsuji Naha-shi, Okinawa	Kiyoshi Tominaga	370
12	Kyokuto Sakurai Soke Rengokai	1787-1 Higashioki Aza Hara Numazu-shi, Shizuoka	Yasuyuki Serizawa	360
13	Fukuhaku-kai	5-18-15 Chiyo Hakata-ku Fukuoka-shi, Fukuoka	Makio Wada	340

14	Kyosei-kai	2-6-5 Nihoshin-machi Minami-ku Hiroshima-shi, Hiroshima	Isao Okimoto	280
15	Sakaume-gumi	2-6-23 Higashi-shinsaibashi Chuo-ku Osaka-shi, Osaka	Kin Zaikaku	280
16	Kyokuryu-kai	4-301-6 Ishimine-cho Shuri Naha-shi, Okinawa	Yoshihiro Onaga	270
17	Goda-ikka	3-14-12 Takezaki-cho Shimonoseki-shi, Yamaguchi	Kanji Nukui	190
18	Kyodo-kai	3-1170-221 Shintakayama Onoichi-shi, Hiroshima	Kazuo Morita	180
19	Azuma-gumi	1-11-8 Sanno Nishinari-ku Osaka-shi, Osaka	Kiyoshi Kishida	170
20	Nakano-kai	12-4 Ikutama-cho Tennouji-ku Osaka-shi, Osaka	Taro Nakano	170
21	Taishu-kai	1314-1 Yugeta Oaza Tagawa-shi, Fukuoka	Raitaro Oma	130
22	Asano-gumi	615-11 Kasaoka Kasaoka-shi, Okayama	Yoshiaki Kushita	120
23	Kozakura-ikka	9-1 Kotuki-cho Kagoshima-shi, Kagoshima	Kiei Hiraoka	120
24	Shinwa-kai	2-14-4 Shiogami-cho Takamatsu-shi, Kagawa	Kunihiko Hosotani	70
25	Yamano-kai	180-1 Hayakawa Oaza Kousa-cho Kamimashiki-gun, Kumamoto	Tetsuo Ikeda	70

Source: Kaplan & Dubro, 2012, pp. 128–129.

eventually evolve into the modern Yakuza (Hill, 2003, chapter 2). However, for the most part, claims about Yakuza benevolence are greatly exaggerated.

Japanese scholars think that modern-day Yakuza emerged in the middle of the 19th century as a coalition between much older groups of *tekiya* (itinerant pedlars) and *bakuto* (gamblers) (see Hill, 2003; Siniawer, 2008). It is this past that seems to be reflected in the Yakuza name, which is a derivation of "eight" (*ya*), "nine" (*ku*), and "three" (*sa*)—the worst possible hand in the traditional Japanese card game *Oicho-Kabu* (a kind of baccarat). The word *Yakuza* is therefore a derisory way of calling someone a *loser*. It's quite offensive to call someone *Yakuza*. However, it's also true that if you encountered Yakuza in 19th century Japan, they'd be more likely to rob and murder you than open their purse and escort you safely home.

A pre-war boom

The Yakuza clans grew steadily throughout the 19th century. This growth accelerated in the early 20th century on the back of the global rise of socialism (Siniawer, 2012). At this point in history, the Yakuza were fairly disparate, disorganized groups. However the clans were beginning to leave behind their bawdy origins and coalesce around ultra-right wing, extreme nationalist ideology.

They shared this ideology with similarly ultra-right wing government officials, with whom they were able to cultivate an unusually intimate relationship (Siniawer, 2012). With socialism on the rise, a weakly disguised tie-up quickly blossomed into a very public partnership in which the Yakuza clans were commissioned to violently progress the fascist political cause. As self-styled protectors of Japanese culture and traditions, the Yakuza were paid huge amounts of money to fight socialist revolutionaries in the streets, forcibly break strikes, and violently disrupt left-wing political protests (Kaplan & Dubro, 2012, p. xxiii).

This collaboration ended abruptly at the start of the Second World War (Siniawer, 2008, 2012). However the pre- and inter-war period had set in motion what would become a globally unprecedented quasi-symbiotic relationship between the Yakuza and the Japanese state (Hill, 2003). This tight relationship re-emerged in the immediate post-war period when the Yakuza got their second big break. This time, courtesy of the Americans.

A post-war expansion

After the Second World War America occupied Japan until 1952. Their official mandate was to rebuild the country. This created a huge opportunity for the Yakuza. The post-war Japanese state was battered, degraded, and disorganized. American occupiers desperately needed help to fill the ensuing power vacuum. In the absence of state institutions, Yakuza clans were widely commissioned to run projects ranging from construction and labor brokering to tax collection and policing (Wildes, 1948).

It's hard to imagine now, but after the war, the Yakuza's civic role grew to such an extent that it was almost impossible to disentangle them from the official government. In many cases, the Yakuza *were* the government. In some areas the police were so weak that the Yakuza just took over entirely. The Yakuza even helped fund their chronically cash-starved counterparts. The police need for cash was so dire that they set up "Police Supporters Associations" and "Crime Prevention Societies" to raise extra funds. Via these associations and societies, the Yakuza paid cash directly into police coffers, enabling them to pay their bills and get back to work (Wildes, 1948, p. 188). Of course, the Yakuza's cash wasn't a gift. In return for money, police agreed to ignore the Yakuza's illicit activities (Hill, 2003, p. 78).

Thus, the Yakuza established themselves firmly at the heart of the Japanese society, from where they were able to project their power and influence for decades. That influence is less visible now, but in the years that followed the war, it was blatantly obvious; for example, the Yakuza successfully lobbied for the mass-pardoning of gang members in 1958. In 1971, an ex-prime minister and education minister guaranteed the bail of a leading Yakuza boss (Kaplan & Dubro 1986, p. 116). In essence, that's like US President Eisenhower and one of his ministerial buddies posting bail for Frank Costello. Or the UK Prime Minister Churchill teaming up with his mate Richard Law to vouch for Ronnie and Reggie Kray.

Uneasy acceptance

In Japanese society, hostility towards Yakuza has traditionally been very restrained. Particularly in the post-war years when it was perceived that the Yakuza had largely lived up to their claims of being a benevolent force in society. For example, during the state-imposed starvation rations on civilians at the end of the war, the Yakuza clans set up a network of over

17,000 black markets that enabled people who were able to buy and sell what they needed to survive (Dower, 2000).

Against this backdrop, the Yakuza garnered tolerance, and even admiration, within sections of the police. They had shown that they could be a useful stabilizing force in the otherwise chaotic criminal underworld (Kaplan & Dubro, 2012, pp. 150–151). The relationship may have been an uneasy one, but a controlled, organized criminal underworld was considered preferable to the disorganized, chaotic, unpredictable alternative.

To a great extent, the Yakuza have actively cultivated a positive image. Until relatively recently they would host police in their offices, update them on their activities, and discuss what is going on in the streets. When violence between clans spilled out onto the streets, the Yakuza would hold press conferences to publicly apologize and beg forgiveness (Kaplan & Dubro, 2012). When an earthquake hit Kobe in 1995, the Yakuza were the first out searching for survivors. Similarly in 2011, when a massive earthquake and tsunami hit Northeast Japan, they were the first to deliver supplies to emergency evacuation centers.

A new future for the Yakuza?

You can still buy Yakuza fan magazines, but public support and government tolerance for the clans is declining. Since the 1990s, the Japanese government has been strengthening laws to constrain the Yakuza, and the Japanese public has become increasingly frustrated by clan violence.

These changing attitudes have forced the Yakuza clans to evolve. Cooperation with law enforcement agencies has been rolled back. Notably, through what has become known as the "three no's policy:" (1) no police allowed into their offices; (2) no evidence offered, or criminals delivered; and (3) no confessing or offering information when arrested (Kaplan & Dubro, 2012, p. 151).

Alongside these changes, the Yakuza has become increasingly secretive about their activities. Operations have been moved underground, and Yakuza ownership of legitimate businesses has become increasingly hidden behind front companies and impenetrable layers of bureaucracy. Yakuza offices have started to disappear with crests removed from walls. Membership too has changed. Via the creation of new, non-regulated "associate" and "freelance" roles, new Yakuza members are increasingly held off the books. Officially, there are now just 24,000 Yakuza, down from 184,091 in 1963.

The Yakuza clans have also begun to consolidate. Small clans are merging with larger clans. The remaining are bigger, more centralized, and more powerful. They are also increasingly diversifying their operations abroad, to places like America, China, South Korea, and Europe (Varese, 2011). The Yakuza might be down, but they're still in the game.

Questions

1. Can a criminal organization ever be good?
2. How can organizations that do bad things still win popular support?
3. Can the Yakuza be considered an organizational success story?
4. The Yakuza's "official" history is different to that recorded by Japanese scholars. What does this tell us about the efficacy of different sources of information?

References

Abadinsky, H. (2012). *Organized Crime*. Cengage Learning.

Adelstein, J. (2018). "The Outsider" scores a few hits among the misses. *Dark Side of the Rising Sun*. Retrieved from https://www.japantimes.co.jp/tag/the-outsider/

Amnesty International (2016). "This Is What We Die For", Human Rights Abuses In The Democratic Republic Of The Congo Power The Global Trade In Cobalt. United Kingdom: Amnesty International, International Secretariat. Retrieved from https://www.amnesty.org/en/documents/afr62/3183/2016/en/.

Anderson, E. (2000). *Code of the Street: Decency, Violence, and the Moral Life of the Inner City*. New York: WW Norton & Company.

Anderson, G. (2010). *Cityboy: Beer and Loathing in the Square Mile*. UK: Hachette.

Baccara, M. & H. Bar-Isaac. (2008). How to organize crime. *The Review of Economic Studies* 75(4), 1039–1067.

Belfort, J. (2011). *The Wolf of Wall Street*. UK: Hachette.

Bell, C. M. (1997). *Ritual: Perspectives and Dimensions*. Oxford: Oxford University Press on Demand.

Bichler, G., A. Malm, & T. Cooper. (2017). Drug supply networks: A systematic review of the organizational structure of illicit drug trade. *Crime Science* 6(1), 2.

Burrow, R., R. Scott, & D. Courpasson. (2022). Bloody suffering and durability: How chefs forge embodied identities in elite kitchens. *Human Relations* 77(1), 111–139.

Campana, P. & L. Gelsthorpe. (2020). Choosing a smuggler: Decision-making amongst migrants smuggled to Europe. *European Journal on Criminal Policy and Research* 27(5), 1–17.

Campana, P. & F. Varese. (2013). Cooperation in criminal organizations: Kinship and violence as credible commitments. *Rationality and Society* 25(3), 263–289.

Catino, M. (2019). *Mafia Organizations*. Cambridge: Cambridge University Press.

Collins, R. (2004). *Interaction Ritual Chains*. Princeton: Princeton University Press.

Cook, K. S., R. Hardin, & M. Levi. (2005). *Cooperation without Trust?* Russell Sage Foundation.

Crane, A. (2013). Modern slavery as a management practice: Exploring the conditions and capabilities for human exploitation. *Academy of Management Review* 38(1), 49–69.

Critchley, D. (2008). *The Origin of Organized Crime in America: The New York City Mafia, 1891–1931*. London: Routledge.

Dahl, F. (2012). Crime one of the world's "top 20 economies": U.N. Retrieved from https://www.reuters.com/article/us-un-crime/crime-one-of-the-worlds-top-20-economies-u-n-idUSBRE83M12P20120423.

Dell, M. (2015). Trafficking networks and the Mexican drug war. *American Economic Review* 105(6), 1738–1779.

Dickie, J. (2005). *Cosa Nostra: A History of the Sicilian Mafia*. London: Macmillan.

Dower, J. W. (2000). *Embracing Defeat: Japan in the Wake of World War II*. New York: WW Norton & Company.

Eck, J. E. & J. S. Gersh. (2000). Drug trafficking as a cottage industry. *Crime Prevention Studies* 11, 241–272.

Economist. (2015). Why the Yakuza are not illegal. September. Retrieved from https://www-economist-com.abc.cardiff.ac.uk/the-economist-explains/2015/09/29/why-the-yakuza-are-not-illegal.

Eisenhardt, K. M. & J. A. Martin. (2000). Dynamic capabilities: What are they? *Strategic Management Journal* 21(10–11), 1105–1121.

Ellis, S. (2016). *This Present Darkness: A History of Nigerian Organized Crime*. USA: Oxford University Press.

Gambetta, D. (1996). *The Sicilian Mafia: The Business of Private Protection*. Harvard: Harvard University Press.

Gambetta, D. (2011). *Codes of the Underworld: How Criminals Communicate*. Princeton: Princeton University Press.

Gill, M. & R. Burrow. (2018). The function of fear in institutional maintenance: Feeling frightened as an essential ingredient in haute cuisine. *Organization Studies* 39(4), 445–465.

Glenny, M. (2009). *McMafia: Seriously Organised Crime*. London: Random House.
Grey, C. (2012). *Decoding Organization: Bletchley Park, Codebreaking and Organization Studies*. Cambridge: Cambridge University Press.
Guerci, M., R. Sferrazzo, F. Cabras, & G. Radaelli. (2022). Organized crime and employment relations: A personal story of 'Ndrangheta control on employment relations management practices in southern Italy. *Work, Employment and Society* 36(4), 758–768.
Hassard, J. S. (2012). Rethinking the Hawthorne Studies: The Western Electric research in its social, political and historical context. *Human Relations* 65(11), 1431–1461.
Higgins, S. (2014). Yakuza past, present and future: The changing face of Japan's organized crime syndicates. *Themis: Research Journal of Justice Studies and Forensic Science* 2(1), 12.
Hill, P. B. (2003). *The Japanese Mafia: Yakuza, Law, and the State* (Vol. 74). Oxford: Oxford University Press on Demand.
Kaplan, D. E. & A. Dubro. (2012). *Yakuza: Japan's Criminal Underworld*. Los Angeles: University of California Press.
Kelly, A. (2019). Apple and Google named in US lawsuit over Congolese child cobalt mining deaths. Retrieved from https://www.theguardian.com/global-development/2019/dec/16/apple-and-google-named-in-us-lawsuit-over-congolese-child-cobalt-mining-deaths.
Machiavelli, N. (1961/1513). *The Prince; Transl. from the Italian*. London: Penguin.
Marshall, D. A. (2002). Behavior, belonging, and belief: A theory of ritual practice. *Sociological Theory* 20(3), 360–380.
Paoli, L. (2002). The paradoxes of organized crime. *Crime, Law and Social Change* 37(1), 51–97.
Paoli, L., V. A. Greenfield, & P. Reuter. (2009). *The World Heroin Market: Can Supply Be Cut?* USA: Oxford University Press.
Porter, B. (2014). *Blow: How a Small-town Boy Made $100 Million with the Medellín Cocaine Cartel and Lost it All*. New York: St. Martin's Griffin.
Radaelli, G., M. Guerci, F. Cabras, & N. Dalla Chiesa. (2019). How are professionals recruited by external agents in misconduct projects? The infiltration of organized crime in a university. *Human Relations* 72(9), 1407–1435. doi: 10.1177/0018726718782616.
Raub, W. (2004). Hostage posting as a mechanism of trust: Binding, compensation, and signaling. *Rationality and Society* 16(3), 319–365.
Reilly Jr, E. F. (2014). Criminalizing Yakuza membership: A comparative study of the anti-Boryokudan law. *Washington Universal Global Studies Law Review* 13, 801.
Reuter, P. (1983). *Disorganized Crime: The Economics of the Visible Hand*. Cambridge, MA: MIT Press.
Saviano, R. (2019). *Gomorrah: Italy's other Mafia*. London: Pan Macmillan.

Schelling, T. C. (1980). *The Strategy of Conflict*. Harvard: Harvard University Press.

Seymour, C. (1996). *Yakuza Diary: Doing Time in the Japanese Underworld*. New York City: Atlantic Monthly Press.

Siniawer, E. M. (2008). *Ruffians, Yakuza, Nationalists: The Violent Politics of Modern Japan, 1860–1960*. New York: Cornell University Press.

Siniawer, E. M. (2012). Befitting bedfellows: Yakuza and the state in modern Japan. *Journal of Social History* 45(3), 623–641.

Skarbek, D. & P. Wang. (2015). Criminal rituals. *Global Crime* 16(4), 288–305.

Thoumi, F. E. (1995). *Political Economy and Illegal Drugs in Colombia* (Vol. 2). Tokyo: United Nations University Press.

Tondo, L. (2021). Italy's largest mafia trial in three decades to begin against 'Ndragheta. Retrieved from https://www.theguardian.com/world/2021/jan/13/italy-mafia-trial-ndragheta-calabria.

Varese, F. (2001). *The Russian Mafia: Private Protection in a New Market Economy*. Oxford: Oxford University Press.

Varese, F. (2011). *Mafias on the Move: How Organized Crime Conquers New Territories*. Princeton: Princeton University Press.

Vitaliano, D. F. (2015). Repeal of prohibition: A benefit-cost analysis. *Contemporary Economic Policy* 33(1), 44–55.

Volkow, N. D., R. D. Baler, W. M. Compton, & S. R. Weiss. (2014). Adverse health effects of marijuana use. *New England Journal of Medicine* 370(23), 2219–2227.

Wildes, H. E. (1948). IV. Underground politics in post-war Japan. *American Political Science Review* 42(6), 1149–1162.

PART 2
HOW ORGANIZATIONS WORK

PART 2

HOW ORGANIZATIONS WORK

6
Record-Keeping, Rules, and the Invention of Bureaucracy

> **Keywords**
>
> bureaucracy; Max Weber; rationality; modernity; Zygmunt Bauman; Alvin Gouldner; goal displacement; mock bureaucracy; bureaucracy and fairness; bureaucracy and morality

> **Consider**
>
> What do the Pyramids at Giza, the Great Wall of China, and your high street bank all have in common?

6.1 Introduction

At the beginning of this book I wrote about Egypt's 4,500-year-old pyramids (Spence, 2000). I also wrote about China's 6,000 km, 7th century (BCE) Great Wall (Waldron, 1990). I asked you to think about the organizations behind these incredible achievements, and what it required, organizationally, to create these monuments.

I'm revisiting these examples because, in terms of how they worked, the organizations that built Egypt's pyramids, and China's Great Wall, actually had a fair amount in common. This might seem surprising.

What could the ancient Egyptians and Qin dynasty Chinese Wall possibly have in common? More to the point, who cares? How could it possibly matter here now, in this book?

The answer is that it matters because both monuments were made possible by (1) a prodigious amount of slave labor; and (2) a system of organization that is absolutely central to our modern world. That system of organization is called bureaucracy. Perhaps you'll remember it mentioned in the previous chapters? As I write these words, nothing is happening on any serious scale in the world without bureaucracy, and it hasn't done for quite some time. Our entire everyday life is harnessed to bureaucracy, and it is the focus of this chapter.

This chapter has three parts. The first establishes some basic theoretical foundations that I think are helpful to understand at this point. Things like what bureaucracy is, where you find it, and where it came from. The second part looks at why we love a good bureaucracy. The third part of this chapter is all about the flaws in the bureaucratic system, and why nobody ever says: "I love all this bureaucracy."

6.2 What is bureaucracy?

If you look up the word "bureaucracy" in the Oxford English Dictionary (OED) you'll see it started being used around 1818. It means "government by bureau." This is quite a complicated concept, because it incorporates a few different ideas. For example, "government" means "the action of ruling; continuous exercise of authority over the action of subjects or inferiors; authoritative direction or regulation; control, rule" (OED). "Bureau" means two things. First, "a chest of drawers with a writing-board; a writing-desk with drawers for papers, etc." Second, a "room full of desks; an office or an agency."

All a bit ambiguous? The point is this: a bureaucracy is a type of organization that is centered on the idea of an office (the bureau) and hierarchical, authoritarian, desk-based working practices. Bureaucracies are grounded in notions of formality, logic, reason, and something called the "division of labor." They are a way of organizing things to accomplish large-scale administrative tasks by systematically coordinating the work of many individuals.

These are complex ideas, so I'll elaborate further. A bureaucracy is a system in which arbitrary practices (doing things because you feel like it) are replaced by prescribed, rule-based ways of doing things. We're talking about a system in which complex tasks are broken down into simple ones, and people spend time working out the best way to do them. Once defined, these "best practices" are recorded in procedures that everyone is expected to follow.

Once written, procedures are not performed by just anyone. In a bureaucracy, work is carried out by people who specialize in doing particular jobs. People do jobs they are properly qualified to do. They are paid for this job and nothing else.

The concept of bureaucracy also denotes a particular form of authority: "systemic" rule. In a bureaucracy, you aren't governed by other people. You are governed by "the system." An easy way to understand this is in terms of "being ruled by rules." This might sound a bit cryptic, but all it means is that you do whatever is written in the rules. You do what is written down, because, well, those are the rules. That's how things are done. Sound familiar? Starting to make sense?

Linked to the concept of a bureaucracy is the concept of a bureaucrat. A bureaucrat is "an official who endeavours to concentrate administrative power in their bureau; they are a member of a bureaucracy" (OED). So, a bureaucrat is someone who practices bureaucracy. Bureaucrats are people who use rules to govern others. They exercise bureaucratic power. Bureaucrats write the rule book(s) and make sure everyone does what is written in them. A bureaucrat is someone who administers the bureaucracy.

Everything I've described previously is summarized in Table 6.1, which is a synthesis of one of the first serious attempts to theorize what a bureaucracy is, and what it's like to work in one. The contents of this table are taken directly from Tribe and Weber (2019, pp. 343–354), which is a new translation of Max Weber's original iconic work (published in 1922)—a portion of which was on bureaucracy.

Table 6.1 The key characteristics of a bureaucracy

(1)	There exists [or can be formulated] legal norms [e.g., laws/rules] that can be specified and followed.
(2)	People in organizations are bound to obey the organization's rules, these [rules] being grounded in rationality [good scientific sense]; these same people are not bound to obey individuals. They are bound to follow the rules.
(3)	Tasks are defined and allocated to people qualified to undertake them.
(4)	Individuals are only appointable to the offices (they are specifically qualified [by specialist training] to do).
(5)	Those who administer the organization [bureaucratic administrators] and those who execute the means of production (the people who make things) are separate. They're two different categories of worker.
(6)	People have no basic right to a particular post within an organization. Official positions in a bureaucracy are not hereditary. You cannot lay claim to a specific post because your mother had the job before you. People are selected to do a particular role because they are the best qualified. People are selected because they have the right qualifications.
(7)	The principle that all administrative work is done in writing is central. Dispositions and instructions are made in writing. "Paperwork" [digital or otherwise] and the "office" are the focal point of action within the organization.
(8)	Those who are employed in a bureaucracy: (a) are personally free and only observe substantive official obligations [the rules]; (b) are placed in a fixed official hierarchy, and therefore have a clearly defined role in the organization; (c) are appointed by contract; (d) possess a specialist qualification—they are qualified through examination and certified as such; (e) are paid by fixed salary, graded according to their position in the hierarchy and level of responsibility; (f) are entitled to a pension; (g) have the right to resign; (h) treat the official appointment as their principal occupation; (i) see themselves as having a career, and will attain promotion according to age or performance or both; (j) work in complete separation from the means of production [e.g., the factory workers]; (k) have no personal, unassailable right to the post they occupy.

Table 6.1 Continued

(9)	Appointment by contract assuming free selection is the essence of modern bureaucracy.
(10)	In a bureaucracy the role of specialist qualification is constantly increasing.
(11)	Appointments should be full-time not part-time. A typical bureaucrat is a full-time one.
(12)	Purely bureaucratic administration is the most formally rational way of ruling over people in an organization. It provides precision, consistency, discipline, rigor, reliability, and predictability for rulers and other interested parties [e.g., workers/employees/staff]. It is the intensity and scope of work done, its formal universal applicability for all tasks, and its very high degree of technical perfection that render it so rational [and therefore so valuable].

Source: Tribe & Weber, 2019, pp. 343–354.

6.3 Where do you find bureaucracy?

If you were suddenly gripped by an urge to find a bureaucracy, where would you look? What would you look for exactly? How would you know when you've got it?

Answering these questions is pretty easy. Think about an organization you've worked for or interacted with recently. Think about the ways your work in this organization was structured by things like procedures. Did you have to work in a certain kind of way? If you had to write down these procedures and describe them to someone, what would you write?

For example, my first ever "proper" job (in the Weberian sense), was in a big high street retail bank in the UK. Let's call it "BigBank." I was what they called a "Customer Advisor." My job at BigBank involved spending precisely 7.5 hours per day following procedures. If someone wanted a bank account, I had to look up the procedure on the intranet and do whatever it said. If someone wanted a loan, I did exactly the same thing. Also with mortgages. If someone wanted one, I looked up how to do it on the intranet and did whatever it said.

Working at BigBank was pretty easy. Fresh out of school, I was pretty good at doing what I was told. There were so many procedures at

BigBank I didn't really have to make any decisions about anything. All I did was fill out forms, enter details into the computer, and wait to be told what to do next.

This is what bureaucracy looks like. It is a tightly controlled, highly regulated system of organization defined by procedures governing pretty much everything. It is grounded in the idea that there is a single best way to do things that you can write down, teach people, and get them to follow time and time again. Consistency and standardization, that's the point. That's bureaucracy.

6.4 Where did bureaucracy come from?

It's actually pretty hard to identify a time, a place, an organization, or a person that invented bureaucracy. It's simply not the case that one day there was no bureaucracy, and the next day there was. A better way to think about bureaucracy is as a way of organizing that people have experimented with at different points in our history. It took the form that we know today during the industrial revolution, but ultimately our first experiments with bureaucracy can be traced back to antiquity (Kalberg, 1980).

The very first bureaucracies weren't big and complex. They looked nothing like today's mega-bureaucracies, such as US's Internal Revenue Service. Instead they were relatively small and simple—remember the storage facility in Chapter 2 (Frangipane, 2016, pp. 10–13)? The first bureaucracies were established in organizations where people were tentatively experimenting with record-keeping, rules governing cooperation, and, generally, just trying to be more prescriptive about how to do things.

One thing that we do know is that the emergence of bureaucracy was intricately linked to our ability to record information in an accurate and permanent way (Mattessich, 1987; Powell, 2009). In fact, some argue that systems of writing actually developed out of arithmetical techniques used in record-keeping (e.g., Nissen, Damerow, Englund, & Englund, 1993, p. x). The implication being that we learnt to write in order to better process, store, and manage information. That is, in order to operate bureaucracies.

According to this theory, the first scribes were among the first bureaucrats. This is an intriguing notion because it suggests the desire to be better organized was what drove us to develop writing. So, what is perhaps the greatest invention in our history was predicated on the desire to keep lists, rather than to record the intricate beauty of our culture (Pollock, 1992, p. 307).

If we take this thesis to be true, which many people do, then it is possible to see bureaucracy emerging and spreading broadly in parallel with our ability to collect, store, analyze, and process information. There is relatively reliable evidence of this happening as long ago as 8,000 BCE (Frangipane, 2016; Keister, 1963; Mattessich, 1987; Mouck, 2004) and potentially even as far back as 35,000–20,000 BCE (Ifrah, 2000, p. 62).

In the case of the latter, we have evidence that 35,000 to 20,000 years ago people in what is now the Democratic Republic of Congo were using notches on bones and stones to quantify and record things like who bought and sold what to whom, and keep track of debts (Ifrah, 2000, pp. 62–63). You can see an example of a notched bone in Photo 6.1. Assuming we're right about these notched bones and stones, then they formed part of an extremely basic bureaucratic system of administration.

Arguably more reliable evidence of fledgling bureaucracy comes from the more recent period of 8000 BCE onwards, and the ancient Sumerians. The ancient Sumerians were a group of people living in a southern area of Mesopotamia (part of modern-day Iraq). Around 8000 BCE the Sumerians were using plain clay tokens to symbolically represent the transfer of commodities from one person to another (you can see examples of these tokens in Photo 6.2).

Like the people using notched bones and stones, it is believed that these Sumerian tokens recorded the transfer (sale) of goods, debts, and the payment of taxes (Basu & Waymire, 2006). Moreover, that these tokens were integral to what was possibly the world's first highly centralized bureaucracy (Farazmand, 1998).

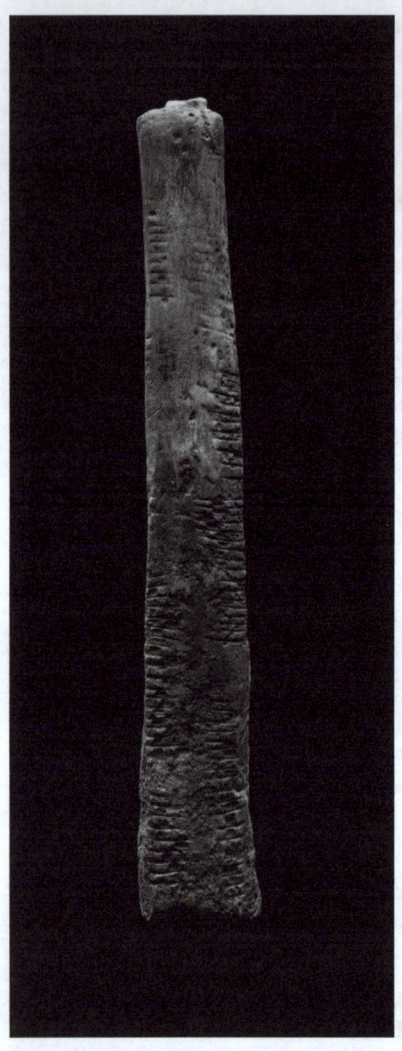

Photo 6.1 The Ishango Bone (discovered in the Democratic Republic of Congo)
Source: Human Origins Program, NMNH, Smithsonian Institution.

The word "possibly" is crucial here. It may well be that other bureaucracies existed before the Sumerian one. We know about Sumerian bureaucracy because they kept records on clay tablets that were preserved by the dry deserts of Iraq. However, in East Asia, Africa, Central and Southern America, there also existed large,

Photo 6.2 Sumerian clay tokens c 8000 BCE
Source: Ziyaret Tepe Archaeological Project.

ancient, flourishing civilizations. Bureaucracy almost certainly existed in these places too. We just don't have any evidence of it because the material they used for record-keeping was organic materials (e.g., bamboo, string, leather, and food). This kind of stuff doesn't last long before it rots away (Yeo, 2021, pp. 12, 20).

This point noted, and sticking with the archaeological record, it seems that over a period of about 5,000 years the Sumerians refined their record-keeping practices. By 4000 BCE Sumerians were using complex engraved tokens to account for manufactured goods (as opposed to simple commodities like sheep and barely). See Photo 6.3. By 3250 BCE these engraved tokens were being sealed in clay balls (called "bullae") to protect against fraud (see Photo 6.4).

Around 3000 BCE, we have the first evidence of cuneiform writing (logo-syllabic script). See Photo 6.5. In fact, one of the oldest known written documents in the world today is believed to be a bureaucratic record written by an administrative official by the name of Kushim. We believe Kushim worked in a brewery, and the document we have seems to be a record of him receiving 135,000 litres of barley over 37 months (Nissen et al., 1993, p. 36).

All this matters because the reliable storage and recovery of information is absolutely central to any bureaucracy. This is true whether the bureaucracy is ancient or modern. Think about it. How does writing things down help you to organize things better? What does it enable you to do that you couldn't do before?

Photo 6.3 Sumerian engraved tokens c 4000 BCE
Source: Denise Schmandt-Besserat, Courtesy Musee du Louvre, Near Eastern Department, Paris, France.

Photo 6.4 Sumerian bullae c 3250 BCE
Source: Denise Schmandt-Besserat, Courtesy Musee du Louvre, Near Eastern Department, Paris, France.

6 | Record-Keeping, Rules, and the Invention of Bureaucracy

Photo 6.5 Sumerian cuneiform writing c 3000 BCE
Source: MET Museum (public dom.).

If you're not sure about the answer to this question, think back to Chapter 5 on criminal organizations. Remember the effect that not being able to write anything down had on an organization's ability to operate? It is virtually impossible to run an organization involving more than just a few people without writing things down. That is, without bureaucracy.

This point stands out in the case of the ancient Sumerians. We're pretty confident that the Sumerian's ability to accurately record and permanently store information enabled massive growth in the size and complexity of organizations like farming estates, temples, palaces, and governments. Moreover, that as the Sumerians got better at organizing, so too their civilization flourished.

How so? Well, we know the Sumerians used their record-keeping skills to manage the communal storage of grain and belongings and the payment of taxes (Basu & Waymire, 2006; Frangipane, 2016).

Record-keeping enabled administrators, like Kushim, to keep track of things, like how much people had contributed to the communal grain silo, and therefore, how much they could expect to withdraw in the future (Schmandt-Besserat, Sasson, & Baines, 1995). We also know that keeping records enabled Sumerians to administer a complex system of taxation. Modern, state-run organizations (such as the government department that deals with taxation) are built around good, reliable, well-administered bureaucracies. This was no different in the time of the Sumerians.

For the ancient Sumerians, as it is for governments now, having accurate, permanent records of things like who had paid what taxes was incredibly important. With these records they could calculate exactly how much tax had been paid and work out what resources were available to pay for things like palaces, temples, irrigation, city defences, and armies (Basu & Waymire, 2006; Schmandt-Besserat et al., 1995). Having records meant that you could do things like set budgets, plan, and organize things in a more sophisticated way. Bureaucracy opened a whole world of possibilities.

Interestingly, it is also believed that tax records enabled Sumerian officials to do things considered to be very advanced (modern), like work out ways of redistributing wealth to make their society fairer (Charvát, 2013, p. 116). Records meant that Sumerian officials knew who owned the most land, and thus who could be taxed the most. It also worked the other way. They also knew who owned very little land, and therefore who should pay less tax. From this, they could also deduce who might potentially benefit from agricultural surpluses and allocate these accordingly (Schmandt-Besserat et al., 1995).

Although we don't have particularly reliable evidence of an ancient Sumerian welfare state, the crucial point is that it becomes possible to do these kinds of things when you have accurate, permanent records. Entire systems of organization could be (and were) built around these records, and they had a massive impact on how ancient societies functioned (Farazmand, 1998; Mattessich, 1987; Steinfeld, 2015). Bureaucracy might sound extremely dull, but it's an absolute game-changer when it comes to organization.

6.5 Why we love a good bureaucracy

Bureaucracy is arguably the dominant system of organization in the world today (Monteiro & Adler, 2022). As the anthropologist David Graeber put it in his book, *The Utopia of Rules*, it's difficult to imagine other ways of setting up organizations that are not "immeasurably worse" (Graeber, 2015, p. 152).

Why is it so hard to imagine organizing in a way that isn't bureaucratic, do you think? Why is it that bureaucracy is so important? There are several ways of answering this question. Perhaps the most obvious is that bureaucracy facilitates large-scale administration by coordinating the work of many individuals in a systematic, predictable, and efficient way (Blau, 1963). What's there not to like about that?

Bureaucracy's allure is also not just confined to efficiency. Bureaucracy also enables organizations to operate in a fair and consistent way. Du Gay (2000) talks at length about this in his book *In Praise of Bureaucracy*, which I recommend you read. Also check out Monteiro and Adler (2022). I've recommended both in "Things to Watch, Things to Read."

Fairness in a bureaucracy derives from the idea that properly run bureaucracies are incredibly good at two things—working out the most efficient way to doing things and figuring out how to put these efficient ways of doing things into practice, in a way that produces the same outcome time and time again.

Let's use an example to understand what I mean by this—the process you went through to get a place at university. As far as UK universities are concerned, the process you went through to get a place probably went a bit like this: an organization [the exam board] assessed your academic performance using a standardized test and gave you a grade. You gave this grade to the university when you applied for a place in your course. The university then used this grade to decide whether or not to give you a place on the course. Simple.

In fact, if you didn't do an interview or submit a personal statement, then the grades submitted were probably the *only* thing the university used to decide whether to give you a place or not. If that was the case, then the entire process might even have been automated. More probably though, someone, somewhere, read your application and used a set of entry criteria [the "rules" for acceptance] to decide whether to offer you a place or not. If you met the criteria, you got an offer letter. End of story.

This might feel horribly impersonal. Years of hard work distilled down into some grades, a list of rules, a bureaucrat, and a binary "yes" or "no" answer. However, in many ways it's a pretty ideal system. When it comes to applying to university, this is precisely what you want. You want this system because it is a fair way of doing things. It is fair because every student's application is assessed against exactly the same set of criteria. In a bureaucracy, everyone gets treated the same.

This is why universities use bureaucracies to allocate students to places. It is also why governments use bureaucracies to allocate benefits and calculate tax, and it is why banks (such as the one I used to work for) use bureaucracies to decide who gets bank accounts, loans, and mortgages. Bureaucracies are an efficient, consistently fair way of doing things.

6.6 The flaws in the system

How do you feel about what I've said about why we love a bureaucracy? Does it all feel a bit celebratory—a bit too good to be true, like it's only part of the story? Well, you're right. It is. A very reasonable question that might be nagging at you is that if bureaucracy is so great, why does nobody ever say: "I love all this bureaucracy," or "it's so reassuring to have to fill out all these forms," or even "it's so much easier having these complex rules to follow?"

6.6.1 Fair enough?

Let's begin by revisiting the example of your application to university. University application systems are actually only fair insofar as everyone's applications are assessed against the same criteria.

However, just because everyone's applications are all assessed using the same criteria, does not mean the criteria being used to make those assessment are fair. If you think about it, the whole point of having assessment criteria is that they privilege certain people (e.g., those with high grades) and discriminate against others (e.g., those with low grades).

This is where things get quite complicated. Assessments must be made about who/what will get the privilege and simple, standardized rules are an incredibly blunt way of doing this. Is it fair, for example, to deny someone a place at university because they were in a car crash on the day of their exam? Is it fair, for example, to deny someone a place at university because the state school they attended provided a poor education compared to the one kids got at the private school down the road?

Ultimately, this is where the argument that bureaucracies are fair reaches its limit and starts to break down. Bureaucracies don't care about context. There is no room for subjective assessments. Rules are rules, and in a bureaucracy, they are all that counts. That's it. End of story.

Except it isn't the end of the story, thankfully. These types of errors can be corrected by building mechanisms into bureaucracies to counter-balance the systematic unfair treatment of certain groups of people. University admission systems have mechanisms that try to level up the playing field by trying to account for students' individual circumstances. Sure, these mechanisms are not perfect, but it's better than the alternative of doing nothing.

6.6.2 Alienation, on a grand scale

Another particularly well-documented flaw in the bureaucratic system is the stultifying effect it has on people. If you work—or have worked—in a bureaucratic organization, you'll know what I mean. Life as a bureaucrat can be frustrating and incredibly boring. There really is only so much fun you can have with a rule book.

Remember my work experience in the bank? It was my first proper job, and it was quite easy to do well. All I had to do was learn the rules and follow them. This done, the job rapidly became the most boring thing I'd ever done in my life. Still today, I've never been more bored than when I was working in the bank.

I'm sure banking can be really exciting. However for me the job I was doing was so bureaucratized, it required absolutely nothing of me. All I did was follow rules and procedures. I didn't think for myself at all. Everything was dictated and prescribed for me. It was horrendous.

This is what critics of bureaucracy mean when we say bureaucracy leaves people feeling "alienated" from their work. It's the sense of being unable to identify with it, of being controlled, exploited, and generally just feeling dehumanized—like a tiny cog in a large, complicated machine. Alienation is one of the major effects of a highly rationalized, bureaucratic system of organization, and it's why many people come to hate it.

6.6.3 There's bureaucracy, then there's real life

To what extent do you think people actually follow rules and procedures in bureaucratic organizations? In most cases the answer is "only to an extent," or sometimes even "not at all." Sound surprising?

In a now-classic study, Gouldner (1954) shows how a bureaucracy in which everyone religiously follows the rules can be little more than a myth—a kind of fiction that only managers believe in. Sure, an organization might have a comprehensive rule book with detailed, well-defined procedures, but sometimes that's as far as it goes.

What Gouldner describes is the reality that within any bureaucratic organization there likely exists a "system within a system," or what he calls a "mock" bureaucracy—a system in which workers only pretend to follow the rules but actually decide amongst themselves how to do everything.

Let's go back to that job at BigBank. The system we used to make lending decisions only approved loans for low-risk things like house renovations. If you wanted a loan to go on holiday, you'd get declined. This was a problem. Customers couldn't go on holidays they couldn't afford. Bankers lost sales bonuses.

The solution to the problem was just as Gouldner described—a secret, subversive system within a system. It worked a bit like this: with a bit of help from bankers, customers would realize the folly of trying to borrow money to go on holiday. With a bit of reflection, they'd decide what they really wanted was a house extension. As if by magic, the loan would be approved.

Put less delicately: customers lied on their loan application forms in order to get the money they wanted. Other customers had their forms rewritten for them by bonus-hungry bankers. Either way, the system was gamed. Customers got their money and bankers got their sales bonuses. Life was good. Or was it?

This particular mock bureaucracy ultimately created massive problems. Huge numbers of people borrowed huge amounts of money to fund lifestyles they couldn't afford. A great many went bankrupt because of it, and a great many banks got into trouble with regulators because of it.

The case of BigBank is a cautionary story. However, paradoxical as it may sound, not following the rules can be a good thing. Sometimes rules need to be broken for the system to work. This might sound weird. In many ways it is. What's the point in a bureaucracy if you have to spend your life working around the rules?

To understand the answer to this question have a crack at writing down the procedure for something simple, like making a coffee. Really think about it. How exactly do you make a coffee? Write down all the steps involved, and then give it to someone. Tell them they can only do whatever you've written down. Nothing more.

If you do this exercise properly, you'll realize it's incredibly hard to write a procedure. In fact, it's almost impossible to properly "bureaucratize" something—even something simple like making a cup of coffee. This is because it's hard to describe even the most basic task in enough detail that someone can do it successfully by simply following the rules. If all you can do is what's written down, it is likely that whatever you are trying to do will come out wrong. Even with the most simple things, there's a huge amount of what's called "tacit skill" involved—things we do intuitively that are difficult (if not impossible) to write down.

For example, making a coffee requires you to know exactly how much coffee granules to use with how much water. You need to know where to get ingredients and the correct order in which to assemble them. Also, other practical things like how long to leave the cafetière before you press the plunger (assuming you're using one), what size cup you'll need, and how hot the water must be.

If you make your own coffee, you'll know all these details intuitively, and you'll know the precise sequence you must follow to make a coffee. You'll also know which parts of the procedure are really important and which aren't.

The question though, is whether you know these details precisely enough to be able to write a procedure that someone who doesn't know what they are doing could follow? And not just follow but follow and create a coffee that is exactly the same as the one you would make. Do you know, for example, the precise volume of water and milk needed to make a coffee down to the milliliter? Do you know, down to the gram, how much coffee and sugar you need? Do you know, down to the degree, how hot the water needs to be? This is the level of detail you need to be able to go into if you really want to properly bureaucratize something.

The point is that bureaucratizing things is really hard. As a consequence, most of the time bureaucracies don't actually work in the way that they are supposed to. In bureaucratic organizations, people have to use their intuition to fill in the gaps. Sometimes, they may do it in ways that support the organization's overall objectives. Sometimes, they may not. Sometimes, people may, as in the case of BigBank, exploit the system for their own gain.

In relation to the latter, Blau (1963) describes how one of the most powerful weapons in the arsenal of a trade union is the "work to rule" instruction. You don't actually need to go on strike to cripple an organization. Workers can cripple an organization simply by following its own rules and procedures. No rule can ever really be detailed enough to capture all the possibilities associated with its enactment. Consequently, working to rule starves an organization of all the discretionary effort needed to operationalize formal rules and procedures. If you're ever frustrated at work give it a go. You might be surprised at the effect it has. You might also get fired. Let me know how you get on.

6.6.4 Just remind me again, why are we doing this?

Have you ever experienced a situation when someone in an organization has asked you to do something absolutely stupid because "those are the rules?"

I have an example. In the midst of the COVID-19 pandemic, I went to a library to pick up a book. Quite reasonably, the library had in place a "one way" system to prevent people from coming into contact with each other and help limit the spread of COVID-19. This is all well and good, except, the system didn't work and we were all blindly following it anyway.

The scenario was this: people could only borrow books if they had made an appointment. Appointments were spaced 20 minutes apart. It takes about 2 minutes to collect a book. I made my appointment and collected my book. All grand, except rather than stepping 2 meters to the right (across an open and empty stretch of carpet) and walking directly out of the library, I was told to exit the library by walking into the very center of the library turning around and walking back out again. This "exit" route was about 100-metres long and took me past lines and lines of students working at desks. Once I reached the heart of the library, I then had to turn 180 degrees and follow a path immediately parallel to the one I had just taken in. Eventually I returned to the reception desk I had just been standing at, but now 2 meters to the right. Then I was allowed to walk out the door.

This is what goal displacement looks like. It is a situation when following rules becomes the only thing that matters, even when doing so goes against everything the rules were intended to prevent.

6.6.5 Out of sight, out of mind

One of the biggest criticisms of bureaucracy is that it disconnects people from the products of their labor and blinds them to what the organization is doing. Bureaucracies, according to Bauman (1989, p. 101), silence "moral inhibitions and, more generally, make(s) people refrain from resistance against evil." Bureaucracies enable "people to do things their nature would otherwise prevent them from doing" (Bauman, 1989, p. 95).

Seems a bit extreme? What does Bauman mean by it, do you think? How could a rule-centered, desk-based way of working erode peoples' moral inhibitions and stop them resisting evil? The answer is that it can, it does, and the history books are full of chilling examples.

Bauman makes his arguments in the context of the Nazi Holocaust and the role that bureaucracy played in this atrocity (see also Arendt, 1963/2006). However, his comments are also not restricted to the Holocaust. Bauman argues that the erosion of moral inhibitions is what happens in *all* bureaucracies. It is a kind of extreme, dysfunctional side effect.

What Bauman argues is that when labor is divided (as it is in bureaucratic organizations) people are physically and mentally distanced from the final product (or service) they are contributing towards. People become buried in large and complex organizational structures in which they only work on narrowly defined decontextualized tasks. The work they perform is experienced as meaningless, regardless of what it ultimately leads too. Bauman's words are better than mine (1989, p. 100):

> it is one thing to give the command to load bombs onto a plane [and to press the button to drop them], it is quite another to take care of the regular steel supply in the bomb factory. The commander [who orders the bomb to be dropped] may have no vivid, visual impression of the devastation the bomb is about to cause. While the steel worker does not even have to think about the uses the bomb will be put to ... for most parties[,] knowledge of the final outcome is more or less irrelevant as far as their own work is concerned. Remember too, that even if the individual was to think about the purposes to which their actions contribute to, it is not they who ultimately make the bombs. It is the factory that does that.

6 | Record-Keeping, Rules, and the Invention of Bureaucracy

So what Bauman is talking about is the capacity of bureaucracies to distance people from the activities of the organization. For Bauman (1989, pp. 99–101) this effect is an outcome of two parallel processes:

> ... [first] the meticulous and functional division of labour (in addition to the linear graduation of power and subordination) and, [second] the substitution of technical for moral responsibility. All division of labour (also such division as results from the mere hierarchy of command) creates distance between most of the contributors of the final outcome of a collective activity, and the outcome itself. Before the last links in the bureaucratic chain of power ... confront their task, most of the preparatory operations that brought about that confrontation have been already performed by persons who had no personal experience, and sometimes not the knowledge either, of the task in question. What such practical and mental distance from the final products means is that most functionaries of the bureaucratic hierarchy may give commands without full knowledge of their effects. ... such is the distance that any judgements that are made are abstract, detached, technical ones. They are certainly not moral ones. They measure and monitor the progress of the work, but say little about the nature of the operations and its morality. ... People may question the morality of tasks within an administrative hierarchy if they are able to see the outcomes. However this possibility disappears as a result of the functional division of labour. When tasks are broken down into their constitutive parts, distance is created. ... Technical responsibility differs from moral responsibility in that it forgets that the action is a means to accomplish something other than itself. As outer connections are removed from the bureaucrat's field of vision, the bureaucrat's own act becomes an end in and of itself. It is something that is only judged according to its own criteria—about whether that particular task was done successfully, or not. Once isolated from their distant consequences, most functionally specialized acts either pass moral tests easily, or are morally indifferent. When unencumbered by morals, acts can be judged on unambiguously rational grounds. This is how technical efficiency supplants morality.

So, perhaps the biggest challenge created by bureaucracy is its ineffectiveness in the context of something called "substantive rationality." Bureaucracies do a good job of calculating the most efficient way of achieving something—of being "instrumentally" rational. However, they are nothing like as good at ensuring the "ends" are sensible in themselves. The point is that people in bureaucracies pay very little attention to the "big picture." They are not concerned with what the organization is *actually* doing, or with whether it is ethical and appropriate. Instead, they are almost exclusively concerned with ensuring things are done in the most efficient way possible. As Grey (2016) puts it: "bureaucracies don't care about the substantively rational. They don't care about ethics, they just care about getting the job done as quickly as possible."

6.7 Summary

What I hope has become clear to you from reading this chapter is that bureaucracy is an invention. It's a way of organizing that can trace its lineage back to antiquity, and the written records of early scribes laboring to inject order and efficiency into the relative chaos of fledgling civilizations.

We've moved a long way since our ancestors first etched notches into bones and stones, carved tokens, and scratched lists into clay tablets. Modern bureaucracies are huge, complex structures often involving large numbers of people. These bureaucracies can be big, unwieldy, and produce horrifying results. However, bureaucracy can also perform an important role in our society. They are integral to key institutions, such as the government departments that deal with taxation and welfare. They're also integral to private, capitalist organizations. They are helpful because they provide an efficient, effective way of getting things done.

Not just this, as the anthropologist David Graeber puts it, "For many of us, much of the time, and for all of us, some of the time, bureaucracies hold a kind of 'covert appeal'" (Graeber, 2015, p. 149). There is, in theory at least, an intuitive logic to a system defined by formalized rules and regulations where there are hierarchies of impersonal officials. Such a system gives you predictable, consistent, and fair outcomes. What more could you want?

Things to Watch, Things to Read

In this table are suggestions for things you can watch and things you can read to learn more about this topic. I've also included a very short commentary, so that you know why I've recommended a particular source and what to look out for.

Read in two to three hours	Weber, M. (author). Keith Tribe (translator). (2019). *Economy and Society: A New Translation*, pp. 343–354. Cambridge, Massachusetts: Harvard University Press.

This is a new translation of Max Weber's iconic, posthumously published book *Economy and Society*. Pages 343–354 are the most relevant for the study of bureaucracy—it's where Weber deals with the subject of bureaucracy. Note that at the point Weber published *Economy and Society*, bureaucracy had already been around for centuries, and that Weber was well aware of this. As such, contra to a lot of sources, Weber didn't invent the concept of bureaucracy. However, Weber was one of the first to make a serious attempt at theorizing it. As one of the defining texts of the modern social sciences, *Economy and Society* is well worth reading—even if you just focus on the section on bureaucracy.

Read in a day or two	Monteiro, P. and P. S. Adler. (2022) Bureaucracy for the 21st century: Clarifying and expanding our view of bureaucratic organization. *Academy of Management Annals* 16(2), 427–475.

This article reviews over a century of organizational research on bureaucracy. It finds that researchers have thought about bureaucracy in three different ways. As: (1) an organizing principle; (2) a paradigmatic form of organization; (3) as (just) one of a great many different ways of structuring organizations. In the article the authors propose a new direction for research into bureaucracy and make suggestions about how we can better understand bureaucracy's various guises as we move into the 21st century.

Read in a week or three	Bauman, Z. (2000). *Modernity and the Holocaust*. New York: Cornell University Press.

This book won the European Amalfi Prize for Sociology and Social Sciences. It is a groundbreaking text that explores the connection between modernity (and bureaucracy in particular) and the Holocaust. At the heart of this book are the profound, chilling consequences Bauman believes bureaucracy has on morality. Bauman's point being that where we have modernity, and bureaucracy in particular, we have the potential moral blindness to events such as the Nazi Holocaust. I quote this book at length towards the end of this chapter, but it's well worth reading—it's an incredible piece of work.

Du Gay, P. 2000. *In Praise of Bureaucracy: Weber, Organization, Ethics.* London: Sage.

This book is another outstanding piece of work on bureaucracy. As the title suggests, it is a defence of bureaucracy. To paraphrase the author: It is an attempt to reclaim the ethical dignity of the bureau and bureaucrat. Amongst other things, it also offers an interesting critique of Bauman's *Modernity and the Holocaust*, tempering some of its key arguments. It is helpful to read *In Praise of Bureaucracy* and *Modernity and the Holocaust* one after the other.

Watch in an evening	Loach, K. (Director). *I, Daniel Blake*. (2016). Sixteen Films.

Winner of the Palme d'Or at the 2016 Cannes Film Festival *I, Daniel Blake* is a powerful drama film that focuses on a man's desperate struggle with the UK welfare state. In the context of a hyper-rationalized, purposefully difficult to navigate bureaucracy, the film shows Daniel being pushed into poverty by a system set up not to care. Based on real peoples' actual experiences, the story told is well familiar to many in the UK and far beyond.

Watch in a week	Lanzmann, L. (Director). *Shoah*. (1985). IFC Films.

This is considered to be one of the best documentaries ever made. Across two parts and over nine-and-a-half hours it undertakes a forensic analysis of the Nazi Holocaust, and of the particular role of bureaucracy within it. The power of this documentary comes from the centrality of interviews and eye-witness testimony. These give a sickening, unapologetically detailed insight into the organization (the bureaucracy), through which one of the most defining events of the 20th century was orchestrated. You should watch this in conjunction with Bauman's *Modernity and the Holocaust*.

Research Insight: A checklist that saves lives

Source: Haynes, A. B., T. G. Weiser, W. R. Berry, S. R. Lipsitz, A. H. S. Breizat, E. P. Dellinger, et al. (2009). A surgical safety checklist to reduce morbidity and mortality in a global population. *New England Journal of Medicine* 360(5), 491–499.

Edited abstract: published in the *New England Journal of Medicine*, this study by Haynes et al. (2009) reports the initial findings of their investigation into the effect of introducing a piece of bureaucracy—the world's first safety checklist—into eight hospitals in eight cities around the world. Set in the context of an estimated 234 million operations performed yearly, the study hypothesizes that a program to implement a 19-item surgical safety checklist designed to improve team communication and consistency of care would reduce complications and deaths associated with surgery. The key findings of the study are that the rate of death of 1.5% (before the checklist was introduced) declined to 0.8% after it had been implemented. It showed that using the checklist reduced inpatient complications from 11% of patients to 7%. The article concludes with the recommendation that the checklist be used to improve the quality and safety of healthcare.

Case Study: The World Health Organization Surgical Safety Checklist

Based on: Gawande, A. (2010). *Checklist Manifesto, the (HB)*. Indi: Penguin Books.

Introduction

The central function of healthcare organizations is to provide safe and effective care to people in need. 90% of the time they do just that. However, researchers estimate that if you are admitted to hospital, there is about a 10% chance you will experience an adverse incident during your stay (Jha et al., 2013). In this case study, we'll look at how often things go wrong in healthcare and why. We'll also look at what is being done to make healthcare safer, and how bureaucracy is helping.

Adverse incidents in healthcare

In healthcare, an adverse incident is the technical term for an event in which a person is harmed as a consequence of medical care that is designed to help them. As a concept, it incorporates incidents that are both preventable (e.g., medical errors) and incidents that are not preventable (e.g., accidental slips and falls).

The global burden of adverse incidents is huge. Every year, there are around 421 million hospitalizations in the world resulting in an estimated 42.7 million adverse incidents (Jha et al., 2013). Of the 42.7 million adverse incidents that occur annually, around 43.5% are preventable (de Vries et al., 2010). This is a staggering statistic, but one that must be kept in perspective. If you are admitted to hospital, it is unlikely that you will suffer an adverse incident. Remember, 90% of the time nothing goes wrong.

If you are unlucky and suffer an adverse incident, the chance of you being seriously hurt is extremely low. Precisely how low your chances of harm are is difficult to know. This is because very few healthcare systems in the world are open and transparent about adverse incidents. As a result, we don't really know exactly how many adverse incidents occur globally or what effect they have. At the moment, we primarily rely on estimates (e.g., Jha et al., 2013; Meara et al., 2015).

An exception is the UK's National Health Service (NHS), which makes data on adverse incidents publicly available. Consider the data from NHS England, which is the healthcare system for one of the four countries that comprise the UK. Between 1 April 2020 and 31 March 2021, NHS staff reported more than 2.1 million adverse incidents across the entire health system (Improvement, 2021b). Of these, 69.3% caused no harm to the patient. 27.1% caused low levels of harm. Just under 4% resulted in higher degrees of harm. 0.3% resulted in the death of the patient.

In NHS England's data, 0.3% equals 6,263 people dying as a consequence of harm caused by an adverse incident. We can contextualize this number further by looking at a particular category of adverse incident called a "Never Event."

Within NHS England a "Never Event" is defined as a serious, largely preventable patient safety incident that should not have occurred if healthcare providers had implemented existing national guidance or safety recommendations (Improvement, 2021a). The definition NHS England uses is wider than the one used in most healthcare organizations. The definition used by NHS England incorporates avoidable incidents that cause harm to patients **and** avoidable incidents that only have the potential for significant harm.

The numbers are as follows. Between 1 April 2020 and 31 March 2021, NHS England staff reported 364 Never Events (Improvement, 2021c). Included in this data are 142 incidents of "wrong site surgery" [e.g., procedures performed on the wrong part of the body]; 80 incidents of "retained foreign object post procedure" [e.g., surgical swabs accidentally left in the body after surgery]; and 30 incidents of "wrong implant/prosthesis" [e.g., a heart patient who had the wrong pacemaker fitted].

Because of the impact of COVID-19 there were less Never Events in 2020–21 than usual. Between 1 April 2019 and 31 March 2020 staff at NHS England reported 472 Never Events (Improvement, 2020). Between 1 April 2018 and 31 March 2019 they reported 496 Never Events (Improvement, 2019).

These numbers might sound shocking. In many ways they are. However, they are consistent with countries with similarly advanced, well-funded healthcare systems. You are not more likely to suffer harm in an English hospital than you are in an Italian, German, Australian, or a US one.

Why do adverse incidents happen and what is being done about them?

The data reported previously reflects the simple reality that trying to care for sick people is hard. Healthcare environments are technically complex and organizationally challenging places. There are a great many things that can go wrong.

For example, vital life-saving equipment can fail or be set up incorrectly. Important information can be lost or poorly communicated. Capable, highly skilled professionals can be easily distracted, forget something, rush, take a shortcut, and make a mistake. Moreover, as M. S. Donaldson, Corrigan, and Kohn (2000) describe, humans simply make mistakes (see also Reason, 1990, 2000).

However there is no escaping the human and economic costs of the 42.7 million adverse incidents that occur annually in the world (Jha et al., 2013). This statistic is one that the world has become increasingly aware of, particularly since the year 2000 (L. Donaldson, 2002). Accordingly, improving the quality and safety of patient care has risen up the priority lists of healthcare organizations, national governments, and non-governmental organizations (NGOs) around the world.

One area that has received particular attention is surgical operating theatres, where 39.6% of all adverse incidents occur (de Vries et al., 2010). Of the more than 313 million surgical procedures that take place annually (Meara et al., 2015), adverse incidents are believed to occur in between 12.5% and 20.1% of cases. Avoidable adverse incidents occur in between 4.2% and 7% of cases (Anderson, Davis, Hanna, & Vincent, 2013; see also Panagioti et al., 2019). So, according to these estimates, there are between 13.1 million and almost 22 million avoidable adverse incidents in surgical operating theatres globally, every year.

Many different approaches have been taken to address the problem of avoidable harm in surgery. One of the most effective was spearheaded by the World Health Organization (WHO) and involved the introduction of a piece of bureaucracy into the operating theatre: a simple, standardized "Surgical Safety Checklist" for use during surgical procedures.

The Surgical Safety checklist

The idea for a surgical safety checklist came from aviation where checklists have played a major role in improving safety since the crash of a Boeing 299 during a demonstration flight to the US Army Air Corps in 1935. Eventually known as the B17 "Flying Fortress," the plane crashed moments after take-off. The subsequent investigation concluded that "pilot error" was to blame. The B17 was found to be "just too much plane for one man to fly." Planes had become too complex, meaning that pilots couldn't fly them safely using skill, memory, and intuition alone.

Boeing's solution to the problem of the growing complexity of flying planes came as a surprise to many. Rather than redesign the plane, they introduced a one-page checklist. This was the world's first pre-flight safety checklist. The checklist is shown in Photo 6.6. On the checklist you can see the most important things pilots needed to do to fly the plane. The checklist didn't replace the skill of flying. Rather, the checklist proceduralized the skill. The checklist set out all the safety-critical things pilots needed to do. It reminded them when they had to do things and in what particular order.

6 | Record-Keeping, Rules, and the Invention of Bureaucracy

RESTRICTED

APPROVED B-17F and G CHECKLIST
REVISED 3-1-44

PILOT'S DUTIES IN RED
COPILOT'S DUTIES IN BLACK

BEFORE STARTING
1. Pilot's Preflight—COMPLETE
2. Form 1A—CHECKED
3. Controls and Seats—CHECKED
4. Fuel Transfer Valves & Switch—OFF
5. Intercoolers—Cold
6. Gyros—UNCAGED
7. Fuel Shut-off Switches—OPEN
8. Gear Switch—NEUTRAL
9. Cowl Flaps—Open Right— OPEN LEFT—Locked
10. Turbos—OFF
11. Idle cut-off—CHECKED
12. Throttles—CLOSED
13. High RPM—CHECKED
14. Autopilot—OFF
15. De-icers and Anti-icers, Wing and Prop—OFF
16. Cabin Heat—OFF
17. Generators—OFF

STARTING ENGINES
1. Fire Guard and Call Clear—LEFT Right
2. Master Switch—ON
3. Battery switches and inverters—ON & CHECKED
4. Parking Brakes—Hydraulic Check—On-CHECKED
5. Booster Pumps—Pressure—ON & CHECKED
6. Carburetor Filters—Open
7. Fuel Quantity—Gallons per tank
8. Start Engines: both magnetos on after one revolution
9. Flight Indicator & Vacuum Pressures CHECKED
10. Radio—On
11. Check Instruments—CHECKED
12. Crew Report
13. Radio Call & Altimeter—SET

ENGINE RUN-UP
1. Brakes—Locked
2. Trim Tabs—SET
3. Exercise Turbos and Props
4. Check Generators—CHECKED & OFF
5. Run up Engines

BEFORE TAKEOFF
1. Tailwheel—Locked
2. Gyro—Set
3. Generators—ON

AFTER TAKEOFF
1. Wheel—PILOT'S SIGNAL
2. Power Reduction
3. Cowl Flaps
4. Wheel Check—OK right—OK LEFT

BEFORE LANDING
1. Radio Call, Altimeter—SET
2. Crew Positions—OK
3. Autopilot—OFF
4. Booster Pumps—On
5. Mixture Controls—AUTO-RICH
6. Intercooler—Set
7. Carburetor Filters—Open
8. Wing De-icers—Off
9. Landing Gear
   a. Visual—Down Right—DOWN LEFT Tailwheel Down, Antenna in, Ball Turret Checked
   b. Light—OK
   c. Switch Off—Neutral
10. Hydraulic Pressure—OK Valve closed
11. RPM 2100—Set
12. Turbos—Set
13. Flaps ⅓—⅓ Down

FINAL APPROACH
14. Flaps—PILOT'S SIGNAL
15. RPM 2200—PILOT'S SIGNAL

RESTRICTED

Photo 6.6 Pre-flight checklist for the Boeing B17 "flying fortress"
Source: AMG (public dom.).

Healthcare's equivalent of the pre-flight checklist was designed, tested, and introduced by the WHO on the 14 January 2009. This surgical safety checklist is shown in Photo 6.7. On the checklist, you'll see 19 checks split into three different sections. The first part is done before the patient is anesthetized. The second part is done after the patient is anesthetized but

Surgical Safety Checklist

World Health Organization — **Patient Safety** (A World Alliance for Safer Health Care)

Before induction of anaesthesia

(with at least nurse and anaesthetist)

Has the patient confirmed his/her identity, site, procedure, and consent?
- ☐ Yes

Is the site marked?
- ☐ Yes
- ☐ Not applicable

Is the anaesthesia machine and medication check complete?
- ☐ Yes

Is the pulse oximeter on the patient and functioning?
- ☐ Yes

Does the patient have a:

Known allergy?
- ☐ No
- ☐ Yes

Difficult airway or aspiration risk?
- ☐ No
- ☐ Yes, and equipment/assistance available

Risk of >500ml blood loss (7ml/kg in children)?
- ☐ No
- ☐ Yes, and two IVs/central access and fluids planned

Before skin incision

(with nurse, anaesthetist and surgeon)

- ☐ **Confirm all team members have introduced themselves by name and role.**
- ☐ **Confirm the patient's name, procedure, and where the incision will be made.**

Has antibiotic prophylaxis been given within the last 60 minutes?
- ☐ Yes
- ☐ Not applicable

Anticipated Critical Events

To Surgeon:
- ☐ What are the critical or non-routine steps?
- ☐ How long will the case take?
- ☐ What is the anticipated blood loss?

To Anaesthetist:
- ☐ Are there any patient-specific concerns?

To Nursing Team:
- ☐ Has sterility (including indicator results) been confirmed?
- ☐ Are there equipment issues or any concerns?

Is essential imaging displayed?
- ☐ Yes
- ☐ Not applicable

Before patient leaves operating room

(with nurse, anaesthetist and surgeon)

Nurse Verbally Confirms:
- ☐ The name of the procedure
- ☐ Completion of instrument, sponge and needle counts
- ☐ Specimen labelling (read specimen labels aloud, including patient name)
- ☐ Whether there are any equipment problems to be addressed

To Surgeon, Anaesthetist and Nurse:
- ☐ What are the key concerns for recovery and management of this patient?

This checklist is not intended to be comprehensive. Additions and modifications to fit local practice are encouraged.

Revised 1/2009 ©WHO, 2009

Photo 6.7 WHO Safe Surgery Checklist
Source: © World Health Organization 2009. All rights reserved.

before the first incision is made. The third part is done when the procedure is over but before the patient leaves the operating theatre.

The checks on the WHO checklist aren't complicated. Like the ones on Boeing's B17, they're the medical equivalent of remembering to tie your shoelaces. However, they represent the things that research has shown are often forgotten, are not done properly, or are done late, but which are absolutely fundamental to complicated procedures, whether performing surgery or flying a plane.

So, if you look at the checklist in Photo 6.7, you'll see references to things confirming the identity of the patient, making sure the site to be operated on is clearly marked, and the team knows what is going on. You'll see reminders to the surgical team to plan ahead, and make sure things like vital equipment, spare blood, and other things are ready and available. You'll also see reminders to the team to introduce themselves and their role to one another and opportunities for everyone to state their concerns about the operation. It's basic but important stuff.

How much help is a simple checklist?

The simple answer to this question is "a lot." Since it was launched in 2009, the WHO Surgical Safety Checklist has done for surgery what Boeing's flight safety checklist did for aviation. It made surgery much, much safer.

Before the WHO Surgical Safety Checklist was launched the team that designed it tested it for three months in eight very different hospitals around the world: Toronto, Canada; New Delhi, India; Amman, Jordan; Auckland, New Zealand; Manila, Philippines; Ifakara, Tanzania; London, England; and Seattle, US. These were hospitals representing a variety of economic circumstances and diverse populations.

Prior to introducing the checklist, the rate of any complication across all the sites was 11%. After the checklist had been implemented the rate of complications dropped to 7%. The total in-hospital rate of death nearly halved, dropping from 1.5% to 0.8%. Rates of surgical-site infection and unplanned reoperation dropped by a similar proportion.

Rates of complication also fell. In high-income hospitals, they dropped from 10.3% before the introduction of the checklist to 7.1% after its introduction. In low-income hospitals they dropped from 11.7% to 6.8%. The rate of death was also reduced. From 0.9% before checklist introduction to 0.6% afterward at high-income sites, and, from 2.1% to 1.0% at lower-income sites. The checklist worked.

Questions

1. Why do you think the surgical safety checklist improved the quality and safety of healthcare so much?
2. Using the WHO Surgical Safety Checklist has been proven to save lives. However, some surgeons have refused to use it. Why do you think that is?
3. Based on what we know about human fallibility, what would you think if a hospital claimed they used the WHO Surgical Safety Checklist 100% of the time?
4. You don't have to be performing surgery to benefit from a checklist. Can you think of how you might use a checklist to improve the quality of your work, or even your life in general?
5. Based on your knowledge of the weaknesses of bureaucracy, do you think there are any risks associated with using the surgical safety checklists?

References

Anderson, O., R. Davis, G. B. Hanna, & C. A. Vincent. (2013). Surgical adverse events: A systematic review. *The American Journal of Surgery* 206(2), 253–262.

Arendt, H. (1963/2006). *Eichmann in Jerusalem: A Report on the Banality of Evil*. London: Penguin.

Basu, S. & G. B. Waymire. (2006). Recordkeeping and human evolution. *Accounting Horizons* 20(3), 201–229.

Bauman, Z. (1989). *Modernity and the Holocaust*. Oxford: Blackwell.

Blau, P. M. (1963). *The Dynamics of Bureaucracy: Study of Interpersonal Relations in Two Government Agencies*, rev ed. Chicago: University of Chicago Press.

Braverman, H. (1998). *Labor and Monopoly Capital: The Degradation of Work in the Twentieth Century*. New York: New York University Press.

Charvát, P. (2013). *The Birth of the State: Ancient Egypt, Mesopotamia, India and China*. Prague: Karolinum Press.

de Vries, E. N., H. A. Prins, R. M. Crolla, A. J. den Outer, G. van Andel, S. van Helden H, et al. (2010). Effect of a comprehensive surgical safety system on patient outcomes. *New England Journal of Medicine* 363(20), 1928–1937.

Donaldson, L. (2002). An organisation with a memory. *Clinical Medicine* 2(5), 452.

Donaldson, M. S., J. M. Corrigan, & L. T. Kohn. (2000). *To Err Is Human: Building a Safer Health System*. Washington (DC): National Academies Press.

Du Gay, P. (2000). *In Praise of Bureaucracy: Weber-Organization-Ethics*. London: Sage.

Farazmand, A. (1998). Administration of the Persian Achaemenid world-state empire: Implications for modern public administration. *International Journal of Public Administration* 21(1), 25–86.

Frangipane, M. (2016). The origins of administrative practices and their developments in Greater Mesopotamia. The evidence from Arslantepe. *Archéo-Nil* 26(1), 9–32.

Gawande, A. (2010). *Checklist Manifesto, the (HB)*. London: Penguin Books.

Gouldner, A. W. (1954). *Patterns of Industrial Bureaucracy*. Glencoe, IL: Free Press.

Graeber, D. (2015). *The Utopia of Rules: On Technology, Stupidity, and the Secret Joys of Bureaucracy*. Melville House.

Grey, C. (2016). *A Very Short Fairly Interesting and Reasonably Cheap Book About Studying Organizations*. London: Sage.

Haynes, A. B., T. G. Weiser, W. R. Berry, S. R. Lipsitz, A.-H. S. Breizat, E. P. Dellinger, et al. (2009). A surgical safety checklist to reduce morbidity and mortality in a global population. *New England Journal of Medicine* 360(5), 491–499.

Ifrah, G. (2000). *The Universal History of Numbers*. London: Harvill.

Improvement, N. (2019). *Provisional Publication of Never Events Reported as Occurring between 1 April 2018 and 31 March 2019*. Retrieved from London: NHS England.

Improvement, N. (2020). *Never Events Reported as Occurring between 1 April 2019 and 31 March 2020 - Final Update*. Retrieved from London: NHS England.

Improvement, N. (2021a). *Never Events Reported as Occurring between 1 April 2019 and 31 March 2020 - Final Update*. Retrieved from London: NHS England.

Improvement, N. (2021b). NRLS national patient safety incident reports: Commentary. London: NHS England. Retrieved from http//:www.improvement.nhs.uk

Improvement, N. (2021c). *Provisional Publication of Never Events Reported as Occurring between 01 April 2020 and 31 March 2021*. Retrieved from London: NHS England.

Jha, A. K., I. Larizgoitia, C. Audera-Lopez, N. Prasopa-Plaizier, H. Waters, & D. W. Bates. (2013). The global burden of unsafe medical care: Analytic modelling of observational studies. *BMJ Quality & Safety* 22(10), 809–815.

Kalberg, S. (1980). Max Weber's types of rationality: Cornerstones for the analysis of rationalization processes in history. *American Journal of Sociology* 85(5), 1145–1179.

Keister, O. R. (1963). Commercial record keeping in ancient Mesopotamia. *The Accounting Review* 38(2), 371.

Mattessich, R. (1987). Prehistoric accounting and the problem of representation: On recent archeological evidence of the Middle-East from 8000 BC to 3000 BC. *Accounting Historians Journal* 14(2), 71–91.

Meara, J. G., A. J. Leather, L. Hagander, B. C. Alkire, N. Alonso, E. A. Ameh, et al. (2015). Global Surgery 2030: Evidence and solutions for achieving health, welfare, and economic development. *The Lancet* 386(9993), 569–624.

Monteiro, P. & P. S. Adler. (2022). Bureaucracy for the 21st century: Clarifying and expanding our view of bureaucratic organization. *Academy of Management Annals* 16(2), 427–475.

Mouck, T. (2004). Ancient Mesopotamian accounting and human cognitive evolution. *Accounting Historians Journal* 31(2), 97–124.

Nissen, H. J., P. Damerow, & R. K. Englund. (1993). *Archaic Bookkeeping: Early Writing and Techniques of Economic Administration in the Ancient Near East.* Chicago: University of Chicago Press.

Panagioti, M., K. Khan, R. N. Keers, A. Abuzour, D. Phipps, E. Kontopantelis, et al. (2019). Prevalence, severity, and nature of preventable patient harm across medical care settings: Systematic review and meta-analysis. *BMJ* 366, l4185. doi: 10.1136/bmj.l4185.

Pollock, S. (1992). Bureaucrats and managers, peasants and pastoralists, imperialists and traders: Research on the Uruk and Jemdet Nasr periods in Mesopotamia. *Journal of World Prehistory* 6(3), 297–336.

Powell, B. B. (2009). *Writing: Theory and History of the Technology of Civilization.* Hoboken: John Wiley & Sons.

Reason, J. (1990). *Human Error.* Cambridge: Cambridge University Press.

Reason, J. (2000). Human error: Models and management. *BMJ* 320(7237), 768–770.

Schmandt-Besserat, D., J. M. Sasson, & J. Baines. (1995). Record keeping before writing. *Civiliations of the Ancient Near East.* 4(4), 2097–2106.

Spence, K. (2000). Ancient Egyptian chronology and the astronomical orientation of pyramids. *Nature* 408(6810), 320–324.

Steinfeld, J. M. (2015). The Achaemenid Empire's Contributions to Public Administration. *International Journal of Public Administration* 38(2), 82–91.

Tribe, K. & M. Weber. (2019). *Economy and Society: A New Translation.* Harvard: Harvard University Press.

Waldron, A. (1990). *The Great Wall of China: From History to Myth.* Cambridge: Cambridge University Press.

Yeo, G. (2021). *Record-Making and Record-Keeping in Early Societies.* London: Routledge.

7
Formality, Rationality, and Organizations

> **Keywords**
>
> formal rationality; modernity; manufacturing services; the division of labor; specialization; standardization; assembly lines; Arsenal of Venice; Henry Ford; Ford Motor Company

> **Consider**
>
> How does rationality define modern, formal organizations?
> Where did it come from and why do we organize in this way?

7.1 Introduction

In this chapter we move on from the topic of bureaucracy ever so slightly. We're sticking with the concept of "formal rationality" (the type of thinking that underpins modern bureaucracies) but we're going to look at how it is applied more generally in organizations.

This chapter has three principal sections. The first establishes some basic theoretical foundations that I think are helpful to understand at this point. The second looks at the spread of rationalized ways of thinking and organizing work in factories. The third looks at the modern services industry, and how the social aspects of work (what people say and even the emotions they show) is also rationalized.

7.2 Theoretical foundations

7.2.1 What we mean when we talk about "formal rationality"

The concept of formal rationality is a "Weberian" one. What I mean by this is that it was invented by Max Weber (remember him from the last chapter?) to describe "spheres of life and a structure of domination that acquired specific, delineated boundaries only with industrialization" (Kalberg, 1980, p. 1158). Consequently, you can understand the concept of formal rationality as a way of thinking about the world that is bound up with the industrial revolution and the "modern" era.

Central to the concept of formal rationality is the idea of doing things in a way that is guided by formal rules that are clearly defined and applied to all. It engenders a rejection of arbitrariness and an insistence that we do things in a way that is formal, proper, rational, logical, and by the [rule] book.

The bureaucracies we discussed in the last chapter are a near perfect example of a formally rational system of organization. This is because bureaucracies are systems of organization defined by formalized rules and highly procedural ways of working. They are places where the aim is to do "nothing more than calculate the most precise and efficient means for the resolution of problems" (Kalberg, 1980, p. 1158). This is essentially what we mean when we talk about formal rationality. It is the bureaucratic spirit we discussed in the previous chapter but applied widely and aggressively.

7.2.2 What we mean when we say something is "modern"?

Something else that's also helpful to understand is the concept of "modernity." When we talk about modernity, about something being "modern," or the "modern era," we're basically talking about two main things. First, we're talking about a particular period in human history: from about 1500 (known as "early modernity") until about 1980 (known as "late modernity").[1] The second thing we mean when we say something is "modern" relates to the ideology of "industrialized civilization" (Giddens & Pierson, 1998, p. 94). That is, the belief in the power of humans to dominate and control the natural and social worlds. Also, a belief in our capacity to create, improve, and reshape the world through practical experimentation and new technology—the ultimate aim being to "discover" what's holding back progress and "fix" the problem.

With the onset of modernity in the 1500s these ideas were widely popularized. In the context of organizations, the effects were profound. In a short space of time, organizations from public bureaucracies to capitalist enterprises underwent a massive expansion, not just in size, but also in terms of scope, sophistication, ambition, willingness, and ability to play a more concerted, coherent role in society (Raadschelders, 2017).

Thus, while we can trace broadly rational systems of organization (such as bureaucracy) back to antiquity, it's fair to say that these were relatively poor examples of the sort of organization that came along during modernity. In the case of early bureaucracies, these only exhibited some of the characteristics described in the previous chapter (see Table 6.1 on "Key Characteristics of a Bureaucracy"), and typically in just a very limited way. The exception here being the public organizations of ancient China which operated in a distinctly modern way several thousand years before any other (Creel, 1964; Kiser & Cai, 2003).

This is not a criticism of our organizational ancestors. It's hardly fair to compare Kushim's clay tablets and fledgling logo-syllabic script with the bureaucracies we have today. The point is that there came a time

---

1 **Note:** there is actually some debate about whether the age of modernity ended in the 1980s or not. For people like Derrida, Foucault, Lyotard, and Rorty, modernity is well and truly over, and we're living in a new, different kind of age. However, for people like Anthony Giddens and Zygmunt Bauman, modernity is still very much in full swing, albeit in a slightly different form. For Giddens, we're currently living in the age of "high" modernity Giddens, A. (2013). *The Consequences of Modernity*. Chichester: John Wiley & Sons. For Bauman, we're living in the age of "liquid" modernity. Bauman, Z. (2013). *Liquid Modernity*. Chichester: John Wiley & Sons.

in our history when we shifted from making basic calculations about how to solve problems, to formulating complex, highly rationalized ways of working that were universally applied and enforced. The point in history when all this happened—when formal, rationalized ways of thinking, working, and organizing came to predominate—is known as the modern era.

7.3 Manufacturing and the birth of modern rational factories

Factories are a great context in which to study and understand the concept of formal rationalized ways of working in organizations. According to the Oxford English Dictionary, the first known uses of words like "manufacturing" (as in "the production of goods") and "factories" (in the industrial sense) came at around 1567 and 1618 respectively. However, we have been manufacturing things (in a fashion) and operating factories (in one form or another) for quite a while. As Roser (2016) describes the fundamentals of manufacturing— (1) cutting, (2) changing material properties, (3) joining, (4) coating, (5) casting and molding, and (6) forming—are ancient.

In this section we're going to explore these ancient fundamentals and follow the path that led us to the modern, highly rationalized factories we have today. The point I want you to get to is an understanding that while modernity was revolutionary in terms of the concentration, application, scale, ambition, and the extent of rationalized organizing, it's not the whole story. We humans have been at it for a while.

7.3.1 The origins of manufacturing

We started cutting things (initially, rocks to make tools) at least 2.6 million years ago, and doing so in an organized way at least 2 million years ago (Plummer, 2004). Possibly as many as 400,000 years ago, we started changing the material properties of things; for example, by heat-treating rocks so they could be made into better tools, and chiseling wooden spears to give them a hard, sharp, pointy end (Brown et al., 2009). We began joining things like wood and stone together to make composite weapons 64,000 years ago (Lombard & Phillipson, 2010). Around 32,000 years ago we started coating things with particular substances to improve their surface properties (Valladas et al., 2001). We began casting and molding (giving formless masses a permanent shape) between 25,000 and 29,000 years ago (Králik et al., 2002). Lastly, we began forming objects—changing the shape of a previously shaped object—around 10,000 years ago (Solecki et al., 2004).

These are the fundamentals of manufacturing, and, until around 3300 BCE, they were artisanal endeavors. So, in the case of things like spears, everyone made their own. With just a few exceptions, the production of things was never centralized (performed in a single place), labor was not divided (people did not undertake different roles in the production process), nor did people really specialize in one particular thing over another. Manufacturing was not organized in anything like the way we know it today.

Between 3300 and 1200 BCE came the first organizations defined by the purposeful division of labor and worker specialization—two concepts that are absolutely fundamental to how virtually all organizations work today. What this meant in practice was two things. First, that people started to be allocated specific jobs in production processes. Second, that people started to specialize in doing one particular job.

The production of bronze is a good example, because it requires planning, organization, and the collaborative working of a subdivided workforce that includes people with specialist knowledge and expertise. In very basic terms, to make bronze you need people out collecting raw materials (e.g., wood, copper, and tin), and other people out foraging, hunting, farming, and digging wells to make sure everyone has food and water (Roser, 2016, pp. 26–27). All these people are there to support the specialist—the person who actually knows how to make bronze. This is what we mean when we talk about the "division of labor" and "specialization."

Around the same time we were learning to divide labor and specialize in particular things, we also started producing standardized products. This didn't happen everywhere, but in some very specific places.

First, in India, then China, and eventually Europe via Italy. Between 2600 and 1900 BCE, Indian Harappans were building entire, uniquely uniform cities from high-quality, fired bricks produced to a standard specification (Danino, 2008). Across an empire the size of Alaska, buildings were made from 10 × 20 × 30 centimetre bricks—a ratio of 1:2:3 (Morley & Renfrew, 2010; Rao et al., 2004). Even the weight of the bricks was standardized (Khan & Lemmen, 2013)—see Photo 7.1.

The next big innovation came between 2000 and 1000 BCE, when we figured out how to create locomotive energy in ways other than using our own bodies or the bodies of animals. In what is now the Irano-Afghan borderlands, the ancient Persians learnt to harness the power of the wind to run, what is believed to be, the world's first mass manufacturing operation (Derry & Williams, 1960; see also Lucas, 2006; Wade, 1974). In an industrial complex that eventually included more than 300, four storey vertical windmills, the Persians milled grains (to make flour) on an absolutely colossal scale (Mishmastnehi et al., 2021). You can still visit these windmills today. Some still work. Some even still have their original parts—see Photo 7.2.

Photo 7.1 A Harappan Brick
Source: exhibit in the Royal Ontario Museum, Toronto, Ontario, Canada, Daderot/Wikimedia Commons (CC0 1.0).

Photo 7.2 Persian vertical windmills on the Irano-Afghan Border
Source: François-Olivier Dommergues/Alamy Stock Photo.

7.3.2 Proto-industrial factories

Organizationally, very little changed until the turn of the 16th century. What I mean by this is that throughout the world people made increasingly prodigious use of the innovations described previously. They rationalized increasingly complex production techniques to ever greater degrees, continuing to subdivide labor and develop greater and greater levels of expertise in relation to specific parts of the production process. We also got much better at standardizing products and using renewable energy sources to power manufacturing operations (Lucas, 2006).

The next step forward we made came in the form of a flourishing, proto-industrial manufactory called the Arsenal of Venice. Initially, a store for naval vessels and armaments, the Arsenal of Venice developed into a massive 60-acre production facility. Employing between 2,000 and 3,000 people, it built everything from small scouting ships to great galleys (Lane, 1973, p. 362)—see Photo 7.3.

Two things are significant about the Arsenal of Venice. First (we think) it was home to the very first production assembly line in history (Lane, 1973, p. 363). Second, in housing the first assembly line in history, the Venetians also became possibly the first to encounter the thorny challenge of "disciplining an army of craftworkers to the

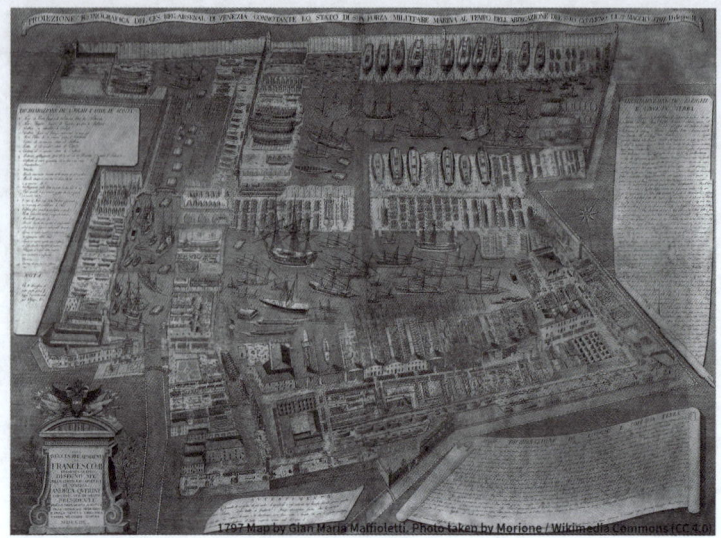

Photo 7.3 The Arsenal of Venice (Venice, Italy) from 1797 map by Gian Maria Maffioletti

Source: 1797 map by Gian Maria Maffioletti. "Christoph Roser at AllAboutLean.com." Photo taken by Morione/Wikimedia Commons (CC 4.0).

demands of factory-style work rhythms" (Davis, 1997, p. 57). You can read more on this in Chapter 8.

The Venetian assembly line was impressively simple. Once they could float, boats in production were moved down a section of the canal past a succession of warehouses on each side. Each warehouse was home to a different group of specialists (a different guild). As one witness recounted, "[at each stop] they handed out to them, from one the cordage, from another the bread, from another the arms, from another the balistas and mortars, and so from all sides everything which was required" (Lane, 1973, p. 363). Standardized, interchangeable masts, spars, planks, benches, and deck fixing were widely used and everything was made on site.

It is claimed that at its productive peak in the spring of 1570, the Arsenal of Venice produced 100 vessels in just 100 days (Lane, 1973, p. 364)—though some have it at 60 days (e.g., Roser, 2016). It is claimed that in the time it took [watching] King Henry III of France to eat his lunch, workers rigged and outfitted an entire galley (Davis, 1997, p. 81; Lane, 1973, p. 140). These particular claims are probably hyped propaganda, but the Arsenal of Venice would nonetheless have been a spectacular sight to behold. Indeed, people, such as the great Dante Alighieri, are known to have traveled great distances to witness the spectacle of ships being mass produced (Lane, 1973, p. 163). The arsenal was literally a 16th-century tourist attraction.

The Arsenal of Venice has an important place in history for at least two more reasons. First, as Roser (2016, p. 87) describes, in pooling workers together and increasing the division of labor, the Arsenal established a basic understanding of what constitutes good practice in the context of industrial manufacturing (see also Davis, 1997, pp. 56–58). Without realizing it, the Venetians set the template for how factories should work, which people around the world have gone on to replicate, develop, and advance (Davis, 2007).

The second reason the Arsenal of Venice is so important is because the Venetians made prodigious use of a type of worker that we today know as "managers" (Davis, 1997, p. 61). To cope with the sheer scale of their operations, the Arsenal established a vertical hierarchy comprising of layers of managers and subordinates. These new managers tracked everything from vessel assemblage and outfitting, to materials, men employed, and monies spent. They audited operations, policed, and even had a crack at motivating the workforce.

7.3.3 The "modern" factory

At the time the Arsenal of Venice was operating, manufacturing operations were generally very simple in nature. Some people were experimenting with how to organize things in an efficient, logical, and broadly rational way, but most organizations were little more than simple cottage industries. They were small, organizationally unsophisticated groups of people (usually families) making things either by hand or using basic machines at home.

With the onset of modernity, small-scale, relatively inefficient cottage industry producers were virtually wiped out. What replaced them was a new and distinct form of organization—the modern, mechanized, highly rationalized factories of the sort we know today. These new factories were a comparatively advanced form of organization. The predecessors of today's sleek, shiny assembly lines, the first mechanized factories were dank, dark, dirty, dangerous places where rationalized thinking and new technologies were blended together. The result was huge organizations in which vast numbers of people were concentrated together in highly regulated, tightly coordinated, extremely efficient ways.

The key attraction of factories was that they enabled the productive capacity of workers to be amplified through the use of machines, further subdivisions of labor, and tight control over the work people were doing. Things that were previously produced very slowly by skilled craft workers on a one-off basis, were now produced much more quickly by people using specially designed machines in carefully-planned, calculated, and rationally organized ways.

Bragging rights for who built the first "modern" factory are highly contested. Darley (2003, p. 103)—along with many others—cites a silk

Photo 7.4 Lombe's silk throwing mill Derby (UK)
Source: eighteenth century print, used by Darley, Gillian (2003). Factory (Objekt). London: Reaktion Books/Wikipedia (public dom.).

throwing mill in Derby (United Kingdom) as "probably the first fully mechanised factory in the world" (see Photo 7.4). Built by Sir Thomas Lombe in 1721, this claim is dubious. Most history books suggest that Lombe actually stole the designs for his factory's machines from another one in Northern Italy (Cipolla, 1972; Roser, 2016, pp. 102–103).

In Italy, machinery had been in use in silk spinning since 1276, albeit on a relatively modest scale (Kuhn, 1981). It is believed that Thomas Lombe traveled to one of these factories, took a job as a night shift worker, and copied the design of the machines. Lombe also apparently hired six Italian engineers to help him build the machines that would eventually go into his Derbyshire factory (Calladine, 1993).

Consequently, we might credit Lombe with building the first mechanized factory in the UK, but the claim his was the first factory in the world is almost certainly wrong. Also, if we credit Lombe with building the first factory in the UK, we should also credit his achievement to industrial espionage. It seems only fair, especially given that, in a curious twist, Lombe was apparently murdered not long after his Derbyshire factory sprang to life. The perpetrator was apparently a mysterious woman from Northern Italy (Roser, 2016, p. 103).

In an even more bizarre twist, Lombe seemingly didn't need to steal the designs for his machines at all. The designs he stole had already been published on three separate occasions—in 1607, 1621, and 1656. They were published in a book called *Novo Teatro di Machine et Edificii* written by the Italian Vittorio Zonca. So, in 1714, when Lombe was sneaking around in Italy, he could actually have been sitting comfortably in Oxford University's Bodleian Library. Or, indeed, in one of the many other libraries in the UK that had a copy of the book (Cipolla, 1972, p. 47; Roser, 2016, p. 102).

Regardless, from around 1700 new mechanized factories were opening all over the world—particularly in Europe and North America. Each claimed new levels of technical superiority and efficiency. Notable amongst these was the construction in the 1780s by an American called Oliver Evans of a new kind of factory based on the idea of a mechanized, moving assembly line. Evans' factory (a flour mill on the Red Clay Creek in Delaware) improved the speed and efficiency of its operations through a system in which materials were

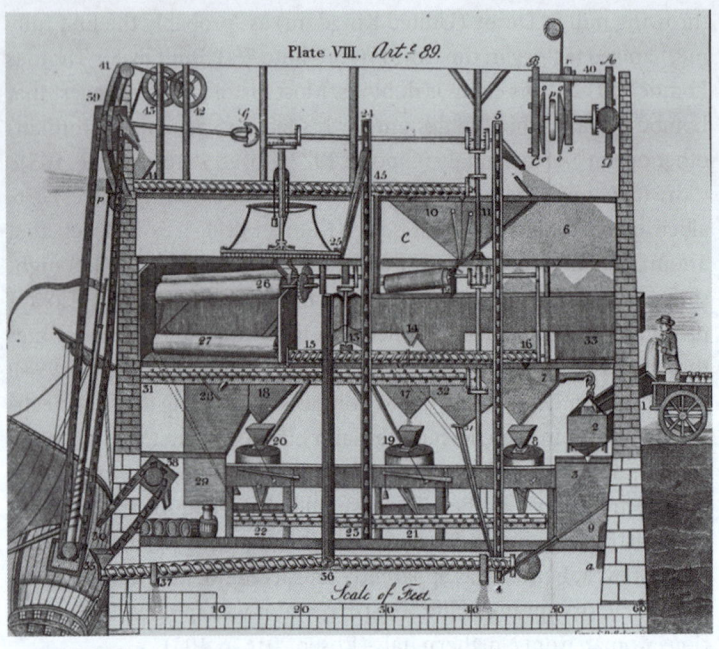

Photo 7.5 Evans' flour factory

Source: United States Library of Congress's Prints and Photographs; id: cph.3c10379/Wikimedia (public dom.).

moved using a series of automated conveyor belts, screws, and drops (Biggs, 1996, p. 8). His system eliminated much of the need for manual labor. Powered conveyor belts (rather than men) moved the grains to different machines that did the work men used to do. You can see a picture of Evans' factory in Photo 7.5.

7.3.4 Ford's *fully mechanized* moving assembly line

Despite the productive efficiency of Evans' mechanized production line, it didn't really take off—except in the Chicago animal slaughter industry (Biggs, 1996, pp. 26–27; Sinclair & Lee, 2003; Standage, 2021, p. 75). More generally it took until the early 20th century for the idea of a mechanized moving assembly line to be (re)discovered and revived in industrial manufacturing. This time by Henry Ford of the Ford Motor Company.

By the time Henry Ford was reinventing Evans' concept of a mechanized moving production line, the principle of organizing work along highly rationalized lines was very common and was producing remarkable results. It was producing not just huge profits, but highly efficient organizations and huge volumes of high-quality, low-cost goods.

The Ford Motor Company is an instructive example. By reintroducing the idea of the moving assembly line, Henry Ford was able to cut the cost of his already keenly priced "Model T" motorcar from $850 USD in 1908 to $298 USD in 1923 (Standage, 2021). In an age when average earnings in American were around $335 USD (in 1914), Ford brought the motorcar within reach of the masses. He did this through a cost advantage created (in part) by Evans' (or was it the Venetians'?) moving production line.

Given that the concept of a moving production line was already 500 years old (and that mechanized versions had been in use for almost 300 years) when Ford put one in his factory, it seems that Ford's real contribution to history was that he set a new benchmark in the aggressive deconstruction of skilled work. He successfully rationalized the complex task of building an entire car into 7,882 separated tasks. Each task was performed by one of his 80,000 (mostly stationary) workers who had been selected, trained, equipped, and paid to perform one specific task and nothing else.

Henry Ford was greatly helped in his work by the famous, self-styled efficiency engineer Frederick Taylor, who is widely (and in some respects erroneously) credited with introducing the world to the concept of "scientific management" (Taylor, 1914). By famous I mean that Taylor's book *The Principles of Scientific Management* was voted the most influential management book of the 20th century by the American Academy of Management (Bedeian & Wren, 2001). By erroneously credited, I mean two things. First, the label "scientific management" was imposed on Taylor by a New York lawyer called Louis D. Brandeis. Taylor called his system "functional management" and, until he met Brandeis, it wasn't all that popular. It was Brandeis who called Taylor's work "scientific management." Brandeis was also the one who popularized it. For a full and very interesting account, read Bridgman and Cummings (2020, pp. 16–34); Cummings et al. (2017); and Tone (2018, pp. 73–78).

The second reason why Taylor is erroneously credited with introducing the world to the concept of scientific management is that many of the ideas he was working with were not especially new. Here, it is important to be very clear. The brand "Scientific Management" was what Taylor (in conjunction with Brandeis) introduced to the world. However, routinized ways of working systematically used to organize labor to [mass] manufacture standardized goods was already in widespread use long before Taylor came along.

So what was so special about Taylor and his system of scientific management? This is actually very hard to deduce, in part because Taylor has been (and continues to be) widely mythologized as a founding-father of both the modern factory and management science as a discipline. Both points are highly contested. We know with certainty that there were other people doing similar things both before and at the same time as Taylor (Bridgman & Cummings, 2020). So the reality is that while Taylor was definitely a proponent of rationalized ways of working, in reality he was just one of a growing crowd of people trying to figure out the best, most efficient way to set up and run organizations such as factories.

Taylor's importance is more about what he, and the concept of scientific management signified. Here there are two important points to note. The first is that Taylor's theory of scientific management was one of the first theories of management practice that was coherently written and widely popularized—see Table 7.1. While the genesis for Taylor's ideas can be traced to other people and earlier times, he defined a methodology (an ideology) that cost-conscious business owners could use to improve the efficiency of their organizations. To see how "Taylorism" translated into "Fordism" see Table 7.2.

Of course, central to Taylor's functional—now scientific—management was the idea of rational thinking applied completely and fully to the management and organization of work. Taylor was a particular proponent of the careful measurement and optimization of workers' time

Table 7.1 The principles of Taylorism

Principle 1: the development of science to replace the old "rule of thumb" knowledge of the workman
Deliberately gather the great mass of traditional knowledge held in the heads of the workmen and in the physical skill and knack of the workmen, which they have acquired through years of experience. Gather this great mass of knowledge, record it, tabulate it, and reduce it to laws and even mathematical formulae. . . . later when these laws, rules and formulae are applied to the everyday work of all the workmen of the establishment through the intimate and hearty cooperation of all those on the management's side, they result, first, in producing a very much larger output per man, as well as an output of better and higher quantity.

Principle 2: the scientific selection of the workman and his development
It becomes the duty of those on the management's side to deliberately study the character, the nature, and the performance of each workman with a view to finding out his limitations on the one hand; and then, as deliberately and systematically to train him.

Principle 3: the bringing of the science and the scientifically selected and trained workman together
We will [all of us] do our work in accordance with the laws of the science, or we will not practice it; we will do our work in accordance with the laws of the science or in our own old way, just as we see fit unless there is someone there to see that we do it in accordance with the principles of the science.

Principle 4: an almost equal division of labor between the management and the worker
Simply, separate those who think, plan, and organize from those who undertake the work.

Source: adapted from Taylor (1947)—see also (Pugh, 2007)—which is itself based on testimony given by Taylor to the House of Representatives in 1912.

Table 7.2 The principles of Fordism

1	Reduce costs so everyone can have one (raise sales, increase profit margins)
2	From craft-based work (build a whole car) to task specialization (division of labor)
3	The efficient organization of labor—parts to people, rather than people to part

Table 7.2 Continued

4	Intensified work by speeding up the pace of work, eliminating workers' breaks between tasks, and adding the crucial innovation of the moving mechanized assembly line
5	Enhanced managerial control over workers (foremen able to regulate the flow of work and keep it moving at a constant speed)
6	Explicitly separate conception from execution—managers think, workers do
7	Standardization replaced craft-based (one-off) manufacturing

and motion. You see this very clearly in the BBC's "People's Century" documentary that I've recommended you watch in "Things to Watch, Things to Read."

Intriguingly, Taylor's theory of scientific management was not actually developed to improve the profitability of organizations like Ford Motorcars. The early part of the 20th century was a time of rampant laissez-faire capitalism and Taylor (or was it Brandeis?) was principally concerned with reducing waste and limiting organizations' ecological impact. Scientific Management was actually designed to conserve effort and resources, rather than increase profit margins (Bridgman & Cummings, 2020, p. 21). This was apparently motivated by two main desires. First, was to ensure products and services remained cheap and affordable to everyone in society. The second desire was to preserve Earth's natural resources for future generations, and limit organizations' impact on the natural environment.

7.4 Rationality and the post-industrial services economy

In the 1950s, there began what would ultimately become a radical shift away from manufacturing in many countries. Europe and North America in particular entered a "post-industrial" age in which the trade in tangible goods began to be supplanted by the trade in intangible services as the dominant form of economic activity.

By services, I mean things like financial services, hospitality, retail, healthcare, information technology, and education. Now worth more than $13.3 trillion (USD) annually, the services economy generates two-thirds of economic output globally, attracts two-thirds of foreign direct investment, and provides almost two-thirds of jobs in developing countries and four-fifths of jobs in developed ones (WTO, 2019).

In this section, we'll look at how the principles of formal rationality are applied in the services economy. What we're interested in here are the new kinds of factories that dominate the world—factories that don't mass produce physical goods, but that mass produce intangible services.

7.4.1 The concept of rationalized services

Do you remember in the last chapter when I told you about my first ever job at "BigBank?" Remember how as a Customer Advisor I spent 7.5 hours every day following rules and procedures other people had written? There is another bit to the story. The process manuals I followed had two parts. The first part told me what I had to *do* to open a bank account or get a loan or a mortgage approved. The second part told me what to *say* to customers while I was doing it. I remember the process for dealing with complaints particularly clearly. If someone made a complaint, I had to write all the details on a special little form and say three things. I had to say these words exactly:

(1) I'm *glad* you told me about this.
(2) I'm *sure* I can sort it out.
(3) I'm *sorry* it happened.

I even got a handy little acronym so I wouldn't forget: "GSS." As in, "glad," "sure," "sorry." My boss would print the acronym on A4 sheets of paper and stick them up all around the office. Everywhere you looked, all you saw were bits of paper with "GSS" written on them.

The point is that the bank was trying to regulate how we treated customers who were complaining. They wanted to guarantee every customer got treated the same, even if different people served them. So, in the same way Henry Ford defined the best, most efficient way to make a motorcar, so BigBank defined what they thought was the best, most efficient way to talk to customers about their complaints. I was the service sector equivalent of one of Henry Ford's assembly line workers (for more on this see Taylor & Bain, 1999).

7.4.2 Rationalized service, in practice

Let's revisit another example from the previous chapter. Remember, I got you to write down the exact process for making the perfect cup of coffee? Now, imagine you're the owner of a coffee shop. If you're thinking rationally about your coffee shop, you'll want your baristas to both make and serve coffee perfectly, every time. Right? To make money, everyone has to get both great coffee and great service. Service matters, so it's important to get it right every time.

The problem though, is how do you get it right every time? Customer service is complex and unpredictable. How do you standardize things? There's a huge amount to think about, even with something as simple as serving coffee. For example, how do you want baristas to greet people. What's the best way? Do you want your baristas to have a crack at upselling? If you do, what's the best way to get someone to buy a coffee *and* a cake? If cake is sold, how do you want it to be handed over? Do you want them to do it in a particular kind of way? If so, what kind of way? Also, how do you want the service to end? Do you want the barista to close things off with a smile and goodbye wave, or just hand over the goods and move on to the next person as quickly as possible?

These are the sort of things rationalized service organizations are concerned with. To really connect with what this means in practice, go back to your protocol for making a perfect coffee. Try adding in the protocol for service. Try writing down the best possible way to **make** and **serve** a cup of coffee. When you've done that, take a look at what you've produced. This is what a rationalized service looks like. See Ritzer (2021) for a wider analysis of how services are rationalized in modern society (see also Leidner, 1993).

7.4.3 Rationalized service and the concept of emotional labor

Now that we have a basic idea of what rationalized service looks like, there is a new, and related concept for you to think about. It's called **emotional labor** and it was developed by the American sociologist Arlie Hochschild (see Hochschild, 1975, 1979; Hochschild, 1983).

At the heart of the concept of emotional labor is a type of work (a type of labor) that is primarily performed in service contexts. Here it helps if you've done some kind of service work before or if you know someone who has. This is because one thing "service" people will know is doing and saying the right things aren't in themselves enough. You can't just read off a script. You must read your script in an authentic way. After all, if you're going to set a script for someone and prescribe what you want them to say, you want them to properly act the part. Right? You want a decent, convincing performance. You want your customer to really believe the words being said are sincere.

At BigBank they were really keen for me to sound genuine, really empathize, and show interest and concern for the customers I was serving. In the case of complaints, they wanted me to earnestly assure the grumpy customer I was genuinely glad they had brought their complaint to my attention; explain with some enthusiasm that I was 110% sure I could fix things; and be forcefully contrite in my groveling apology. I had to do all this even if I wasn't at all glad they were complaining to me, wasn't at all sure I could fix the problem, and, to be honest, wasn't at all sorry it had happened.

This is what emotional labor is. It is, in Hochschild's words, the labor required "to induce or suppress feelings in order to sustain the outward countenance that produces the proper state of mind in others" (Hochschild, 2012, p. 6). This "proper state of mind" being, in the case of my complaining customers, their belief that I was truly "glad," "sure," and "sorry" about stuff even if I wasn't.

Creating the "proper state of mind" in others was, without a doubt, the very hardest bit about working at BigBank. Luckily for me, I got loads of training. Not just in what to say, but also in how to say it.

I went on a course that taught me what to say to customers and how to suppress or fake emotions to create the right impression. They taught me what Hochschild (2012) calls **surface acting**. This being, the ability to act the part, suppress the emotions I felt (if they were the wrong ones), fake emotions I didn't feel (the ones they wanted from me), and just put on a good show of things.

The point with surface acting is to suppress the emotions you do feel (if they're not the right ones), so that you only show the "right" ones. To be sure I kept up the performance, BigBank had weekly (and even daily) conference calls on which I was taught the latest innovations in how to talk to customers. There was even the joy of people covertly checking up on me. Calls were recorded and listened to by my boss. "Mystery shoppers" regularly visited the bank to check I was doing and saying what I was supposed to. If I said or did anything wrong, bonuses were lost and reprimands were dished out.

Although it was never openly discussed at BigBank, most front line customer service staff, such as me, were clearly not emotionally invested in the work they were doing. Consequently, authenticity was always a problem. To "fix" the problem, BigBank invested a lot of time and money in trying to get people to not just act the part, but seriously, really, deeply care. They wanted employees to be genuinely glad someone was complaining to them, genuinely sure they could fix the problem, and genuinely sorry to the customer complaining.

We're going to talk more about how organizations motivate workers in Chapter 8. For now though, I just want you to know that what I'm talking about here is called **deep acting** (Hochschild, 2012) and it's the sort of performance put on by people who make the effort to experience emotions in the way the organization wants them to. It's a step above and beyond simply pretending to act the part (**surface acting**). As far as the organization goes, deep acting is really the holy grail of customer service. What could be more valuable than customer service workers who are genuinely, truly emotionally invested in their work?

At this point, it's worth stressing that while my account of emotional labor is quite critical, emotional labor in itself is not necessarily a bad thing. Emotional labor is simply just another kind of labor. It is the sort of work one does in a service-type role. Where workers on an assembly line perform physical labor, people in a call center do emotional labor. So, where factory workers screw components onto a circuit board, service workers thank customers for their complaints, reassure them they'll fix things, and offer up apologies.

Emotional labor is also not restricted to the sort of minimum wage service work I was doing. All service workers perform emotional labor, in one form or another. Barristers perform emotional labor (Harris, 2002). Doctors (Rogers et al., 2014) and nurses (Riley & Weiss, 2016) perform emotional labor. School teachers perform emotional labor (Constanti & Gibbs, 2004). Academics perform emotional labor (Bellas, 1999).

7.5 Summary

What I hope has become clear from reading this chapter is that rational organizations are an invention. They represent a corollary of ideas emphasizing efficiency, calculability, predictability, and control within organizations. This corollary of ideas didn't spring into existence at a particular point in time, but was developed, refined, and advanced over time.

Accordingly, what I have shown in this chapter is that organizations that run along rationalized lines have a rich and complex history. Elements can be traced to points in our very early history and to different places around the world. For example, to bronze age smelters, Harappan brick kilns, Persian millers, Venetian shipbuilders, and the industrialists of modern Europe and North America.

This latter group are of particular importance because of the sheer extent to which they forcefully, aggressively, and systematically institutionalized what we see today as a distinctly modern system of organization. They used new technologies to rationalize, to an extreme degree, organizational practices that ultimately replaced, simplified, and intensified the productive capacity of human labor.

The results have been astounding, literally defining the societies we live in, the jobs we do and how we do them. There are very few (formal) jobs on the planet that have not been rationalized to one degree or another.

Things to Watch, Things to Read

In this table are suggestions for things you can read and watch to learn more about this topic. I've also included a very short commentary so that you have a sense of why I've recommended a particular source, and what to look out for.

Read in two to three hours	Bandinelli, C. & A. Gandini. (2022). Dating Apps: The uncertainty of marketized love. *Cultural Sociology* 16(3), 423–441.

This article is about dating apps and how they work. It'll tell you about how dating apps rationalize the search for love [through datafication and algorithmic matching]. You also see how dating apps create challenges for would-be lovers. Look out for the gaps in the supposedly perfect world of online dating (also discussed in this chapter's Case Study "McLove"). Also look out for how the authors cast online daters as self-branding "entrepreneurs." Think about what this means in practice.

Read in a day or two	Hochschild, A. R. (2003). *The Managed Heart: Commercialization of Human Feeling*. Los Angeles: University of California Press.

First published in 1982, *The Managed Heart* is an iconic piece of work written by the sociologist Arlie Hochschild. In this book, Hochschild describes the concept of emotional labor, which I elaborated on in the latter sections of this chapter. She goes into incredible detail, and the book itself is very interesting, and readable. It will help you make sense of the service economy, and the sort of labor performed by people employed in it.

Read in a week or three	Ritzer, G. (2013). *The McDonaldization of Society*. Los Angeles: Sage.

Now in its 10th edition, this book offers a forensic analysis of how modern society has become, what Ritzer calls "McDonaldized." As you read the book, you'll realize very quickly that Ritzer is basically talking about the complete and total application of Weber's principle of *formal rationality* to people, work, and organizations across society. He explores how we have become a society obsessed by the ideas of calculability, efficiency, predictability, and control. In many ways it's quite bleak, but it does also help you to see and understand how the world works.

	Ahluwalia, A. (Director). *John and Jane* [Documentary]. (2005). Future East Film.

This documentary follows the stories of six "call agents" that answer American 1-800 numbers in a Mumbai call center. What you see is the lived experience of hyper-rationalized service work. You will see how young Indians [are forced to] don false aliases (American names, identities, and accents) and participate in American "culture training" to help them keep up the act. As well as foregrounding the realities of hyper-rationalized service work, this documentary raises disturbing questions about the nature of personal identity and what it means to be human in today's hyper-globalized world. To be watched in conjunction with Jenkins & Delbridge (2017); Hochschild (2012); and Ritzer (2021).

Listen in an evening	Dmitrijs, M. (12 October 2015). Episode 1: *Principle of Scientific Management—FW Taylor's One Best Way* in *Talking about Organizations*, Podcast. Retrieved from https://www.talkingaboutorganizations.com/e01/.

To be listened to, rather than watched, this podcast explores the thinking of F. W. Taylor, who is widely regarded as an iconic figure in the field of management science. The podcast deals with what Taylor thought, why he made the claims he did, and whether he was in fact the "first" to do what he did. The podcast also considers the significance of Taylor's ideas today—how modern management practices are indebted to the legacy of Scientific Management, and whether this is a good thing or not.

Watch in a week	Elsley, B. [Writer] & Maybury [Director]. Released 10 June–3 July 2013. Season 1. *Dates*. Balloon Entertainment Ltd.

This British romantic drama series contains a lot of adult content. In graphic detail it follows the trials and tribulations of daters in London as they struggle to find love in the imperfect world of online dating. While the specific dating apps they use to connect with each other don't feature prominently in the series, the consequences of using them does. What you see is the phenomenon of "self-branding" described by Bandinelli & Gandini (2022) and how people massage the truth, gloss over certain details and, in some cases, lie outright as a way of painting a particular picture of who they are. What you see is that despite the unprecedented amount of information available to online daters—as per the promise of rationalized love—it is actually very hard to make informed, rational choices based on that data. What you see is daters struggling to know how to act in a fundamentally uncertain world, and how they navigate the challenges thrown up by their dates (and by their own) economies with the truth.

> **Research Insight: Normalized lying at work**
>
> **Source:** Jenkins, S. & R. Delbridge. (2017). Trusted to deceive: A case study of "strategic deception" and the normalization of lying at work. *Organization Studies* 38(1), 53–76.
>
> **Edited abstract:** this article won the Roland Calori Prize in 2019. It is about how people lie at work. Its focus is an organization where they assign the pseudonym "VoiceTel," which is a market leader in the "virtual reception" business. As such, this article is about service organizations, rationalized service work, and how people are paid to engage in "strategic deception." The lies told by the virtual receptionists that this study focuses on aren't especially naughty ones. The virtual receptionists *just* conceal the fact that they're not physically located in their clients' premises. Yet the point remains, lying is an intrinsic and enduring feature of their work. What Jenkins and Delbridge (2017) therefore reveal is how lying can become a legitimate and integral part of someone's job. Look out for the part in which they describe how employees get recognition for their proficiency in deception, and derive satisfaction, self-esteem, and even social standing as employees who are "trusted to deceive."

Case Study: McLove

As I write these words there are an estimated 1,500 online dating apps in the world. Collectively, they serve about 430 million users (Statista, 2021). The most popular dating app in the world is *Tinder*. It is downloaded about 6.5 million times per month, has approximately 6.2 million subscribers and 75 million monthly active users.

For those that don't know, *Tinder* works a bit like a video game. In fact, like many other dating apps, it was designed to be just like one. *Tinder* gamifies dating and enables users to shop around for love and relationships in a fun, exciting, and playful way (Bandinelli & Gandini, 2022, p. 4; Heino et al., 2010). It is highly addictive.

Consistent with the corollary of ideas that define modern organizations, dating apps afford their users a highly rationalized shot at love. Internet dating is a highly efficient, calculated, predictable, and controlled way of searching for love. Never before has it been so easy to find someone you like and hookup.

Efficiency

As a concept, efficiency is all about finding the best possible way to do something. The route I drive to work is efficient because there is literally no quicker or cheaper way for me to get there. Believe me, I've tried.

Online dating apps are purposefully designed to efficiently connect time-starved people looking for love. Regardless of whether you want a lusty hookup, a romantic latte, or a mind-bending chat about the merits of modern art, there is an app that will enable you to do it quickly and easily.

Take *Tinder*, for example. The world's most popular dating app works by showing you photos of available singles in your area. If you don't like the look of the person in the photo, you swipe left, and you'll never see them again. Alternatively, if you do like the look of them, you swipe right. If that person has also swiped right on a picture of you, you're matched together, and you can start chatting. If you really, really like the look of someone, you can "super like" them and, as Hodgson (2017, p. 213) puts it, "properly hammer home your infatuation."

This ultra-efficient way of searching for love is no accident. *Tinder*'s entire business model is built around making it quick and easy for people to connect. In the case of *Tinder*, you can download the app at the breakfast table, upload a photo on the train to work and be swiping through photos over your mid-morning coffee. If you swipe enough and are attractive enough, you could be on a date by lunch time. People can connect, meet up, get to know each other, and start a relationship in just a few days. Consistent with their advertising "Match. Chat. Date." *Tinder* screams efficiency. As Bandinelli and Gandini (2022) put it, "in three easy steps, romance can be realized."

If *Tinder* is not your thing, don't worry. There are plenty of other apps out there to help you efficiently play the dating game. Launched in 2014, *happn* will help you connect with hotties you've crossed paths with on the street and start chatting to them instantly. No more having to pull a u-turn and chase someone down on your way to work.

If you're after a more cerebral and less carnal chance at love, apps like *Match.com*, *eHarmony*, and *mysinglefriend* are the ones for you. They work by getting you (or a friend) to complete long questionnaires and write detailed essays about yourself. These then get analyzed by complex algorithms, which compile a list of potential suitors. It'll even help you to figure out exactly which ones you should date.

If all that seems like too much work, you could just leave it to the government. In the Chinese city of Jiangxi, the state-sponsored dating app *Palm Guixi* uses data on single residents to help match people together. It'll even set you up on a blind date with one of your single neighbors, if you really want (Hawkins, 2023).

Online dating apps are efficient because they exponentially expand your romantic network. They give you access to a huge pool of strangers to ogle over, chat to, and flirt with. All without having to leave your house. They also help make things more efficient by helping you sift through and organize all your new connections. By bringing you together with like-minded people, they reduce uncertainty, speed things up, and make dating less stressful.

Calculability

When we talk about calculability, we're talking about our ability to quantify and measure things, and make rational decisions based on the results. So, my decision about how to get to work is guided by a calculated cost-benefit analysis of the different types of transport available to me. Things like how long it takes to get to and from the office by car, bus, or bike and how much it costs.

In the context of online dating, calculations are constantly being made by everyone involved. At *Tinder* headquarters, app developers track a huge range of metrics. Everything that happens on the app—from what you look at and click on to how long you look at profiles versus pictures—is watched and analyzed to see if there are better ways of creating those lasting connections.

For the lonely heart, online dating is also full of calculations. Most obviously, the decision to start online dating is often a very calculated one.

Do you hang around bars, libraries, or coffee shops in the hope of bumping into your next beau? Or do you hop online and take things into your own hands? When it comes down to it, the latter is much, much quicker, cheaper, and easier.

A considerable amount of calculation also goes into the process of building and reviewing dating profiles. The information you put on your profile dictates the sort of person that's going to be interested in you, and dating apps are specifically designed to make this information readily available. The point is to give people access to the information they need to make an informed, rational dating decision. So, apps show you what someone looks like, what they're looking for, what hobbies they're into, what sort of job they do, where they're located, and whether they want kids. All the important things. All users have to do is figure out what they want and run these criteria through the app's filter.

For a small fee, most apps will also enable you to increase the amount of information available to you. More information means more calculated, more rational, and therefore fundamentally better dating decisions. On *Tinder*, a platinum subscription will get you the chance to chat to people *before* you waste time swiping left/right on their profile. On *mysinglefriend*, a premium subscription gets you data on who's viewed your profile and the ability to sort search results according to a range of different variables. When it comes to online dating, calculations about who is likely to be the best for you is all part of the game.

Predictability

Things are predictable when they unfold in a way that we expect. I can predict with relative certainty that it'll take me 26 minutes to drive to work, 55 minutes to cycle there, and 90+ minutes if I go by train. Because these journey times are relatively consistent, I can make more informed decisions about how to get to work.

When it comes to online dating—as with most things in life—people like predictability. No surprises are generally best. We like our dates to look like the pictures on their profile and to be as old as they say they are. We also like our dates to have the jobs they say they have and be as single as the act of online dating usually implies.

As such, one of the big draws of dating apps is that they provide an element of predictability. Sure, people might lie on their profile, but most of the time you can be relatively certain that you're going to be matched with the sort of person you want to be matched with. That's the whole point of algorithms. They're there to connect you with people matching the criteria you think are important.

Control

Control is all about the exercise of power to direct, regulate, govern, and generally determine behavior in one way or another. It might sound weird to talk about control in the context of online dating, but it is an important element. In fact, control is one of the biggest attractions of online dating. Apps enable you to take control of your romantic future. No more waiting around for the perfect partner to show up—your life, your choice, your date.

Dating apps also enable you to get to know people before you decide whether you want to spend an afternoon with them in a coffee shop or an evening in a pricy restaurant. They enable you to control the expense of time and money. They also enable you to control personal risk. By interacting with someone over an app, you can get to know them a bit before you run the risk of meeting them in person.

In fact, research shows that before a first date most people will engage in quite a lot of risk management strategies. According to Gibbs et al. (2011), they check whether the things potential dates have told them are actually true. Did they really run the Berlin marathon? Are they really a famous Parisian professor? Most people's digital footprints are so big that most things can be checked, cross-referenced, and corroborated online. Again, all without leaving the house.

Some apps, like *Bumble*, are specifically sold on the basis of the control they afford to users. On *Bumble* in 2024, it's the women who get to initiate contact—men aren't allowed. For men on *Bumble*, the work is in crafting elaborate and enticing profiles that will attract the kind of attention they're looking for.

Conclusion

Despite all the tools on offer, internet dating is not as easy as it sounds. As you can guess if you watch the mini-series *Dates* I've recommended in "Things to Watch, Things to Read," the search for love on the internet is not an easy one. Users may have access to an unprecedented amount of information on the available singles around them, but in practice it is actually very hard to make informed, rational choices based on that data. As Bandinelli and Gandini (2022) describe, there is not a direct and unproblematic translation of data into technologically facilitated love. Just because you have the data does not mean you will actually get what you want. In practice, users act in a fundamentally uncertain social environment, navigating an inherent lack of information about others. They may have access to peoples' pictures and biographies, but the answer to the questions of who they truly are and whether they are "the one" remains elusive.

Questions

1. How has online dating rationalized the search for love?
2. To what extent do you think dating apps have actually made finding a partner easier?
3. Is Tinder the most efficient way to find love? Why or why not?

References

Bandinelli, C. & A. Gandini. (2022). Dating apps: The uncertainty of marketised love. *Cultural Sociology* 16(3), 423–441. doi: 17499755211051559.

Bauman, Z. (2013). *Liquid Modernity*. New Jersey: John Wiley & Sons.

Bedeian, A. & D. Wren. (2001). Books of the 20th Century. *Organizational Dynamics* 29(3), 221–225.

Bellas, M. L. (1999). Emotional labor in academia: The case of professors. *The Annals of the American Academy of Political and Social Science* 561(1), 96–110.

Biggs, L. (1996). *The Rational Factory: Architecture, Technology, and Work in America's Age of Mass Production*. Baltimore: Johns Hopkins University Press.

Bridgman, T. & S. Cummings. (2020). *A Very Short, Fairly Interesting and Reasonably Cheap Book about Management Theory*. London: SAGE.

Brown, K. S., C. W. Marean, A. I. Herries, Z. Jacobs, C. Tribolo, D. Braun, et al. (2009). Fire as an engineering tool of early modern humans. *Science* 325(5942), 859–862.

Calladine, A. (1993). Lombe's Mill: An exercise in reconstruction. *Industrial Archaeology Review* 16(1), 82–99.

Cipolla, C. M. (1972). The diffusion of innovations in early modern Europe. *Comparative Studies in Society and History* 14(1), 46–52.

Constanti, P. & P. Gibbs. (2004). Higher education teachers and emotional labour. *International Journal of Educational Management* 18(4), 243–249.

Creel, H. G. (1964). The beginnings of bureaucracy in China: The origin of the Hsien. *The Journal of Asian Studies* 23(2), 155–184.

Cummings, S., T. Bridgman, J. Hassard, & M. Rowlinson. (2017). *A New History of Management*. Cambridge: Cambridge University Press.

Danino, M. (2008). New insights into Harappan town-planning, proportions, and units, with special reference to Dholavia. *Man and Environment* 33(1), 66–79.

Darley, G. (2003). *Factory*. London: Reaktion Books.

Davis, R. C. (1997). Venetian shipbuilders and the fountain of wine. *Past & Present* 156(Aug), 55–86.

Davis, R. C. (2007). *Shipbuilders of the Venetian Arsenal: Workers and Workplace in the Preindustrial City* (Vol. 109). Baltimore: John Hopkins University Press.

Derry, T. K. & T. I. Williams. (1960). *A Short History of Technology from the Earliest Times to AD 1900* (Vol. 231). North Chelmsford: Courier Corporation.

Gibbs, J. L., N. B. Ellison, & C.-H. Lai. (2011). First comes love, then comes Google: An investigation of uncertainty reduction strategies and self-disclosure in online dating. *Communication Research* 38(1), 70–100.

Giddens, A. (2013). *The Consequences of Modernity*. John Wiley & Sons.

Giddens, A. & C. Pierson. (1998). *Conversations with Anthony Giddens: Making Sense of Modernity*. Stanford: Stanford University Press.

Harris, L. C. (2002). The emotional labour of barristers: An exploration of emotional labour by status professionals. *Journal of Management Studies* 39(4), 553–584.

Hawkins, A. (2023). State-sponsored matchmaking app launched in China. *The Guardian*, 20 March. Retrieved from https://www.theguardian.com/world/2023/mar/20/state-sponsored-matchmaking-app-launched-in-china.

Heino, R. D., N. B. Ellison, & J. L. Gibbs. (2010). Relationshopping: Investigating the market metaphor in online dating. *Journal of Social and Personal Relationships* 27(4), 427–447.

Hochschild, A. R. (1975). The sociology of feeling and emotion: Selected possibilities. In M. Millman & R. M. Kanter (eds.), *Sociological Inquiry*, pp. 280–307. Anchor Books.

Hochschild, A. R. (1979). Emotion work, feeling rules, and social structure. *American Journal of Sociology* 85(3), 551–575.

Hochschild, A. R. (1983). *The Managed Heart: The Commercialization of Human Feeling*. Los Angeles: University of California Press.

Hodgson, N. (2017). *The Curious History of Dating*. London: Robinson.

Jenkins, S. & R. Delbridge. (2017). Trusted to deceive: A case study of "strategic deception" and the normalization of lying at work. *Organization Studies* 38(1), 53–76.

Kalberg, S. (1980). Max Weber's types of rationality: Cornerstones for the analysis of rationalization processes in history. *American Journal of Sociology* 85(5), 1145–1179.

Khan, A. & C. Lemmen. (2013). Bricks and urbanism in the Indus Valley rise and decline. Retrieved from https://d1wqtxts1xzle7.cloudfront.net/84111194/b9608f33f7870bfa-libre.pdf?1649922096=&response-content-disposition=inline%3B+filename%3DBricks_and_urbanism_in_the_Indus_Civiliz.pdf&Expires=1732119415&Signature=g5i5dU6flzjqXCHXfizzNoXlSqJLU5OTgLzy4Pf8cuwp.

Kiser, E. & Y. Cai. (2003). War and bureaucratization in Qin China: Exploring an anomalous case. *American Sociological Review* 68(4), 511–539.

Králik, M., V. Novotny, & M. Oliva. (2002). Fingerprint on the Venus of Dolní Věstonice I. *Anthropologie (1962–)* 40(2), 107–113.

Kuhn, D. (1981). Silk technology in the Sung period (960–1278 AD). *T'oung Pao* 67(1/2), 48–90.

Lane, F. C. (1973). *Venice, a Maritime Republic*. Baltimore: JHU Press.

Leidner, R. (1993). *Fast Food, Fast Talk: Service Work and the Routinization of Everyday Life*. Los Angeles: University of California Press.

Lombard, M. & L. Phillipson. (2010). Indications of bow and stone-tipped arrow use 64 000 years ago in KwaZulu-Natal, South Africa. *Antiquity* 84(325), 635–648.

Lucas, A. (2006). *Wind, Water, Work: Ancient and Medieval Milling Technology*. Leiden: Brill.

Mishmastnehi, M., R. Milke, & R. Bernbeck. (2021). A forgotten technology: The production of artificial millstones for windmills in Sistan, southeastern Iran. *Journal of Archaeological Science* 133, 105440.

Morley, I. & C. Renfrew. (2010). *The Archaeology of Measurement: Comprehending Heaven, Earth and Time in Ancient Societies*. Cambridge: Cambridge University Press.

Plummer, T. (2004). Flaked stones and old bones: Biological and cultural evolution at the dawn of technology. *American Journal of Physical Anthropology* 125(S39), 118–164.

Pugh, D. (2007). *Organisation Theory: Selected Classic Readings*. London: Penguin Books.

Raadschelders, J. C. (2017). *Handbook of Administrative History*. London: Routledge.

Rao, L., N. B. Sahu, P. Sahu, U. Shastry, & S. Diwan. (2004). Unearthing Harappan settlement at Bhirrana (2003–04). *Puratattva* 34, 20–34.

Riley, R. & M. C. Weiss. (2016). A qualitative thematic review: Emotional labour in healthcare settings. *Journal of Advanced Nursing* 72(1), 6–17.

Ritzer, G. (2021). *The McDonaldization of Society*. Los Angeles: Sage.

Rogers, M. E., P. A. Creed, & J. Searle. (2014). Emotional labour, training stress, burnout, and depressive symptoms in junior doctors. *Journal of Vocational Education & Training* 66(2), 232–248.

Roser, C. (2016). *Faster, Better, Cheaper in the History of Manufacturing: From The Stone Age to Lean Manufacturing and Beyond*. New York: Productivity Press.

Sinclair, U. & E. Lee. (2003). *The Jungle: The Uncensored Original Edition*. New York: Sharp Press.

Solecki, R. S., R. L. Solecki, & A. P. Agelarakis. (2004). *The Proto-Neolithic Cemetery in Shanidar Cave*. Texas: A&M University Press.

Standage, T. (2021). *A Brief History Of Motion: From the Wheel, to the Car, to What Comes Next*. London: Bloomsbury.

Statista. (2021). *Online Dating Worldwide—Statistics & Facts*.

Taylor, F. W. (1914). *The Principles of Scientific Management*. New York: Harper.

Taylor, F. W. (1947). *Scientific Management*. New York: Harper & Brothers.

Taylor, P. & P. Bain. (1999). "An assembly line in the head": Work and employee relations in the call centre. *Industrial Relations Journal* 30(2), 101–117.

Tone, A. (2018). *The Business of Benevolence: Industrial Paternalism in Progressive America*. Cornell: Cornell University Press.

Valladas, H., J. Clottes, J.-M. Geneste, M. A. Garcia, M. Arnold, H. Cachier, et al. (2001). Evolution of prehistoric cave art. *Nature* 413(6855), 479.

Wade, N. (1974). *Windmills: The resurrection of an ancient energy technology*. Science 184(4141), 1055–1058.

WTO. (2019). *World Trade Report 2019. The Future of Services Trade*.

8
Power, Control, and the Motivation to Work

Keywords

motivation; control; money; industrial paternalism; cognition; affect; action; tunneling

Consider

How do you get people in an organization into line and happily working as hard as they possibly can?

8.1 Introduction

Do you remember in Chapter 6 when I described my first job at BigBank? Do you remember the utter boredom I felt working in an organization where everything was so bureaucratic? What about the Venetians' struggle with "disciplining an army of craftworkers to the demands of factory-style work rhythms" at the Arsenal of Venice (Davis, 1997, p. 57)? Do you remember that?

What I'm scratching at here is the vexing question of *__motivation__*. This is the question of how to get people in an organization into line and working as hard as they possibly can. As far as questions go, it's one of the classics. It's one of the first things organization theorists have ever studied. And not just excitable academics, either. How to motivate people to work has sparked the interest of everyone from ancient Qin bureaucrats to sharp-suited modern executives.

When it comes to peoples' motivation to work, the story is a complex one. This chapter will help you to start piecing things together. It begins with some basic theoretical foundations, such as what we mean when we talk about "motivation" and why it is linked to notions of "power" and "control." From there, the focus shifts to the motivational effects of money and how it's leveraged in organizations. The last section looks at welfare-orientated approaches to motivation and how these are used to drive productivity and ensure discipline in organizations.

8.2 Theoretical foundations

The concept of **motivation** is all about the "energetic forces that originate both within as well as beyond an individual's being, to initiate work-related behaviour and determine its form, direction, intensity[,] and duration" (Latham & Pinder, 2005, p. 486; Pinder, 2014, p. 11). It's all about what drives people to be productive at work.

People began to think seriously about motivation—by which I mean research and build theories about it—from around the 18th century onwards. It's not fair to say people didn't think about motivation before then, but as you'll remember from the previous chapters, the 18th century was an important turning point in world history. The modern social sciences were in their infancy, capitalist economies were taking root, and society was becoming more liberal.

The point about society liberalizing is particularly important because it brought a shift in peoples' understanding of "right" and "wrong" ways of running organizations. Specifically, this liberalizing eroded the perceived legitimacy of direct, coercive forms of control (e.g., Siméon, 2017, pp. 85–86), and triggered the search for new, more subtle ways of getting people to do things. Put bluntly, violence and slavery were on the way out, and people were trying to figure out better, more humane ways of motivating people to work (Burawoy, 1982, p. 27; Cummings et al., 2017, pp. 46–80).

The concepts of **power** and **control** sit at the heart of research into motivation. It's important not to be bashful about this. When we talk about motivation, we're largely talking about how people (managers) get other people (workers) to do what they want them to do (as in Dahl, 1957). It's about how people are variously compelled to do work that, quite possibly, they'd rather not—or at least not do so much, for so long, in quite that way, or for such a small share in the rewards.

The critical point here is that "power springs up whenever people get together and act in concert" (Arendt, 1970, p. 1970). Within this context the Oxford English Dictionary defines power as the "ability to act or affect something," to "control or [exert] authority over others; dominion, rule; government, command, sway." And the "capacity to direct or influence the behaviour of others; personal or social influence." The notion of control is defined in broadly similar terms. It is "the action or fact of holding in check or restraining; restraint."

8.3 Motivating the workforce

In this next section, I'm going to give you a broad overview of two different tactics used to motivate people to work in organizations. I'll begin with the most obvious tactic: paying them money. Drawing on research into human psychology, I'll tell you a bit about the nature of the power money has over us, and how it is leveraged in organizations to get us to do things. In Section 8.5.1, I'll introduce you to what I'm calling welfare-type approaches to motivation and how they have historically been leveraged.

8.3.1 Pay me money

One of the strongest motivations of humans in modern (capitalist) societies is the desire to obtain money (Lea & Webley, 2006, p. 161; Rynes et al., 2004). There are no two ways about it. Rich or poor, people are motivated by money (Ahuvia, 2008). If we think we are going to get money by doing something, we're probably going to do it. Similarly, if we've done something in the past that has resulted in us getting money, we're probably going to do it again. Giving people money, or at least giving them the opportunity to get money, is one of the most reliable ways of getting them to do something.

The nature of money's hold over us is complicated, and research in this area has produced a range of interesting insights. Amongst other things, it reveals money's effect on **cognition** (what we think), **affect** (how we feel), and **action** (what we do).

8.3.1.1 Money and cognition

In relation to cognition—that is, to our thought processes—research seems to show two main things. The first is that when we don't have enough money our cognitive functioning—our ability to think clearly—is diminished. As Mullainathan and Shafir (2013) put it, scarcity leads to something called **tunneling**. That is, "to a laser focus on resources that are lacking to the detriment of other issues that might require cognitive effort" (Leana & Meuris, 2015, p. 62). Put another way, when we don't have enough money our brains become preoccupied by (distracted with) this scarcity making it difficult for us to think about other things.

Based on this theory, researchers specifically connect money scarcity with things like poor decision making. The argument here is that when people don't have enough money, they tend to make worse decisions than normal (Carvalho et al., 2016; Shah et al., 2012; Spears, 2011). Specifically, research suggests that money scarcity leads to people getting locked into cycles of poor decision making, particularly about things to do with money. The effects of these poor decisions accumulate, compound, and amplify one another. The result is a self-perpetuating downward spiral in which the poor get poorer, and poorer, and poorer (Mullainathan & Shafir, 2013).

Other effects relate more directly to organizational behavior. For example, studies suggest that the cognitive load created by money scarcity can impede creativity, make people less likely to voice their ideas, and trigger diminished perceptions of their own self-efficacy (Butler, 2016).

Other studies suggest that money scarcity can reduce cognitive functioning to such an extent it becomes noticeably harder for people to learn new skills (Kanfer & Ackerman, 1989).

The second thing that research into money and cognition has found is that valuing time in monetary terms causes something called a "market-pricing mindset" (Fiske, 1992). This is a relatively straightforward concept, which DeVoe and Pfeffer (2007b) articulate beautifully. Essentially, the concept of a market-pricing mindset pertains to the idea that if we're paid by the hour or day, then two things happen: (1) we become conscious that our time has a specific value, and (2) the decisions we make about how to spend our time become subject to direct monetary evaluation.

An example. As a cash-starved postgraduate, I did some work as a self-employed management consultant, for which I was paid a pretty decent "day rate." As well as refilling my chronically overdrawn bank account, having a day rate meant I could quite literally put a price on time spent working/not working. Theoretically I could go on holiday whenever I wanted, but it would cost me a multiplication of my standard day rate (lost income) plus the cost of the actual holiday. So, about £10,000 GBP for a two-week camping trip.

As it happens, I did in fact evaluate the only holiday I took during this period in my life in precisely these terms. As I tramped the peaks of the Spanish Pyrenees, I wondered whether the climb and the frosty chat with my girlfriend was actually worth it. Would I rather the £10k or the hike with my grumpy partner? When she dumped me part way through the trip, I decided I'd rather have the money. We ditched the mountains and scampered home. Back to work I went.

What I'm driving at with this particularly inglorious example is that directly valuing time has a range of significant effects, one of which is to pull us back to work. Relatedly, studies also show that a market-pricing mindset reduces the chance of us volunteering in our community (DeVoe & Pfeffer, 2007a, 2010), limits our enjoyment of non-work activities, and triggers a decline in our general happiness (DeVoe & House, 2012). It also makes us prone to overworking, and increases work-related stress and burnout (Cooper et al., 2001). So, as far as our brain works, paying people money is a good way to get them to do things.

8.3.1.2 Money and affect

Research suggests that money also seems to have a big impact on how we feel. It affects our subjective wellbeing, which is a complicated psychological concept that broadly refers to our sense of how happy we are (Diener et al., 2018). Research in this area is relatively straightforward. It centers on two distinct propositions.

The first proposition is that we're "happy when our income situation is in line with our aspirations" (Leana & Meuris, 2015, p. 65). So, we're happy when we can afford to do the things we want to do and can buy the things we want to buy.

The second proposition is that as soon as we realize our material aspirations (through working hard and earning money), our material aspirations increase. In effect, as we get richer our material aspirations rise in line with our income. New found (material) wealth becomes the "new normal" and we aspire to (own) bigger and better things.

Kahneman et al. (2000) call this the "satisfaction treadmill." As a concept, it captures the empirical reality that for many of us, working harder and earning more and more money, actually has very little impact on how happy we are (Easterlin et al., 2010). The argument here is that all that happens is that we get used to our new luxuries and want more and more, and have to work harder and harder to get it.

There is a certain intuitive logic to this argument. However it is not uncontested. Cantor and Sanderson (2003) argue that the reason we're not happier when we earn more money is not because our material aspirations increase but because the extra work we do leaves us more stressed out and short of time to enjoy our lives. So, it's not that money doesn't make us happy, just that the extra work we have to do to earn it starves us of time in which to enjoy it.

Easterlin et al. (2010) argue something slightly different. Their argument is that earning more money does in fact make us happier, but that the happiness we feel is only very short lived. Sacks et al. (2012) also correlate money with happiness, but their argument is that happiness only increases up to a certain point (see also Haushofer & Fehr, 2014). $75,000 USD per year (in the USA in 2010) seems to be the magic number. So, according to Sacks et al. (2012), we're happier earning $75,000 than we are earning $50,000. However, earning $95,000 doesn't make us much happier than when we were earning $75,000.

Perhaps the most crucial point arising from these studies is that regardless of whether or not money actually makes us happier, people generally behave as though it does (Ahuvia, 2008). In the context of work and organizations, a minority of people will, as Kahneman et al. (2006) suggest, ease off the pursuit of material wealth once they've reached a certain level of earnings; however, most won't. In fact, for most of us, most of the time, money's motivational effect is consistently strong even though it doesn't really have much of an effect on how happy we are. Go figure.

8.3.1.3 Money and action

Although money is something that organizations can leverage to motivate particular kinds of behavior, it's worth noting that money also motivates unethical behavior. The precise role that money plays in motivating unethical behavior is fiendishly difficult to establish and remains frustratingly poorly understood. The little we do know is mostly derived from laboratory-based studies that have produced results that have mostly proven difficult to replicate (Stajkovic et al., 2022).

Let's look at some examples. First, lab-based studies (e.g., Côté et al., 2013; Piff et al., 2010) have found that people who perceive themselves to have high socioeconomic status are "less likely to behave prosocially, more likely to cheat, and more likely to be utilitarian in their decision making" (Leana & Meuris, 2015, p. 65). As Piff et al. (2010) put it, it seems that those "with more" tend to act less prosocially. They give less and hold themselves to lower moral standards than those who self-identify as members of lower socioeconomic classes (Côté et al., 2013).

Before you get too carried away with this theory, note the caveat laden nature of the arguments. These studies are not arguing that all rich people are antisocial cheaters, and it would be very wrong to draw this conclusion.

Consider other studies (e.g., Gino & Pierce, 2009) that argue the mere presence of wealth—i.e., being surrounded by great riches—increases the frequency of peoples' cheating, particularly amongst those who don't identify as wealthy. The argument here is that poor people in lavish surroundings cheat more than they would in more austere surroundings. Specifically, Gino and Pierce (2009) argue that abundant wealth provokes feelings of envy that in turn lead to unethical behavior.

Again, it's important to note the caveat laden nature of these arguments. Gino and Pierce (2009) are not arguing that if you surround poor people with wealth, they'll be overcome by envy and start lying and cheating all the time. Again, it would be very wrong to draw this conclusion.

Perhaps the most important insight arising from these studies is the suggestion that you don't need to pay people money to motivate them to do something. What these studies suggest is that simply exposing people to money can prime (that is, subconsciously trigger) certain behaviors (Vohs et al., 2006). Money priming can, as Kouchaki et al. (2013) argue, trigger unethical behavior (see also Mok & De Cremer, 2016, 2018). Other studies have shown that it can also diminish cooperative attitudes (Pfeffer & DeVoe, 2009), reduce people's willingness to volunteer (Gasiorowska et al., 2016), and make people less likely to help each other (Guéguen & Jacob, 2013).

It's worth re-emphasizing at this point that arguments relating to the money priming effect are subject to great debate. Research in this area is provocative and has attracted a lot of attention. However, very little of it has ever been replicated—despite many attempts to do so (Stajkovic et al., 2022). So, what we have are individual studies that provide evidence of the effects of money priming, but little that actually counts as irrefutable hard scientific "fact." That's worth keeping in mind.

8.3.1.4 Money matters in organizations: Ford's Five Dollar Day

What I've outlined previously has clear implications. If you want to motivate people then paying them money, or giving them a chance to earn money, is a pretty good way of doing things. In practice, this is precisely what most organizations do to secure some level of commitment and motivation from their workforce and to exert a degree of control over them. There is little subtlety or nuance to it. It's simply a case of: "do X and you'll be paid Y" or "do X and you *might* be paid Y."

There are few better illustrations of the effectiveness of this approach to motivation than Meyer's (1981) excellent account of the "Five Dollar Day" introduced by Henry Ford, at the Ford Motor Company in 1914. The concept of Ford's Five Dollar Day was really simple: pay workers $5 USD per day. Set in the context of most factory workers earning about $11/week, this was an incredible proposition, because it effectively doubled workers' take-home pay.

The initiative itself was based on some pretty rudimentary science. Ford believed that money was all-important to his workers, that and his colleagues literally daring him to do it. Yes, you read it right. Ford's famous Five Dollar Day initiative was triggered by a boardroom dare.

In practice, Ford's Five Dollar Day did not actually double workers' basic wages. These stayed the same, but were supplemented by a profit-sharing plan. Under the plan, all workers received their normal wages, but only those who explicitly met "Ford standards" were given a share of company profits.

Precisely what "Ford standards" entailed was ambiguous and subject to change. Crucially, it also extended far beyond what workers were supposed to do at work. To get a share in company profits, workers had to observe a certain, company-defined set of behavioral prescriptions both at work *and* at home. Working on the basis that a "sound home environment produces an efficient worker," the Five Dollar Day was an attempt to regulate all aspects of workers' lives. Or, as Ford put it, tackle "poor attitudes" and "bad habits" at source, through a unique "character building proposition" (Meyer III, 1981, pp. 110–114).

To get their five dollars, workers had to convince representatives of Ford Motor Company they wouldn't "debauch the additional money," be of good character, and work efficiently (Meyer III, 1981, p. 115). Moreover, they were only allowed onto the program once they'd been "carefully looked up" (ibid.) by the company's specially created "sociological department" (later rebranded the "education department").

As Meyer III (1981, p. 116) describes, it was the sociological department's job to learn the nationality, the religion, the bank savings, whether the man owns or is buying property, how he amuses himself, [and] the district he selects to live in. Also, whether this individual was married? If married, how many depend on you? If single, how many are dependent upon you and to what extent? Relationship of dependents? Residence of dependents? Married men: do you live with your wives? Have you ever had any domestic troubles? Are your habits good or bad? Have you a bank account? The questions went on, and on, and on.

What Ford's sociological department were ultimately looking for was evidence of "thrift and good service and sobriety." They wanted assurances that workers were living the kind of lives the Ford Motor Company wanted them to live (Meyer III, 1981, p. 110). Where evidence of this wasn't found, it was the sociological department's job to "straighten them out" by instituting "better living generally" (Meyer III, 1981, p. 113).

Workers who failed to live up to Ford standards, didn't lose their jobs. Instead they were given six months to "mend [their] ways" (Meyer III, 1981, p. 112). To bring about this change, the profit-sharing element of workers' pay was withheld, and the lost amount was noted on their pay envelope. As time went by, "the company enticed the worker to meet its requirements by offering him a proportion of the accrued profits in a single lump sum. In order to hasten the workers change in life and habits, the amount they could claim decreased as time passed" (Meyer III, 1981, pp. 112–113).

Consequently, with "each payday the worker was reminded of their obstinacy" (Meyer III, 1981, p. 112). As the amount withheld grew so did the pressure to conform. In the end most workers traded their "pride and privacy for the economic security of a job with high pay" (Meyer III, 1981, p. 113). Ford got his compliance—and also staggering efficiency gains. Company estimates put the effect of the Five Dollar Day at around a 15–20% improvement in efficiency. There are few better illustrations of the power of money to get people to do things.

8.3.2 Show me love

The previous section, and Ford's Five Dollar Day in particular, are vivid illustrations of money's power to "initiate work-related behavior and determine its form, direction, intensity and duration" (Latham & Pinder, 2005, p. 486; Pinder, 2014, p. 11). However, while undoubtedly important, money is not the only thing that motivates people to work in organizations. Workers really are motivated by other things, as well.

This is the point I was driving at in this chapter's "Introduction" when I asked you to think about the Venetian's struggle with "disciplining an army of craftworkers to the demands of factory-style work rhythms" (Davis, 1997, p. 57). If you skip ahead to this chapter's "Research Insights", you'll see that one way the Venetians "disciplined" their workforce—that is, motivated them to stay on station and working hard—was through some very rudimentary welfare provisions. They supplemented workers' wages, not with extra money but with something safe to drink.

The significance of this simple provision is grounded in the reality that, for much of its history, fresh water in Venice (as in much of Europe), was completely undrinkable. On the advice of doctors, people drank wine instead (Phillips, 2014, p. 42). It seems nuts today, but it's true. To keep the workforce hydrated and stop them from constantly disappearing in search of drink, managers of the Arsenal of Venice installed free-flowing fountains of wine. It's hard to imagine anything getting done with fountains of free-flowing vino about the place. Certainly not the legendary 100 ships in 100 days. However, the fountains of wine existed—see Photo 8.1.

The practice of supplementing monetary remuneration with "something beyond wages" (Tone, 2018, p. 1) has historically been known as **industrial paternalism**, but also **welfare work**, and **welfare capitalism**. The people who practice it have been variously known as **welfare capitalists** or **paternal industrialists**. In what follows, I'll explain what all this means, why it matters in the context of power, control, and motivation, and what it looks like in practice.

8.3.2.1 The concept of industrial paternalism

Visible today in things like corporate benefits packages, the concept of industrial paternalism has a long history that certainly predates our Venetian fountains of wine. In very general terms, it refers to a system in which organizations (rather than state governments) provide welfare services to the people who work for them. By welfare services, I mean safe drinking water, but also things like decent education, nutritious food, and vital healthcare. It's about things done by the corporation to improve workers' health and wellbeing, and, by extension, their capacity and willingness to work.

Here there are a number of things to make clear. The first is that industrial paternalism comes in all sorts of different shapes and sizes. It varies significantly across time and between different contexts. Consequently, industrial paternalism in the 14th, 17th, and 20th centuries all look very different. Similarly, industrial paternalism in French manufacturing, looks quite different to industrial paternalism in German, British, and Australian manufacturing. There is no single, universal type.

Second, industrial paternalism is not philanthropy. History's great paternal industrialists—such as the Cadburys and Frys of Great Britain—did not simply give their wealth away. Much like the Arsenal's free-flowing wine, the welfare services they gave workers came with a catch. The quid pro quo was the expectation of increased productivity and greater control over the workforce for their deferential obedience.

Third, throughout history, industrial paternalism has generally been compelled by business logic (e.g., belief in the power of its motivational effect) coupled with a strong sense of religious and/or ideological conviction. Paternal industrialists were moved to improve workers' welfare for much the same reason Henry Ford paid his workers $5 a day—because it seemed like the "right" thing to do, for both workers and the organization.

In Europe (and in Britain in particular) this belief can be understood as a permeation of classic Christian-inspired notions of charity and centuries-old feudal vassalage rules. In relation to the latter,

Siméon (2017, p. 12) describes how the medieval feudal system imposed on the wealthy a moral obligation to provide for their workers "as a father should towards his children." Thus, paternal industrialists were traditionally concerned with all aspects of their workers' lives. Anything that impacted on peoples' ability and willingness to work mattered, was scrutinized, and improved.

Paternal industrialists also weren't just compelled by the modernist idea of "fixing" deficiencies in workers' personal, social, and moral wellbeing. It was widely held—though not always observed—that those who failed in their paternalistic duty towards their workforce not only stymied the success of their organization, but risked hell and damnation in their own right. For the ecclesiastically minded, industrial paternalism was as much about booking their own place in heaven as anything else.

The next thing to note is that advocates of industrial paternalism (particularly the enterprising Quakers) seemed genuinely concerned with figuring out how capitalism and social welfare can be made to coexist. They were not hard (neo)liberals. They were business-minded, religious socialists, of a sort. Quakers in particular, while ardent capitalists in their own right, were (generally) appalled by the consequences of unchecked capitalism (but see Williams, 2021). Stemming from their religious beliefs, they extolled the idea that capitalists don't have to choose between profits and workers' welfare. Their argument was that the two are in fact interdependent—that social welfare actually drives profits, and that any other system is doomed to fail. For more on this you can read accounts of Quakers in the manufacturing industry from Cadbury (1912); Raistrick (1950); and Windsor (1980).

8.3.2.2 The traditional focus of paternal industrialists

The precise motivational effects of industrial paternalism are notoriously difficult to quantify. They undoubtedly exist, but are hard to prove and put a price on (Oreopoulos & Salvanes, 2011). Indeed, precisely why history's great paternal industrialists embarked on their ambitious welfare projects and what they got in return, is subject to great debate (Tone, 2018, p. 2). However, there are some defining practices engaged in for their clear motivational effects and obvious benefit to the organization.

8.3.2.2.1 Health, wellbeing, and increased productivity

Arguably the first and primary concern of paternal industrialists throughout history has been with improving workers' health and wellbeing, ostensibly so they can work harder and longer than would otherwise be the case. Here it helps if we set things in the context of early modernity and the rise of mechanized manufacturing organizations in industrializing Europe. Famously labeled "satanic" by the poet William Blake (see Blake & Bloom, 1982), the sort of early mechanized manufacturing organizations I talked about in the previous chapters were truly shitty places to work. As mentioned previously, they were dank, dark, dirty, and very, very dangerous. Gowland et al. (2023) reveals in clinical detail the sort of brutal hardships workers were characteristically subject to (see also Siméon, 2017, pp. 40–41).

The thing about the "satanic" factories of early modern Europe is that they wreaked havoc on the workforce—as Gowland et al. (2023) and Siméon (2017) both describe. Their productive efficiency was incredible, but so was their capacity to churn out legions of unhealthy, sick, and maimed workers. The moral imperative for owners and managers of the organizations to take better care of their workforce was clear. As was the business case for doing so. Even the most dispassionate industrialist could see that masses of unhealthy, sick, and maimed workers were good for very little—certainly not the rigors of industrial manufacturing.

Within this context, welfare initiatives to improve health and wellbeing were conceived as an efficient method for "lessening human waste" and improving organizational efficiency (Tone, 2018, p. 80). Such initiatives broadly fell into one of three different categories. The first category incorporates initiatives concerned with ensuring that the workforce is, at a minimum, physically capable of working. Early initiatives of this kind focused on things like food, nutrition, and healthcare. Think not only of company-funded hospitals, sick rooms, and first aid stations, but also subsidized grocery stores, canteens, and dining rooms. That kind of thing.

In the context of factories with high accident and mortality rates, hospitals, sick rooms, and first aid stations helped fix workers' physical injuries and improve their health in general. Similarly, in the context of general and acute malnourishment amongst the working classes, subsidized grocery stores, canteens, and dining rooms were a great way of making sure people had the energy they needed to work. They were also a surprisingly good way of keeping workers out of pubs and bars at lunch time.

A second category of health and welfare initiatives targeted the causes of injury at work. Here, think about the sort of training courses you do when you join a new organization to stop you hurting yourself. These training courses are the evolved product of several hundred years of work to limit the physical toll of labor on the workforce. In the 21st century, we teach people how to pick up pens, give them ergonomic chairs, and training courses on how to use them. In the 17th, 18th, and 19th centuries, people got stools to sit on, fans to remove toxic gasses, and lighting so they could see what they were doing.

In relation to the latter, electrification during the 19th century is particularly notable for the massive improvement in safety it effected. For even the most tight-fisted employers, illuminating dark workplaces was well worth the expense. Things got even better with the invention of reinforced concrete. From the turn of the 20th century, industrialists could build not only cheaper factories but buildings with larger windows than had ever been possible before. Workers could not just have light but *free* light.

The third category focuses on employees' emotional health and wellbeing. A hot topic of conversation today, paternal industrialists were also concerned with how people felt about their work. Today, we have company counselors, psychologists, and mental health nurses. In the 19th century, industrialists poured money into grandiose buildings and fancy gardens, convinced of the positive emotional impact they'd have on the workforce and the increases in productivity that would ensue.

Illustrative of such beliefs, the June 1910 edition of the American industrial magazine *Factory* was dedicated almost entirely to the question of how to "make factory buildings attractive." Amongst a great many other suggestions, contributors advocated planting Wisterias, Boston Ivy, and Periwinkles. These flowers in particular, it was argued, would do a great job of softening the utilitarian blandness of factory buildings, encouraging people to feel happier and more enthusiastic about their work.

8.3.2.2.2 Leisure, relaxation, and lifestyle regulation

A second traditional area of concern for paternal industrialists was with the lives people lead once work ended. Here, concerns were split along two interrelated lines. First, religiously orientated industrialists were particularly concerned with their workers' moral proclivities and spiritual health. That is, with whether they were God-fearing and righteous. Second and relatedly, they were concerned about how and with whom workers were living their lives—whether workers were living squalid, vice-filled lives or holding down an altogether more wholesome existence.

At best, such concerns were only ever partially about workers spiritual and personal wellbeing. What paternal industrialists were mostly interested in was the extent to which their workers' social lives were impacting on their productive efficiency. Workers' leisure time was of great interest because it was widely perceived that what "workers [do] after hours affect[s] their work performance" (Tone, 2018, p. 71). And because "drunk, financially strapped, or fatigued from indulgence, the 'merry' worker was a sorry substitute for the robust, efficient human machine employers desired" (Tone, pp. 93–94).

Within this context, it was common for industrialists, particularly those with a penchant for controlling forms of paternalism, to use welfare-type initiatives to exert an often-considerable degree of control over workers' non-working lives. Maintaining the productive efficiency of the organization was paramount, as was the need to save workers from themselves and protect their mortal souls. The risk of failing to do so was that workers "would succumb to the perilous thrill of cheap amusements" (Tone, pp. 93–94) and generally debauch themselves.

It was precisely this kind of thinking that underscored Henry Ford's staggeringly intrusive invasions of his workers' privacy previously described. Egregious by today's standards, these types of initiatives and programs weren't uncommon at the turn of the 20th century. Indeed, across Europe and America a considerable number of other organizations also made company welfare contingent on the outcomes of very similar practices. Things like regular home inspections, round-the-clock monitoring of workers, and ongoing assessments of how they lived their lives informed company decisions about everything from pay and remuneration to access to cheap housing and education.

Not all the tactics used to regulate workers' lives were so obviously intrusive and controlling. Indeed, some forms of industrial welfare were only controlling in really quite subtle ways. For example, company-sponsored social venues (such as social clubs and dance halls) seemed innocuous enough, but were actually set up to railroad employees into healthy, wholesome, and industrious pursuits. For workers, such facilities provided much-needed places to meet, socialize, and relax. For the company, the same facilities gave them an insight into workers' social lives and a degree of control over them. In providing the facilities, organizations could decide what they were used for—academic lectures, reading, and billiards rather than boozing, raucous partying, and gambling.

The provision of sports facilities was a similarly efficacious form of corporate welfare. By sponsoring things like tennis clubs, swimming pools, and athletics tracks, companies could direct their employees towards more healthy pursuits. This enabled them to not only keep their workers out of bars, brothels, and gambling dens but also made sure they were literally "fit" for work. Indeed, it wasn't uncommon for companies to specifically fund sports that directly improved peoples' ability to work.

Such social initiatives, as well as those designed to improve workers' health and wellbeing, played a really important role in improving workers' capacity and willingness to work. They also played an important, wider political role by diminishing the threat of trade unions. Many organizations successfully forestalled worker unionization through a kind of crushing kindness directed at the workforce. For many employers, welfare capitalism was a good line of defence against socialism, unionism, and welfare statism.

8.3.2.2.3 Industrial paternalism in organizations: Robert Owen's workers' utopia

One of the earliest, perhaps the best, illustration of industrial paternalism in practice can be seen in the work of the utopian socialist visionary, Robert Owen (1771–1858). Siméon (2017) provides an excellent account of his New Lanark "experiment." That is, Robert Owen's attempt to engineer "the labouring classes material, moral, and intellectual environment" in order to address the "social and economic upheavals of the new industrial age" (Siméon, 2017, p. 12).

Now a museum, hotel, and spa, the former pioneering cotton milling enterprise ran during the 18th and 19th centuries. Built just south of Glasgow (UK) by a man called David Dale, New Lanark was organized along enlightened, progressive, humanitarian lines. From the outset it was a business set up with the aim of (profitably) improving the poor's position in industrial Britain.

Owen acquired New Lanark from his father-in-law, David Dale, in 1799 having worked alongside him for several years. At the point he bought New Lanark, it was a well-established industrial town, known for its benevolent, charitable style of management (Siméon, 2017, p. 12). Despite initial opposition from his co-investors, Owen's aim was to expand and systematize the work that his father-in-law had started. He wanted to create a blueprint for humane industrial practice, which could be taught and replicated elsewhere in order to bring about his utopian vision for society. The point was to facilitate the progression of humanity, by scientifically deducing a way to mitigate the "nefarious effects of the factory system" and, where possible, eradicate them altogether (Siméon, 2017, p. 29).

The welfare needs of the worker (and their family) were at the heart of the system Owen envisaged. His vision was multifaceted, a major element of which concerned working conditions in the factory. Here Owen introduced a range of reforms. First amongst these was a reduction in the length of the working day, for both adults and children—from 12 to 10 hours per day. A keen believer in workers having time for work, rest, and leisure, Owen wanted to "fix" the problem of excessive fatigue among his workers by giving them a more balanced (and thus more sustainable) working day.

Like David Dale, Robert Owen employed considerable numbers of children in his New Lanark mill (Siméon, 2017, pp. 40–41). However, he was also a vocal critic of this practice, and eventually restricted the use of child labor in his factories. He also advocated laws that would protect children from exploitation. Rather than working in factories, Owen wanted children to stay in school and established free ones at New Lanark to provide for their intellectual and moral development.

Owen also prioritized the safety and wellbeing of his workers, implementing a range of initiatives to prevent accidents and injuries. These included improving the design and maintenance of machinery and providing training on how to operate machines safely. He also improved sanitation in his mill, giving workers access to washrooms, clean dining rooms, and drinking water.

Beyond the factory walls, another of Owen's concerns was with social welfare and relations between his workers, the vast majority of whom lived onsite. To improve these, he established a welfare system that included cheap modern housing and a store selling heavily discounted food. He also organized social activities, such as free concerts and dances to promote integration and cooperation among residents.

Through David Dale, and Robert Owen's work, New Lanark gained an international reputation for its progressive approach to industrialization and social reform. Between 1815 and 1825, it was a popular tourist destination (Donnachie, 2005) with people traveling from across Europe to see it (Siméon, 2017, p. 10). More recently, in 2001, the mill's significance in the history of modern ideas was recognized by the United Nations Educational, Scientific, and Cultural Organization (UNESCO). As a place where profitable business was made to coexist with fair treatment of workers, it was entered onto a list of World Heritage sites.

8.4 Summary

This chapter has provided an elementary introduction to the concept of motivation, which was defined initially in terms of the "energetic forces that originate both within as well as beyond an individual's being, to initiate work-related behavior and determine its form, direction, intensity[,] and duration" (Latham & Pinder, 2005, p. 486; Pinder, 2014, p. 11).

Having established this initial definition, motivation was then framed as being about the exercise of power and control in organizations—how managers get workers to do what they want them to do. The study of motivation was then set in the context of early modernity, the decline in the legitimacy of violence and slavery, and the search for better ways of getting things done in organizations.

The two sections that followed outlined, first, the motivational effects of money. That is, the effects of money on what we think, do, and feel in the context of work and organizations. It also showed how Henry Ford, through his Five Dollar Day initiative, used money to exert quite an incredible degree of control over workers at the Ford Motor Company.

The second section focused on welfare-orientated approaches to motivation and how non-monetary rewards are used to drive productivity and ensure discipline in organizations. This section closed with an account of Robert Owen's work (with David Dale) on a 19th century socialist utopia at an industrial cotton mill in New Lanark, Glasgow. Taken together, these sections introduce the big sticks and juicy carrots used to keep people committed and working hard in organizations.

Things to Watch, Things to Read

Notes: in this table are suggestions for things you can read and watch to learn more about this topic. I've also included a very short commentary so that you have a sense of why I've recommended a particular source, and what to look out for.

Read in two to three hours	Leana, C. R. & J. Meuris. (2015). Living to work and working to live: Income as a driver of organizational behavior. *The Academy of Management Annals* 9(1), 55–95.

This is a fascinating, thought-provoking review of the role that income (money) plays in motivating different forms of behavior in organizations. Although its primary focus is the interplay between money and organizational behavior, it also covers the effects of money on behavior in society more generally. To be read in conjunction with the initial sections of this chapter.

Read in a day or two	Kanfer, R., M. Frese, & R. E. Johnson. (2017). Motivation related to work: A century of progress. *Journal of Applied Psychology* 102(3), 338.

This wide-ranging review examines what we know about the psychology of motivation related to work. It covers the major advances of the last 100 years, and will broaden and deepen your understanding of this topic. The initial sections, which focus on state-of-the-art research into the psychology of motivation, are the most relevant. The latter sections on methodology and recommendations for future research are primarily targeted at academics.

Read in a week or three	Tone, A. (2018). *The Business of Benevolence: Industrial Paternalism in Progressive America*. New York: Cornell University Press.

This book provides a comprehensive introduction to the concept of industrial paternalism in early 20th century America. It'll help you to understand what industrial paternalism is, and to see this phenomenon in the context of early 20th century conflicts between capitalists and workers (labor and the labor movement). It also engages with the debate about the role the state should play in welfare provision. What emerges is an understanding of the nature of paternalistic business practices, but also how these practices are used to derail worker unionization and welfare statism.

Watch in an evening	*Experimenter* (2015). Written and directed by Michael Almereyda. Production companies: BB Film Productions; FJ Productions; Intrinsic Value Films; Jeff Rice Films; 2B Productions.

While not an artistic masterpiece, this relatively recent movie gives a chilling, detailed, and deeply uncomfortable insight into Stanley Milgram's obedience experiments, which were conducted at Yale University in 1961. The movie reveals how the experiments unfolded, both in a practical sense and in terms of the clear distress they caused the study's participants. What stands out is not just the distressing nature of Milgram's discoveries, but the thorny issue of research ethics and the complexities of doing deceptive research. To be watched in conjunction with the following "Case Study."

Research Insight: Motivation, Venetian-style

Source: Davis, R. C. (1997). Venetian shipbuilders and the fountain of wine. *Past & Present* 156, 55–86.

Edited abstract: the article is about how those charged with running the late-medieval Arsenal of Venice maintained order in what was (at the time) "the biggest industrial establishment in all Christendom" (Lane, 1973, p. 362). The article is concerned with how the Venetians managed to manufacture up to 100 ships every 100 days, and how they did this in an age when manufacturing was more typically done on a very, very small scale. The answer Davis gives to this question concerns the social contract that was in place at the Arsenal. Venetian managers gave decent wages, but also provided their workers with prodigious quantities of wine. Davis argues that this unlikely business practice was the secret of the Venetians' success. Read the article to find out more.

Case Study: The greatest experiment of all time?

Introduction

Perhaps the darkest, rawest form of motivation comes from the direct application of coercive power. Here, a rudimentary distinction can be made between: (1) people compelled to do something through literal, physical violence; and (2) people compelled to do something through softer, but no less damaging, forms of violence, such as threats, bullying, and the blunt exercise of power.

This Case Study is concerned with the latter of these distinctions. It is all about one of the most famous human science experiments of all time: Stanley Milgram's "obedience experiments" (Milgram, 1963, 1965, 1974). NB: this Case Study can be read in conjunction with the movie *Experimenter*, which is recommended in the "Things to Watch, Things to Read" feature of this chapter.

Who was Stanley Milgram?

Stanley Milgram (1933–84) was a prominent social psychologist who studied and earned his PhD in social psychology from Harvard University in 1960. He later served as an assistant professor at Yale University, where the obedience experiments took place.

Milgram's obedience experiments

Starting in August 1961, Milgram's obedience experiments investigated the extent to which individuals would obey an authority figure even when their actions conflicted with their personal conscience. The experiment involved three key participants: the authority figure (Experimenter), the participant (Teacher), and a confederate (Learner). The procedure went like this:

1. Participants were recruited through newspaper adverts that invited them to take part in a study of memory and learning.
2. Upon arrival at the laboratory, people were paid a small amount of money for their participation in the study.

3. Having been paid their money, study participants, along with a confederate of Milgram, took part in a mock selection process to allocate roles in the experiment. Study participants were always assigned the role of "Teacher" in the experiment. Confederates were always assigned the role of "Learner."

4. The Teacher and Learner were then shown an electric shock generating machine with switches ranging from 15 volts to 450 volts. These were labeled with descriptions such as "slight shock" to "danger: severe shock." At this stage, the Learner would disclose that they have a heart condition.

5. The Experimenter explained that the Learner would be attached to the shock generator and then asked a series of questions by the Teacher. It was the Teacher's job to administer electric shocks whenever the Learner made a mistake.

6. To demonstrate the authenticity of the shocks, the Experimenter attached the Teacher to the shock machine, and gave them a shock of 45 volts.

7. The experiment began with the Teacher sitting in front of the shock generator. The Learner, in the adjacent room, was wired to the shock machine but then secretly detached from it before the experiment started.

8. The Teacher would then start asking the Learner questions. For each wrong response, the Teacher was instructed to administer an electric shock, increasing the voltage with each subsequent error.

9. If the Teacher hesitated or expressed concern about continuing, the Experimenter provided a series of standardized prompts to encourage them to proceed. These prompts included statements like, "Please continue," or "The experiment requires that you continue."

10. As the Learner got more and more questions wrong, they became more and more vocal in their complaints. Their complaints got increasingly loud, and as the voltage got higher, they started to scream in pain.

11. Once the (fake) shocks rose above a certain voltage, Learners would stage a heart attack. They would fall to the floor screaming and crying out for help and stop responding to instructions from the Teacher. The Teacher was instructed to continue regardless.

12. The experiment typically ended when the Teacher reached the maximum shock level of 450 volts, or when they refused to administer any further shocks. At this point, the true nature of the study was revealed, and participants were debriefed about the purpose and rationale of the experiment.

The study's findings

The study findings were extremely surprising and highly controversial. Milgram and his team found:

1. A significant proportion of participants displayed a high degree of obedience to the Experimenter's instructions. In Milgram's original study (Milgram, 1963), approximately 65% of participants administered the highest level of shocks (450 volts) to the Learner.

2. Most Teachers would continue shocking Learners even as their cries of pain became audibly louder. Some would also continue shocking the Learner long after they had suffered a (staged) heart attack and stopped responding altogether.

3. The proximity of the Learner to the Teacher had an impact on obedience. When the Teacher and Learner were in the same room, obedience rates decreased. Conversely, when the Experimenter was physically present and exerted authority, obedience rates were higher.

4. When participants saw others obeying the Experimenter's instructions, they were more likely to comply as well. Conversely, when participants witnessed dissent from others, their obedience decreased.

The study's implications

Milgram's study triggered significant debate about the apparent fragility of human agency. His findings seemed to suggest that our capacity to think and act freely, making independent moral judgements, was nowhere near as strong as was previously thought. He challenged the belief that only innately evil people would commit acts of harm, and presented the possibility that there was a shocking automaton in all of us (see also Bauman, 1989; Zimbardo et al., 1972).

Hannah Arendt's study of the war criminal Adolf Eichmann, and the detached efficiency with which he organized Nazi death camps, seemingly informed Milgram's analysis (see Arendt, 1963/2006). Inspired by Arendt's "*Banality of Evil*" thesis, Milgram argued that participants in his study did what they did because they entered what he called an "agentic state."

For Milgram, his study's participants yielded to authority and became immersed in the work of educating the Learner. They failed to grasp the true nature of what they were doing because of the way labor was divided within the experiment and its hierarchy of power. Because study participants were following the instructions of a powerful authority figure, they stopped thinking for themselves. They became, as Milgram put it, alienated from their own actions (Milgram, 1974).

This theory is how Milgram's findings are primarily understood today. Yet, alternative theorizations are available. Notably, Haslam et al. (2015) argue that what Milgram found was not simply a case of passive obedience—of people blindly carrying out the will of others. Their argument is that Milgram's findings can be explained in terms of something they call "engaged followship."

Central to the notion of engaged followship is the idea that Milgram's Teachers continued to shock Learners so extremely because they were inculcated in the behavioral norms of experimentation and the idea of "advancing science" (Haslam et al., 2015, p. 60). Viewed this way, Milgram's findings were not a true reflection of human nature. Rather, they were the result of how the experiment was set up and explained to the study's participants by the Researchers.

So, according to this argument, the conformity that was observed in Milgram's study is attributed to participants feeling "obligation(s) to, and identification with, the Experimenter" (Haslam et al., 2015, p. 60). In effect, then, participants delivered their shocks because they didn't want to muck up the study's findings, not because they were overwhelmed by the power and authority of the people running the experiment.

Conclusion

Today Milgram's obedience experiments are considered amongst the greatest of all time. The insights they gave fed into a growing post-war body of research that was concerned with nature and causes of evil. They revealed something shocking about humanity and enhanced our knowledge of how events such as the Holocaust were possible. Remember this also connects to the detachment of human beings from their doings as mentioned in Chapter 6.

However, it wasn't just Milgram's findings that were significant. The ethics of his practices attracted huge criticism (e.g., Baumrind, 1964). The duplicitous nature of the experiment, the clear and obvious psychological suffering participants were exposed to, and the potential for this to have lasting effects were all widely criticized. These would, ultimately, dog and curtail Milgram's career until his early death in 1984 at the age of 51.

Questions

1. What do you think about Milgram and Haslam et al.'s competing explanations for why the people who participated in Milgram's experiment acted in the way they did? How else could we explain ordinary peoples' apparent willingness to shock other people to death?
2. Do you think Milgram's agentic state theory still applies today?
3. What do Milgram's findings reveal about power relations in organizations?
4. To what extent do you think people in organizations are blindly obedient to the power and authority of others?
5. Can you think of any examples of when people in organizations have improperly used their authoritative power to compel other people to do things they may not have wanted to do?

6. What do Milgram's findings tell us about peoples' ability to challenge power and authority in organizations?
7. On the basis that Milgram's experiments were highly traumatic for participants, are the insights he gave worth the trauma inflicted?

References

Ahuvia, A. (2008). If money doesn't make us happy, why do we act as if it does? *Journal of Economic Psychology* 29(4), 491–507.

Arendt, H. (1963/2006). *Eichmann in Jerusalem: A Report on the Banality of Evil*. London: Penguin.

Arendt, H. (1970). *On Violence*. London: Allen Lane.

Bauman, Z. (1989). *Modernity and the Holocaust*. Cambridge: Polity Press.

Baumrind, D. (1964). Some thoughts on ethics of research: After reading Milgram's "Behavioral Study of Obedience". *American Psychologist* 19(6), 421.

Blake, W. & H. Bloom. (1982). *The Complete Poetry and Prose of William Blake*. Los Angeles: University of California Press.

Burawoy, M. (1982). *Manufacturing Consent: Changes in the Labor Process under Monopoly Capitalism*. Chicago: University of Chicago Press.

Butler, J. V. (2016). Inequality and relative ability beliefs. *The Economic Journal* 126(593), 907–948.

Cadbury, E. (1912). *Experiments in Industrial Organization*. London: Longmans, Green, and Company.

Cantor, N. & C. A. Sanderson. (2003). 12 life task participation and well-being: The importance of taking part in daily life. In D. Kahneman, E. Diener, & N. Schwarz (eds.), *Well-Being: Foundations of Hedonic Psychology*, 230–243. London: Russell Sage Foundation.

Carvalho, L. S., S. Meier, & S. W. Wang. (2016). Poverty and economic decision-making: Evidence from changes in financial resources at payday. *American Economic Review* 106(2), 260–284.

Cooper, C. L., Dewe, P., & M. P. O'Driscoll. (2001). *Organizational Stress: A Review and Critique of Theory, Research, and Applications*. London: Sage Publications, Inc.

Côté, S., P. K. Piff, & R. Willer. (2013). For whom do the ends justify the means? Social class and utilitarian moral judgment. *Journal of Personality and Social Psychology* 104(3), 490.

Cummings, S., T. Bridgman, J. Hassard, & M. Rowlinson. (2017). *A New History of Management*. Cambridge: Cambridge University Press.

Dahl, R. A. (1957). The concept of power. *Behavioral Science* 2(3), 201–215.

Davis, R. C. (1997). Venetian shipbuilders and the fountain of wine. *Past & Present* 156, 55–86.

DeVoe, S. E., & J. House. (2012). Time, money, and happiness: How does putting a price on time affect our ability to smell the roses? *Journal of Experimental Social Psychology* 48(2), 466–474.

DeVoe, S. E. & J. Pfeffer. (2007a). Hourly payment and volunteering: The effect of organizational practices on decisions about time use. *Academy of Management Journal* 50(4), 783–798.

DeVoe, S. E. & J. Pfeffer. (2007b). When time is money: The effect of hourly payment on the evaluation of time. *Organizational Behavior and Human Decision Processes* 104(1), 1–13.

DeVoe, S. E. & J. Pfeffer. (2010). The stingy hour: How accounting for time affects volunteering. *Personality and Social Psychology Bulletin* 36(4), 470–483.

Diener, E., S. Oishi, & L. Tay. (2018). Advances in subjective well-being research. *Nature Human Behaviour* 2(4), 253–260.

Donnachie, I. (2005). Historic tourism to New Lanark and the Falls of Clyde 1795–1830. The evidence of contemporary visiting books and related sources. *Journal of Tourism and Cultural Change* 2(3), 145–163.

Easterlin, R. A., L. A. McVey, M. Switek, O. Sawangfa, & J. S. Zweig. (2010). The happiness–income paradox revisited. *Proceedings of the National Academy of Sciences* 107(52), 22463–22468.

Fiske, A. P. (1992). The four elementary forms of sociality: Framework for a unified theory of social relations. *Psychological Review* 99(4), 689.

Gasiorowska, A., L. N. Chaplin, T. Zaleskiewicz, S. Wygrab, & K. D. Vohs. (2016). Money cues increase agency and decrease prosociality among children: Early signs of market-mode behaviors. *Psychological Science* 27(3), 331–344.

Gino, F. & L. Pierce. (2009). The abundance effect: Unethical behavior in the presence of wealth. *Organizational Behavior and Human Decision Processes* 109(2), 142–155.

Gowland, R. L., A. C. Caffell, L. Quade, A. Levene, A. R. Millard, M. Holst, et al. (2023). The expendables: Bioarchaeological evidence for pauper apprentices in 19th century England and the health consequences of child labour. *Plos one* 18(5), e0284970.

Guéguen, N. & C. Jacob. (2013). Behavioral consequences of money: When the automated teller machine reduces helping behavior. *The Journal of Socio-Economics* 47, 103–104.

Haslam, S. A., S. D. Reicher, K. Millard, & R. McDonald. (2015). "Happy to have been of service:" The Yale archive as a window into the engaged followership of participants in Milgram's "obedience" experiments. *British Journal of Social Psychology* 54(1), 55–83.

Haushofer, J. & E. Fehr. (2014). On the psychology of poverty. *Science* 344(6186), 862–867.

Kahneman, D. (2000). Experienced utility and objective happiness: A moment-based approach. In D. Kahneman and A. Tversky (eds.), Choices, Values and Frames, 673–692. New York: Cambridge University Press and the Russell Sage Foundation.

Kahneman, D., A. B. Krueger, D. Schkade, N. Schwarz, & A. A. Stone. (2006). Would you be happier if you were richer? A focusing illusion. *Science* 312(5782), 1908–1910.

Kanfer, R. & P. L. Ackerman. (1989). Motivation and cognitive abilities: An integrative/aptitude-treatment interaction approach to skill acquisition. *Journal of Applied Psychology* 74(4), 657.

Kouchaki, M., K. Smith-Crowe, A. P. Brief, & C. Sousa. (2013). Seeing green: Mere exposure to money triggers a business decision frame and unethical outcomes. *Organizational Behavior and Human Decision Processes* 121(1), 53–61.

Lane, F. C. (1973). *Venice, a Maritime Republic*. Baltimore: JHU Press.

Latham, G. P. & C. C. Pinder. (2005). Work motivation theory and research at the dawn of the twenty-first century. *Annual Review of Psychology* 56, 485–516.

Lea, S. E. & P. Webley. (2006). Money as tool, money as drug: The biological psychology of a strong incentive. *Behavioral and Brain Sciences* 29(2), 161–176.

Leana, C. R. & J. Meuris. (2015). Living to work and working to live: Income as a driver of organizational behavior. *The Academy of Management Annals* 9(1), 55–95.

Meyer III, S. (1981). *The Five Dollar Day: Labor Management and Social Control in the Ford Motor Company, 1908–1921*. New York: State University of New York Press.

Milgram, S. (1963). Behavioral study of obedience. *The Journal of Abnormal and Social Psychology* 67(4), 371.

Milgram, S. (1965). Some conditions of obedience and disobedience to authority. *Human Relations* 18(1), 57–76.

Milgram, S. (1974). *Obedience to Authority: An Experimenntal View*. New York: Harper Row.

Mok, A. & D. De Cremer. (2016). When money makes employees warm and bright: Thoughts of new money promote warmth and competence. *Management and Organization Review* 12(3), 547–575.

Mok, A. & D. De Cremer. (2018). Too tired to focus on others? Reminders of money promote considerate responses in the face of depletion. *Journal of Business and Psychology* 33, 405–421.

Mullainathan, S. & E. Shafir. (2013). *Scarcity: Why Having too Little Means so Much*. New York: Times Books.

Oreopoulos, P. & K. G. Salvanes. (2011). Priceless: The nonpecuniary benefits of schooling. *Journal of Economic Perspectives* 25(1), 159–184.

Pfeffer, J. & S. E. DeVoe. (2009). Economic evaluation: The effect of money and economics on attitudes about volunteering. *Journal of Economic Psychology* 30(3), 500–508.

Phillips, R. (2014). *Alcohol: A History*. Chapel Hill: UNC Press Books.

Piff, P. K., M. W. Kraus, S. Côté, B. H. Cheng, & D. Keltner. (2010). Having less, giving more: The influence of social class on prosocial behavior. *Journal of Personality and Social Psychology* 99(5), 771.

Pinder, C. C. (2014). *Work Motivation in Organizational Behavior*. New York: Psychology Press.

Raistrick, A. (1950). *Quakers in Science and Industry: Being an Account of the Quaker Contributions to Science and Industry during the 17th and 18th Centuries*. Exeter: David and Charles.

Rynes, S. L., B. Gerhart, & K. A. Minette. (2004). The importance of pay in employee motivation: Discrepancies between what people say and what they do. *Human Resource Management* 43(4), 381–394. https://doi.org/10.1002/hrm.20031.

Sacks, D. W., B. Stevenson, & J. Wolfers. (2012). The new stylized facts about income and subjective well-being. *Emotion* 12(6), 1181.

Shah, A. K., S. Mullainathan, & E. Shafir. (2012). Some consequences of having too little. *Science* 338(6107), 682–685.

Siméon, O. (2017). *Robert Owen's Experiment at New Lanark: From Paternalism to Socialism*. Basingstoke: Springer.

Spears, D. (2011). Economic decision-making in poverty depletes behavioral control. *The BE Journal of Economic Analysis & Policy* 11(1) Contributions, Article 72, 1–42.

Stajkovic, A. D., J. M. Greenwald, & K. S. Stajkovic. (2022). The money priming debate revisited: A review, meta-analysis, and extension to organizations. *Journal of Organizational Behavior* 43(6), 1078–1102.

Tone, A. (2018). *The Business of Benevolence: Industrial Paternalism in Progressive America*. Cornell: Cornell University Press.

Vohs, K. D., N. L. Mead, & M. R. Goode. (2006). The psychological consequences of money. *Science* 314(5802), 1154–1156.

Williams, E. (2021). *Capitalism and Slavery*. Chapel Hill: UNC Press Books.

Windsor, D. B. (1980). *The Quaker Enterprise: Friends in Business*. London: Muller.

Zimbardo, P. (2011). *The Lucifer Effect: How Good People Turn Evil*. London: Random House.

9
Resistance and the Informal Side of Organizations

Keywords

power; control; resistance; contest; personal emancipation

Consider

How does power work, and how do people resist it?

9.1 Introduction

In the last chapter I introduced you to the basic concept of power. The idea I progressed was that peoples' motivation to work is created, at least in part, through the powerful effects of managers' motivational strategies. I explained how both monetary and non-monetary rewards are leveraged to drive productivity and ensure discipline in the workplace.

One thing I didn't talk so much about was the possibility of resistance. That is, the possibility that managers' directives and motivational strategies might not actually be all that popular or effective. In this chapter I'm going to balance things up a bit. I'm going to explain the concept of resistance and show you what it looks like in practice.

The chapter begins with some basic theoretical foundations. I'm going to explain the concept of resistance, and then progress your understanding of power a couple of steps further. With a better understanding of the concept of power, I can then map some of the different forms resistance to power can take. I'll tell you where you can find these different forms of resistance and how effective they're believed to be.

You'll ultimately get to an understanding that organizations are what Fleming and Spicer (2007) call "contested" spaces. You'll see that organizations are not cutesy places stuffed full of docile workers diligently working towards the same centrally prescribed goal, but gritty, argumentative places characterized by struggle, strife, and myriad forms of contestation.

9.2 Theoretical foundations

9.2.1 The concept of resistance

The concept of **resistance** is fairly straightforward. If you look it up in the Oxford English Dictionary (OED) you'll see it defined as: "opposing, or withstanding someone or something." It's about pushing back against some ruling power. It's about people who, for one reason or another, object to the way things are (or are going), and decide to do something about it (Fleming, 2016, p. 106).

One very broad way of thinking about resistance is as a mechanism (a tool) people leverage in the pursuit of something called "personal emancipation" (Alvesson & Willmott, 1992). Emancipation being related to ideas around freedom—it's the "action or process of setting free" (OED). In the context of organizations, resistance is how workers contest the domineering logic of management—to transform peoples' productive potential into actual goods produced—and the omnipresent, concomitant necessity of domineering forms of power and control.

Resistance then is also about the realization of freedom from different forms of tyranny and oppression. Classically understood, it's about agency (Bristow et al., 2017, p. 1188), and the maintenance (or reclamation) of acceptable working conditions (Gagnon & Collinson, 2017, p. 1255; see also Prasad & Prasad, 2000). The latter—acceptable working conditions—being something that are traditionally eroded as managers seek to achieve ever-greater productivity, through ever-greater levels of control.

In practice, resistance can take many different forms. This is one thing you'll see very clearly as you read through this chapter. Another thing you'll see is that resistance is absolutely everywhere (Lukes, 1974/2021; Scott, 1990). As Foucault (1990, p. 95) puts it, "where there is power, there is resistance" (see also Jermier et al., 1994). It's not an isolated, unusual, idiosyncratic phenomenon.

9.2.2 Power, revisited

To recap very briefly: in the last chapter I noted the OED definition of power as being the "ability to act or affect something," to "control or [exert] authority over others; dominion, rule; government, command, sway." And the "capacity to direct or influence the [behavior] of others; personal or social influence." In this section, I'll elaborate on this definition in a bit more detail. Drawing on Lukes (1974/2021)—a well-regarded "classic" text on the subject of power—I'll talk you through three different ways of seeing and thinking about power.

One thing to note at this point is that Lukes' (1974/2021) "three dimensions" of power is just one framework that you can use to understand and make sense of power. There are other quite excellent frameworks out there. Examples include: Clegg (1989); Clegg et al. (2006); Fleming & Spicer (2007, 2014); and Scott (1990). In some areas, these different frameworks overlap. In others they don't. Think of them as different "takes" on the same thing.

Note that my aim here is not to give you a definitive account of power. This would be impossible in the space I have available. Power is a vast and complex phenomenon, and research into it would easily fill quite a few books. So rather than try and cover everything, the aim of this chapter is simply to encourage you to think more deeply about the concept of power by showing you some of the different forms it can take and what these forms look like. With that in mind, Lukes (1974) is a great place to start.

9.2.3 The one-dimensional view of power

In his iconic analysis, the first form of power Lukes (1974/2021) identifies is the "one-dimensional view" of power.[1] This is the sort of power you saw exercised in the Milgram experiment featured in Chapter 8's Case Study feature. Do you remember that? When it's used it conforms to what Dahl calls an "intuitive" idea of power (Dahl, 1957, p. 201). Neatly summarized it's: "A has power over B to the extent that he can get B to do something B would otherwise not do" (Dahl, 1957, p. 203).

Characteristically, this form of power is *direct* and *causal*. What this means is that when it's exercised it produces very particular effects. You can literally see this form of power in operation. It's visible and obvious. Peoples' behavior changes. As Dahl describes, people who are subject to this kind of power do things they wouldn't otherwise have done. For example: Jane gets John to walk to Starbucks to get her a coffee. John doesn't want to go to Starbucks—the coffee is rank and it's raining—but he goes anyway. That sort of thing.

This form of power is also what's called *episodic*. So, the exercise of power is an event. It's something you can see happening in a particular time and particular place. Sticking with the Jane-John example, you could say that Jane gets John to walk to Starbucks to get her a coffee at 9 am on Monday morning, before their meeting at company headquarters in Tangier.

Another characteristic of this form of power is that it's *situational*. This means that it works in some situations but not in others. For

---

1 Confusingly, other people use different labels for this kind of power. You might also see it called the "pluralist" view of power Dahl, R. A. (1957). The concept of power. *Behavioral Science* 2(3), 201–215; Polsby, N. (1963). *Community Power and Political Theory*. Yale: Yale University Press; Wolfinger, R. E. (1971). Nondecisions and the study of local politics. *American Political Science Review* 65(4), 1063–1080. Or as Fleming, P. & A. Spicer. (2007). *Contesting the Corporation: Struggle, Power and Resistance in Organizations*. Cambridge: Cambridge University Press call it, simply "coercion," see pages 13–16 particularly.

example: Jane gets John to buy her a coffee during office hours, because she manages the office he works in. Jane is John's boss, and she has power over him because of where she sits in the organizational hierarchy (as in Gouldner, 1954). John is paid to do what Jane tells him to do. However, when the working day ends, like magic, Jane loses all her power over John. She can't call him up on a Sunday and get him to jog down to Starbucks for her.

For a particularly good illustration of the situated nature of power, read Blau (1963). Alternatively, watch the dark comedy *Triangle of Sadness* (2022). You'll see I've recommended it in "Things to Watch, Things to Read." Pay particular attention to Part 3—the scene where everyone realizes Abigail is the only one who knows how to make fire and catch and cook food. What you'll see in this scene is the "basis" of power shifting (e.g., French & Raven, 1968), and it's a masterful, award-winning piece of cinema (see also Mechanic, 1962; Thompson, 1956).

9.2.4 The two-dimensional view of power

The sort of power described above—Lukes' (1974/2021) "one-dimensional" view of power—is quite straightforward. To reiterate, it's "A has power over B to the extent that he can get B to do something B would otherwise not do" (Dahl, 1957, p. 203). In contrast, Lukes' (1974/2021) "two-dimensional" view of power is far less obvious. Centered on the notion of a "non-decision," it incorporates the sort of power that is exercised when decision-making processes are manipulated.[2]

Very briefly: Lukes' (1974/2021) two-dimensional view of power captures the kind of power that is exercised when the scope of decision making is confined to "relatively 'safe' issues" (Bachrach & Baratz, 1962, p. 948). So, when the sort of things people discuss and make decisions about are regulated by those who devote "energies to creating

---

2 Again, other people use different labels for this form of power. Bachrach, P. & Baratz, M. (1962). Two faces of power. *American Political Science Review* 56(4), 947–952. call it the "second face" of power. Fleming, P. & A. Spicer. (2007). *Contesting the Corporation: Struggle, Power and Resistance in Organizations*. Cambridge: Cambridge University Press call it "power as manipulation."

or reinforcing social and political values and institutional practices" (Lukes, 1974/2021, pp. 24–25).

This form of power can show up in a range of different scenarios. Consider, for example, this scenario: John emails Jane and asks her to add an item to the agenda for their team meeting. He wants to talk about a rota for buying coffee. There are other people in the team, and he doesn't see why he has to buy her coffee every day. Jane sees the email and deletes it. The meeting happens. John's item isn't discussed. The end.

In this scenario, the form of power Jane exercises is manipulative, insidious, and sneaky. However, it's not coercive. Jane reads John's email and just ignores it. His item isn't put on the agenda, and he's not given the chance to talk about it. Jane purposefully denies him that opportunity. On this occasion doing precisely *nothing* is an expression of power—can you see that?

For another illustration of Lukes' (1974/2021) two-dimensional view of power, consider this second, slightly different scenario: John is annoyed that Jane makes him buy her a coffee every morning. He's not the only one in the team, and he thinks other people should do it from time to time. He thinks about writing an email to Jane to ask for the issue to be discussed at a team meeting. Then he remembers that Jane believes the youngest person in the team should always buy her coffee. She was quite clear about that. Faced with this well-established belief, John gives up on his idea. He goes back to work and never sends the email. The end.

The form of power Jane exercises in this second scenario also isn't coercive. Quite the opposite. It's virtually imperceptible. In fact, it can hardly be said to exist at all. After all, once again, Jane doesn't actually *do* anything. That's how subtle it is. However, as with the previous scenario, power is in fact in operation. It shows up in John's decision *not* to email his boss. You can see it in what he decides *not* to do.

The cumulative point here is that according to Luke's two-dimensional view, power can be said to be working when people consciously adjust what they think and do in order to fit in with an established value system. People, like John, only do the things they know will fit existing social frameworks and accord with the dominant group's way of thinking.

9.2.5 The three-dimensional view of power

Lukes' (1974/2021) third form of power—his "three-dimensional" view of power—is more elusive still. For the critical reader, it's also more insidious. Drawing on Baruch Spinoza (1632–77), and particularly Michel Foucault (1926–1984), it concerns the most "hidden, least visible forms of power" (Lukes, 1974/2021, pp. 91 & 94). It's also grounded in the idea that power is only ever tolerable when "it mask[s] a substantial part of itself," and that "its success is proportional to its ability to hide its own mechanisms" (Foucault, 1990, p. 86).

Very briefly: Lukes' (1974/2021, p. 93) three-dimensional view of power is all about what he calls the "micro-physics of power." Or as Foucault puts it: "power in its capillary forms" (Foucault, 1980, p. 39). We're talking about the kind of power that "reaches into the very grain of individuals, touches their bodies and inserts itself into their very actions and attitudes, their discourses, learning processes and everyday lives" (Foucault, 1980, p. 39).

This might seem quite convoluted and confusing. In many ways it is—what does Foucault mean? Helpfully, Lukes gives us a quite neat summary that clears things up a bit:

> "A" may exercise power over "B" by getting her to do what she does not want to do, but he also exercises power over her by influencing, shaping, or determining her very wants. Indeed, is it not the supreme exercise of power to get another or others to have the desires you want them to have—that is, to secure their compliance by controlling their thoughts and desires? Lukes (1974/2021, pp. 31–32)

One way of thinking about this kind of power is as "ideational domination" (Fleming & Spicer, 2007, p. 22), or more radically, as "thought control" (Lukes, 1974/2021, p. 166). It's about the "basic and unquestioned group rules that actors refer back to as their bed-rock reality" (Fleming & Spicer, 2007).

One characteristic of this form of power is that conflict simply doesn't happen. The argument here is that conflict never happens because the dominant power regime is incredibly well established. In fact, it's so well established that nobody can even see it in operation. It's so deeply engrained in the social fabric that its different manifestations—in the normative practices that structure how people think and live their lives—are regarded as normal and natural (Barley & Kunda, 1992).

In essence, according to this view of power, the affected are so immersed in (and aligned with) the normative (normalized) understanding (view) of the world that they see nothing obviously wrong with it. This matters because, for Lukes, these individuals are impeded "from living as their own nature and judgement dictate" (Lukes, 1974/2021, p. 90). They are unaware of the domination they are subject to and the radical possibility that alternatives may exist.

Viewed this way, power is expressed through the production of compliant subjects. It's about the people trained/socialized/normalized/institutionalized into particular patterns of behaviors and ways of thinking about the social world. This to the extent that while individuals may see and believe in their own autonomy, the decisions they make invariably betray their own interests. They betray their own interests because they are largely guided by hegemonic power relations.

This is incredibly heavy stuff. Try this example to crystallize things: in our Jane-John scenario, Luke's three-dimensional view of power shows up when John doesn't even question Jane's demands because he can't see them as problematic in the first place. So, we're talking about a scenario in which John may actually *want* to get Jane's coffee every morning because he recognizes and accepts his role as office errand boy. And, moreover, because he fundamentally believes that, as the youngest member of the team, it is natural and normal for him to spend his time getting cups of coffee for his boss. For sure, this is not what he thought he would be doing when he took the job, but he does it anyway. He performs this thankless task believing that he has to pay his dues to his elders and betters. This is what Lukes' three-dimensional view of power looks like in practice.

9.3 Forms of resistance

With your now more nuanced understanding of power, it is possible to move on to the topic of resistance. This we're going to do with particular reference to Mumby et al. (2017), who very helpfully distinguishes between four principal forms of resistance. They distinguish between different combinations of "hidden" and "overt," "micro" (meaning "involving individuals") and "macro" (meaning "involving groups of people") forms of resistance.

One thing to keep in mind as you read this section is that resistance is actually far more complex than Mumby et al's four neat categories suggest. I'm only using them for illustrative purposes, and to kick-start your thinking about the concept of resistance. In reality, resistance comes in all sorts of different shapes and sizes, and Mumby et al.'s system of classification is just a tool we can use to simplify things. Simplicity is helpful because resistance, like power, is an extremely complex social phenomenon. You'll see what I mean in the pages that follow.

9.3.1 Hidden forms of micro-resistance

> When the great lord passes, the wise peasant bows deeply and silently farts—Ethiopian Proverb (cited in Scott, 1990, p. v)

The Ethiopian proverb I've cited previously is a great example of Mumby et al.'s (2017, p. 1165) first form of resistance, which they call "hidden forms of micro resistance" (see also Fleming & Spicer, 2007, pp. 5 & 59; Mumby, 2005). Scott (1985) calls it "everyday forms of resistance," and latterly "infrapolitics" (Scott, 1990).

As well as silently farting, hidden forms of micro-resistance can also comprise things like "petty forms of sabotage, foot dragging, feigned ignorance, character assassinations, gossip, rumour and idle threats" (Mumby et al., 2017, pp. 1165–1168; see also Scott, 1990). Also employee absenteeism and pilferage (meaning the appropriation of work and company products (Ditton, 1977)) are forms of this.

In practice, what "counts" as hidden forms of micro-resistance is pretty much limitless. The crucial point is that we're talking about [ultra] low-profile acts of resistance that are hidden from view (Scott, 1990). So, acts of resistance that are "underground," "unofficial," "offstage" (Contu, 2008), but also "soft," "discreet," "disguised," and "ambiguous" (Courpasson, 2017, p. 1278). We're talking about resistance that can only be seen if you pay very, very close attention (Bleiker, 2000).

Hidden forms of micro-resistance are traditionally understood as the go-to tactic for people in highly repressive contexts (as in Dawson & Bencherki, 2022). They're how people resist when more overt, public forms of confrontation would endanger their "economic or even physical survival" (Courpasson, 2017, p. 1279). They're also regarded as the go-to tactic when conflict first kicks-off. In such scenarios, there's an obvious imperative to operate quietly and away from view. Rao and Dutta (2012) provide an excellent illustration of what I mean by this.

The power of hidden forms of micro-resistance comes from the uncertainty and ambiguity it creates. It works because it's unsettling, and because not much can be done about it. After all, hidden forms of micro-resistance don't "quite make the mark as a direct challenge" (Mumby et al., 2017, p. 1166). Think about it: when is a fart truly oppositional? When does it becomes an act of resistance? How do you know? What kind of response does it necessitate? How do you respond to an employee's belligerent farting?

What really matters is how the act is carried out—how and when the fart is released, how loud it is, and how much it smells. Context is everything. A fart becomes resistance only when it disrupts the somber moments of a team meeting or echoes around the room in response to a senior manager's demand for unpaid overtime.

Alternatively, the employee could keep their arse silent. They could do the overtime that's demanded of them, but then take the equivalent amount of time off sick. They could also show up for work, but absent themselves from the labor process. That is, withhold the productive capacity of their labor by engaging in what Paulsen (2014) calls "empty labour" (see also Paulsen, 2015). So, they could come to work, but not actually do anything useful while they're there.

Perhaps you have some experience of this form of resistance? Have you ever purposefully loafed about on the job? I certainly have. As an undergraduate, I spent my summers working in an office with a bunch of other temps. The permanent staff detested us and gave us the dullest, most boring work imaginable. Literally, the dregs—the mind-numbing rubbish nobody else could bring themselves to do. We survived by taking extra-long lunch breaks and cruising the internet looking for entertainment (Thompson et al., 2020). https://darwinawards.com/ was a particular favorite.

For Scott (1990), hidden forms of micro-resistance are a highly effective way of resisting power. Courpasson et al. (2012) argue much the same (see also Courpasson, 2016). Courpasson describes how hidden forms of micro-resistance are "all the more efficient [because they are] less detectable and can conceal [their] political potential" (Courpasson et al., 2017, p. 1278).

Certainly, one can imagine the undermining potential of a well-timed fart. It's not going to topple a regime, but as Mumby et al. (2017, p. 1167) point out "thousands of petty acts of resistance, rather like snowflakes on a steep mountainside, can set off an avalanche" (Scott, 1990, p. 192). Have you ever seen this happen? It's quite rare, but when it does, the results can be quite spectacular.

The point here is that if enough people engage in enough acts of micro-resistance, then things *might* change. Even if they don't, these acts in their multiplicity lay the foundations for future, stronger, more overt challenges to those in charge. They might seem banal and inconsequential, but such acts can (and do) provide "the stubborn bedrock upon which other forms of resistance can grow" (Scott, 1985, p. 273).

At least, that's the basic argument. Others, such as Contu (2008), argue slightly differently (also Kelley, 1993). Their critique of hidden forms of micro-resistance is uncompromising. For them, it's really just "decaf resistance" (Contu, 2008). It's all a bit vanilla. You could call it belligerence, but not resistance with any serious force or intent behind it. Their argument is that resistance that's imperceptible, covert, and micro in nature is precisely that—hidden away, small scale and weak. It'll achieve very little, certainly not any real, meaningful, lasting changes.

Contu (2008) also argues that hidden forms of micro-resistance can actually be counterproductive in the long run. They argue that rather than laying important foundations other forms of resistance can build on, the quiet resistor is duped by bogus notions of self-determination and a fantasy of autonomy (Bristow et al., 2017, p. 1195). The quiet resistor may believe they're progressing some lofty cause, but in reality their actions never seriously threaten existing power relations (Thompson, 2016). More problematically, their actions may stop more serious forms of resistance from taking root and coming to any kind of fruition.

If you follow Contu's (2008) line of argument, hidden forms of micro-resistance are better conceptualized as a kind of release valve or coping mechanism (Fleming, 2005, p. 47; 2013). They function, not by changing the status quo but by dissipating workers' frustrations and making it possible for them to continue with their work (see also Cederstrom & Fleming, 2012; Fleming & Spicer, 2008).

I think there is a certain truth to this argument. My own loafing during my undergraduate summer temp work didn't really achieve much. All it gave me was a break from my work and an opportunity to recharge my mental batteries. I loafed to kill time and summon the energy to go back to the banal tasks my office manager had set for me. Perhaps if I had stayed for longer, and more people had loafed with me, things would have turned out differently.

Either way, there is logic and plausibility to both arguments. So what do you think? Are hidden forms of micro-resistance powerful? Are they powerful enough to bring about social change in an organization, or anywhere else for that matter?

9.3.2 Hidden forms of macro-resistance

This next form of resistance is similarly "beneath the threshold of political detectability" (Mumby et al., 2017, p. 1167). It concerns not the lone recalcitrant resistors, but them and all their mates. It's about the unruly as a collective (as in Courpasson, 2016). Think: groups of people resisting together in more or less purposeful, systematic, and well-organized ways (Alcadipani et al., 2018). Or, as Mumby et al. (2017, p. 1167) put it, "forms of collective, yet quiet, disguised, hidden or anonymous resistance" (see also Prasad & Prasad, 2000).

For examples of this kind of resistance, look at the Guerrilla Gardeners who quietly, covertly and collectively cultivate illegal greenery in towns and cities across the world (Baudry & Eudes, 2016; Hardman et al., 2018; Mckay, 2011). Also look at the bands of disaffected employees using online forums to meet, share stories, and organize resistance to oppressive employers' regimes.

The beauty of hidden forms of macro-resistance is threefold. First, as Gouldner (1954) describes, hidden forms of macro-resistance can be uniquely powerful. After all, what could be worse (for those in charge) than bands of covert resistors secretly running about the place creating disruption and organizing dissent from within? The notion of people purposefully, systematically, and quietly orchestrating rebellion is uniquely powerful—and indeed, cinematic. I'm sure you can think of plenty of movies based around this form of resistance—in organizations but also more widely.

Second, the concept of hidden forms of micro-resistance also adds weight to Scott's (1985, 1990) point that individual resistors can establish strong foundations upon which more overt challenges to dominant power relations can be built (see also Courpasson, 2017). Hidden forms of macro-resistance can be understood as precisely the types of resistance that emerge out of hidden forms of micro-resistance. It's the kind of resistance that happens when others are enlisted into the cause—when small scale, covert acts multiply, intensify, gain traction, and have an effect. For example, when one frustrated individual enlists the help of others, and together they work to undermine whatever it is that they're frustrated about.

Thirdly, hidden forms of macro-resistance also connect us to, and quite vividly illustrate, a concept I talked about briefly in Chapter 7. Specifically, the idea that there exists an informal side to all formal organizations. That there are entire, coherent, informal organizations *within* formal organizations. Do you remember the secretive, subversive, "mock" bureaucracies described by Gouldner (1954), in which workers pretended to follow prescribed rules, but actually decided amongst themselves how to do everything? Their subversion can be understood as a really great example of hidden forms of macro-resistance in action.

9.3.3 Public forms of micro-resistance

Next in Mumby et al.'s classificatory system are public forms of micro-resistance. This category incorporates resistance that's small-scale—meaning just involving individual people—but overtly confrontational, combative, and self-sacrificial in nature (Courpasson, 2016; Courpasson et al., 2012; Mumby et al., 2017, p. 1169; Thomas & Davies, 2005; Thomas et al., 2011). The public—rather than secretive—nature of this form of resistance is what distinguishes it from the previous two forms of resistance already described.

To understand and make sense of this form of resistance, think "direct action" (Spicer & Böhm, 2007, p. 1677) and "non-compliant behaviour" (Ackroyd, 2007). Think about what Vardi & Weiner (1996, p. 151) call "misbehaviour," meaning "any intentional action by members of organizations that violates core organizational and/or societal norms" (see also Robinson & Bennett, 1995; Vardi & Weitz, 2003).

Overt acts of resistance that directly and explicitly target dominant power relations might sound a bit extreme, but they are in fact quite common (Alcadipani et al., 2018; Ezzamel et al., 2001; Taskin et al., 2023). Keep in mind that we're not necessarily talking about physical acts of resistance, or such acts of sabotage that have an element of destructive violence to them. Employees ranting about their employers on *X*, *Instagram*, or other social media platforms also count as public forms of micro-resistance. Viewed this way, I'm sure you can think of many, many examples?

As far as the research goes, relatively modest examples of public forms of micro-resistance can be seen in Bristow et al.'s (2017) study of early career researchers (ECRs). What this study shows is how ECRs responded to overt hostility toward their academic discipline and the commercialization of higher education in general. The study shows ECRs enacting a wide range of different, gentle forms of overt, direct resistance. It describes how, amongst other things, ECRs would enact a strategy called "playing a newbie" (Bristow et al., 2017, p. 1193). This involved leveraging their early-career status—feigning ignorance and naivete—in order to press senior management on difficult, challenging issues. As a newbie, they could ask the kind of questions others couldn't.

For more extreme examples, think whistleblowing (Weiskopf & Tobias-Miersch, 2016; Weiskopf & Willmott, 2013) and the (initial) hunger strikes described by Courpasson (2017). Also think about the utterly tragic case of the Tunisian Mohamed Bouazizi's self-immolation, that catalyzed the 2011 "Arab Spring" in 2011 (Salih, 2013). Destitute, powerless, and in desperate protest at ruinous police corruption, Mohamed Bouazizi doused himself in petrol and set himself alight. His lonely, very public, and ultimately fatal protest triggered waves of civil unrest across the Middle East and North Africa. It eventually resulted in direct action that forced ruling elites from power in Tunisia, Egypt, Libya, and Yemen, and triggered civil wars that persist to this writing.

9.3.4 Public forms of macro-resistance

Mumby et al.'s (2017) last form of resistance is called public forms of macro-resistance. It concerns "collective, owned, and publicly declared forms of resistance that aim to challenge or unsettle" (Mumby et al., 2017, p. 1170). As Courpasson (2017, p. 1278) puts it, we're talking here about "hard-liners engaging in heroic rebellions, demonstrations and strikes against authority figures" and "brick-throwing students and fasting dissidents ready to sacrifice their lives for a given cause" (see also Bleiker, 2000, p. 256; Courpasson, 2016).

Visibility, scale, and organization are the principal distinguishing characteristics of this kind of resistance. However, the degree of organization varies from "loosely networked groups of people, to highly visible, large scale mass marches enacted by bureaucratic and formal social movement organizations" (Mumby et al., 2017, p. 1170).

Public forms of macro-resistance can therefore take many different forms (Juris & Khasnabish, 2013). Unsurprisingly, most tend to stand out quite a lot—these forms of resistance are the kind that make the news. Think mass civil and industrial unrest, occupations, and boss kidnapping (Chatterjee et al., 2018; Fantasia, 1989; Hyman, 1989; Korpi, 2018).

One relatively recent example would be the violent protests (riots) that rocked France in 2023. Catalyzed by the police's shooting of 17-year-old Nahel Merzouk (Lough, 2023), protests resulted in huge amounts of disruption and destruction, but ultimately, this act of macro-aggression was the response to longstanding complaints about police brutality and systemic racism. Nightly, over more than a week, 40,000 police were deployed in towns and cities across France in an attempt to maintain law and order. Despite this mobilization, in less than a week protestors had attacked more than 250 police stations and gendarmeries, looted widely, and burned at least 5,000 vehicles, 10,000 bins, and 1,000 houses (Albertini & Bronner, 2023).

In relation to organizations, public forms of macro-resistance are often a sign of the breakdown of industrial relations. For a current example, look at the British Higher Education sector. Since 2018, the University and College Union, representing around 120,000 staff at UK universities, has run a series of highly disruptive strikes. Initially over massive cuts to pensions, and latterly over pay, pay equality, workload, and casualization, the strikes have resulted in over 575,000 teaching hours being lost in 2018 alone and disrupted the education of over 1,000,000 students (Inge, 2018).

9.4 A few final points

My account of power and resistance in this book is quite critical. For the thinking reader, it might well come across as quite dystopic. I have, after all, talked quite a lot about oppressive notions of all-powerful authorities and weak underdogs locked in never-ending battles over everything and anything. There is some truth to this narrative, but the bleakness of this vision can also be tempered. I think it's worth noting and keeping the following in mind as you come to the end of this chapter and with it, this book.

First, power is an omnipresent social phenomenon. As Arendt (1970, p. 44) puts it, power "springs up whenever people get together and act in concert." Power shouldn't be a terrifying concept. Any form of organized society depends on it—as in nothing gets done on any serious scale without it. What matters is who has what power, how much of it do they have, and what they do with it?

Second, and building on what I've said previously, it's important to note and remember that power can be generative. Power can be, as Lukes (1974/2021, p. 114) puts it, "productive, transformative, authoritative and compatible with dignity." Thus what also matters is whether or not people use the power they have to bring about good in the world or whether they are cynically progressing their own self-interests.

Third, in much the same way that power can be productive, so can resistance (Ford et al., 2008). Although resistance is by its very nature combative and oppositional, it doesn't have to be socially destructive (Thomas & Davies, 2005). Resistance can have hugely positive effects (Courpasson et al., 2012). Gagnon and Collinson (2017, p. 1270) provide a great illustration of this third point (as do McCabe et al., 2020). The team at the center of Gagnon and Collinson's (2017, p. 1270) study outrightly rejected the divisive managerial prescriptions that were imposed on them, and decided to work together in a quite different way. Through their resistance, what they achieved was a more inclusive, much happier working environment. They also outperformed all the other teams.

Lastly, nobody ever has absolute power. This is the stuff of movies. For sure, some people or organizations may seem all-powerful. The reality though, is that they're not. There is always scope for some form of resistance. As this chapter has shown, resistance can come in all sorts of different shapes and sizes. Even the most apparently feeble forms of resistance can produce surprisingly powerful effects. It may take time, but resistance is never futile.

9.5 Summary

In this chapter I've introduced you to the idea of organizations as contested places (as in Fleming & Spicer, 2007). I've also introduced the concept of resistance and nuanced your understanding of power. Specifically, I've introduced you to Lukes' (1974/2021), one-, two-, and three-dimensional views of power. I've explained what these are and what these different forms of power look like in practice.

After that I've introduced you to Mumby et al.'s (2017) four principal forms of resistance:

(1) Hidden forms of micro-resistance;
(2) Hidden forms of macro-resistance;
(3) Public forms of micro-resistance; and
(4) Public forms of macro-resistance.

As well as describing what these are, I've given examples and shown you where to find them in organizations and wider society.

In the final subsection, I emphasized the points that power is an omnipresent social phenomenon and that both power and resistance can be productive (generative) in social contexts. I've also (re)emphasized the point that power is never absolute but is always contestable (resistible) in one way or another.

Things to Watch, Things to Read

In this table are suggestions for things you can read and watch to learn more about this topic. I've also included a very short commentary, so that you have a sense of why I've recommended a particular source and what to look out for.

Read in two to three hours	Bristow, A., S. Robinson, & O. Ratle. (2017). Being an early-career CMS academic in the context of insecurity and "excellence": The dialectics of resistance and compliance. *Organization Studies* 38(9), 1185–1207.

This article is based on interviews with 24 early career Critical Management Studies (CMS) academics. It describes how they cope with and resist challenges to their academic identities by proponents of neoliberalism in business schools around the world. Bristow and her colleagues don't report any grand acts of resistance in their article. However, you will read about the simple ways through which resistance is orchestrated and what they achieve. This article is also useful in relation to Chapter 2 of this book, which looks at public organizations—the sections on neoliberalism and the Case Study in particular.

Read in a day or two	Barker, J. R. (1993). Tightening the iron cage: Concertive control in self-managing teams. *Administrative Science Quarterly* 408–437.

This is another article that combines themes and topics discussed in different chapters in this book. It builds on what I've told you about power and control, through an ethnographic study of how a manufacturing organization's control system evolved in response to a managerial change. It describes the shift within the organization from hierarchical, bureaucratic forms of control to "concertive" forms of control in the form of self-managing teams. What stands out beautifully well is how the organization's members developed a system of value-based normative rules that controlled their actions more powerfully and completely than the former (bureaucratic) system. The point Barker gets to is a chilling one. He shows that concertive control did not free the workers in his study from Weber's iron cage of rational control. Instead, it appeared to draw the iron cage tighter and to constrain the organization's members more powerfully.

Read in a week or three	Lukes, S. (2021). *Power: A Radical View*. London: Bloomsbury Publishing.

First published in 1974, and now in its 3rd edition, Lukes' book *Power: A Radical View* is a classic text in the social sciences. It is particularly iconic in the field of organization studies. It informs much of our contemporary understanding of power and continues to be widely read, used, and cited. The book itself is fairly short and functions as a good primer on the subject of power. It's generally quite easy to read but is quite technical in a few places. It is well worth making the effort to read this book.

Watch in an evening	Östlund, R. (Director). (2022). *Triangle of Sadness* [Film]. BBC Films

This Palme D'or-winning movie (in 2022) was directed by Ruben Östlund. It's an adult-themed dark comedy distinguished by dramatic portrayals of power and its shifting basis. Parts 1 and 2 are interesting, but the real action comes in Part 3. Here, pay particular attention to the scene where everyone realizes Abigail is the only one who knows how to make fire, catch, and cook food. What you'll see in this scene is the "basis" of power shifting. You'll see Abigail moving from a position of near powerlessness, to being the most powerful in the group.

> **Research Insight:** Beyond the hidden/public resistance divide: How bloggers defeated a big company
>
> Source: Courpasson, D. (2017). Beyond the hidden/public resistance divide: How bloggers defeated a big company. *Organization Studies* 38(9), 1277–1302.
>
> **Edited abstract:** this unique piece of research analyses the four-and-a-half-year struggle of a group of dismissed employees against their former employer. Its shows their transition from isolated, disenchanted individuals to an organized collective on hunger strike. It progresses our understanding of resistance by showing that the development of public resistance is nourished by discrete individualistic and non-confrontational expressions of dissent. Second, it shows how the efficacy of resistance is influenced by the meaningfulness of the resisting space constituted by the blog.

Case Study: What people do when resistance is risky

Based on: Rintamäki, J. & M. Alvesson. (2023). Resisting whilst complying? A case study of a power struggle in a business school. *Academy of Management Learning & Education* 22(2), 257–273.

Introduction

Universities in general, but specifically university business schools, are increasingly caught between two competing logics. On the one hand, the old logic of academia. On the other hand, the new logic of the market. The new logic of the market is winning. It has been for quite some time now (Alakavuklar et al., 2017; Clarke & Knights, 2015; Fleming, 2021; Giroux, 2002; McCann et al., 2020; Rintamäki & Alvesson, 2023; Shore, 2010).

According to the new logic of the market, education is conceptualized as a commodity that is there to be sold according to its exchange value. Students are viewed as consumers and academics are viewed as services providers. The value of an academic is directly proportional to their ability to impart knowledge (measured by student satisfaction scores), produce sizable publication portfolios (n = ?), and generate research income (measured in £, $, and €). Business academics are highly regulated, primarily by layers of powerful, hierarchically organized professional managers. They are an increasingly quintessential example of "knowledge economies governed by technical administrators" (McCann et al., 2020, p. 432)—managers whose primary concern is with profit, competition, and league table rankings.

By contrast the old logic of academia is centered on a quite different set of values—things like collegiality, cooperation, freedom, and opportunity. The quality of academic output is valued above volume, and people are given the time they need to do difficult, complex projects and bring that work to fruition. The school's academics work in self-managing organizations. They operate in a polycentric way, on a horizontal (rather than a hierarchical) basis. Rules, when they are defined, come from within the academic community. They're also agreed democratically, and in accordance with inclusive, emancipatory principles.

The wider context

To give you a sense of how things have changed, jokes now circulate on the internet about how academic greats, such as Albert Einstein, wouldn't have survived in modern academia. Einstein specifically, because he took far too long to produce any work. He'd have got the sack long before anything he wrote hit the press.

Adam Smith would have been in much the same boat. His books took ages to write, and he only produced two of them. To be fair, at least Adam Smith's students seemed to like him (see Norman, 2018). If he couldn't hold down a research position, perhaps he could have been a university teacher or an adjunct.

For the modern academic, permanent jobs are only possible when you've published a journal article or two. This can take years. In the case of Valentine et al. (2023), five and a half years to be precise—and that's just the time it took to get their article accepted into the journal *Organization Science*. What's not included is the time it took to conduct the research and write the article in the first place. That's extra. In some cases, such as

Harding et al. (2022), it can take 10+ years for research to go from inception to publication.

In this context, it's perhaps not surprising that a survey by the UK's prestigious Royal Society found that only around 3.5% of PhD students ever make it into a salaried job in academia (*The Scientific Century: Securing Our Future Prosperity*, 2010). Of those who get through the front door of a university, only 12% (or 0.45% of the total number of people who gained a PhD), survive long enough to join the professoriate (ibid.). That was in 2010. Things are worse now.

All this matters because it is indexical of the massive power asymmetry that exists in modern universities. In a great many cases, universities are places where academics have very little power and even less power to do anything about it. Simply getting a job is a massive achievement. If an academic wants to keep their job, they have to do it really, really well. The consequences of failure can be dire. Mental and physical health suffers, as does hard-fought-for career longevity (Parker, 2014). For many, academia does indeed "suck" (Korica, 2022, p. 1523). Thus the imperative to push back, to balance things up, and change the way things are is a powerful one (Jones et al., 2020).

The case of BSE

The Business School of Economics (BSE) is a pseudonym given by Rintamäki & Alvesson (2023) for a real academic business school based in Europe. The school has around 150 academics and is particularly "corporatist" in its orientation (as in Alajoutsijärvi et al., 2018). Basically, it's a good example of somewhere the market logic predominates.

Of interest in Rintamäki and Alvesson's (2023) study is the state of industrial relations within the business school. In particular, the events that played out following the university's appointment of a new Dean with a mission to "improve BSE's position in national rankings, which had been deemed subpar by university management" (Rintamäki & Alvesson, 2023, p. 4).

Based on their interviews with 19 faculty members, Rintamäki and Alvesson (2023) described what happened when the new Dean started (see pages 8–9). They describe how, once appointed, the Dean moved quickly to consolidate his power in the organization. In a manner akin to a "coup d'etat," he replaced the school's senior management team with loyalists before anyone really knew what was going on. With the backing of the university, he centralized power at the top, limiting peoples' access to budgets, and constraining their ability to act autonomously.

The new dean's coup d'etat was coupled with a harsh style of management. This was extremely intimidating and left no ambiguity about who was in charge. He also introduced a new system of micro-management—a workload allocation system that focused academics' minds on a very narrow range of tasks. First and foremost, writing articles was made everyone's number one priority, and these had to be published in a very, very small number of highly elite journals. Nothing else was acceptable.

To ensure success, individual academics performance was closely monitored and aggressively managed. Those who failed to deliver were performance managed out of the organization. As part of this they were made to account for what work they did, every day, and explain why publications weren't forthcoming. As one of Rintamäki and Alvesson's (2023, p. 9) interviewees said: "People who are sick, people who have got, you know, partners dying, people who have cancer themselves are being told, 'you are not meeting your [performance] matrix.'" In a very literal sense, they had to "publish or perish" professionally (De Rond & Miller, 2005).

Resisting when resistance is risky

Set in the context of (a) extreme job insecurity; and (b) hyper-aggressive, highly muscular forms of (micro)management, the scope for academic resistance to the Dean's totalitarian autocracy was limited. Rintamäki and Alvesson (2023) describe two principal ways through which resistance was orchestrated. Both can be understood as what Mumby et al. (2017) call "hidden forms of micro-resistance." They describe academics adopting: (1) a "mercenary mentality;" and/or (2) engaging in what Rintamäki & Alvesson (2023) call "resipliance."

Mercenary mentality is a resistance strategy

For Rintamäki and Alvesson (2023), the concept of "mercenary mentality" pertains to "an approach to work where personal advancement is emphasized over community matters" (p. 9). It incorporates, essentially, two things. First, the paradoxical notion of resisting by quitting (as in

Hirschman, 1970). That is, refusing to participate in the organization and simply walking away from it entirely.

According to the participants in Rintamäki and Alvesson's (2023) study, in a school comprised of 150 people, more than 100 quit. Senior academics with strong CVs went first (as in McCann et al., 2020). These were the people who could most easily get new jobs, which they did, and then made their escape. Those with weaker CVs had to make sacrifices in order to get new jobs. These included sometimes large pay cuts, demotions, and/or moving long distances to find new jobs.

Some academics adopted a kind of middle-ground strategy. They stayed for a while, to publish more work and generally build up their CVs. When their CVs were strong enough, and an appropriate position had opened up somewhere, they quit and moved on to a new university.

The second component of Rintamäki and Alvesson's (2023) mercenary mentality involved academics disengaging from the school to the greatest extent possible. People who adopted this mentality didn't quit their jobs, but to escape the toxic atmosphere at BSE, they simply stopped coming into the office. They worked from home instead. For example, one person in Rintamäki and Alvesson's (2023) study reported coming in just once every couple of weeks and only during term time. This equated to around ten times a year. In this way the offices and corridors of the school emptied out. The previously vibrant academic community became a passive, disengaged, barely present one.

Rescipliance as a resistance strategy

The second form of resistance Rintamäki and Alvesson (2023, p. 11) identify is called "rescipliance," which they define as "demonstrating resistance attitudes to one's self and one's peers while complying with management demands regarding work outputs." Much more simply put, the word is clearly a portmanteau of resistance and compliance.

For Rintamäki and Alvesson (2023), rescipliance has two principal elements: people both *resist* and also *comply* with the demands that are made of them. So rather than engaging in a tempered form of compliance/resistance (as in Bristow et al., 2017), academics did both. They wholeheartedly resisted the new dean's initiatives and actively tried to undermine them. And they did exactly what was demanded of them.

Reflecting the "hidden" and "micro" nature of this form of resistance (Mumby et al., 2017), this form of resistance was therefore characterized by academics doing things like working from home and trying to publish in highly elite journals. In effect, the former (working from home) functioned as a form of restorative escape (Jones et al., 2020, p. 13). Like the release valves and coping mechanisms described by (Fleming, 2005, p. 47), it enabled academics to protect and distance themselves from the toxicity of the school, and focus on doing what they needed to do to keep their jobs.

Conclusions

The resistance strategies described by Rintamäki and Alvesson (2023) enabled academics at BSE to navigate and survive the workplace. It also enabled them to avoid being singled out as a problematic trouble maker and becoming a target. Adopting mercenary mentality and resipliance functioned as good survival tactics. Yet, neither accomplished much. Their weak, highly individualized nature meant that their power was muted. Little change was effected. The toxic status quo persisted, until the Dean eventually left to work his magic on a new business school.

Questions

1. To what extent do you think "mercenary mentality" and "rescipliance" constitutes resistance?
2. Based on the Case Study, how did academics engage in rescipliance?
3. Can you think of other examples of how people might "resist" and "comply" at the same time?

References

Ackroyd, S. (2007). Organizational misbehavior. In G. Ritzer (ed.), *The Blackwell Encyclopedia of Sociology*. Singapore: Wiley-Blackwell. doi: 10.1002/9781405165518.wbeoso040.

Alajoutsijärvi, K., K. Kettunen, & S. Sohlo. (2018). Shaking the status quo: Business accreditation and positional competition. *Academy of Management Learning & Education* 17(2), 203–225.

Alakavuklar, O. N., A. G. Dickson, & R. Stablein. (2017). The alienation of scholarship in modern business schools: From Marxist material relations to the Lacanian subject. *Academy of Management Learning & Education* 16(3), 454–468.

Albertini, A. & L. Bronner. (2023). Riots in France: The appalling toll of days and nights of looting, fires, assaults. *Le Monde*, 3rd July 2023. Retrieved from https://www.lemonde.fr/en/france/article/2023/07/03/looting-fires-assaults-the-appalling-toll-of-five-days-and-nights-of-rioting-in-france_6042014_7.html

Alcadipani, R., J. Hassard, & G. Islam. (2018). "I shot the sheriff": Irony, sarcasm and the changing nature of workplace resistance. *Journal of Management Studies* 55(8), 1452–1487.

Alvesson, M. & H. Willmott. (1992). On the idea of emancipation in management and organization studies. *Academy of Management Review* 17(3), 432–464.

Arendt, H. (1970). *On Violence*. London: Allen Lane.

Bachrach, P. & M. Baratz. (1962). Two faces of power. *American Political Science Review* 56(4), 947–952.

Barker, J. R. (1993). Tightening the iron cage: Concertive control in self-managing teams. *Administrative Science Quarterly* 37(3), 363–399.

Barley, S. R. & G. Kunda. (1992). Design and devotion: Surges of rational and normative ideologies of control in managerial discourse. *Administrative Science Quarterly* 37(3), 363–399.

Baudry, S. & E. Eudes. (2016). Urban gardening: Between green resistance and ideological instrument. In Courpasson, David, and Steven Vallas (eds.), *The SAGE Handbook of Resistance,* 476–494. London: Sage.

Blau, P. M. (1963). *The dynamics of bureaucracy: Study of interpersonal relations in two government agencies*, Rev. Chicago: University of Chicago Press.

Bleiker, R. (2000). *Popular Dissent, Human Agency and Global Politics* (Vol. 70). Cambridge: Cambridge University Press.

Bristow, A., S. Robinson, & O. Ratle. (2017). Being an early-career CMS academic in the context of insecurity and "excellence": The dialectics of resistance and compliance. *Organization Studies* 38(9), 1185–1207.

Cederstrom, C. & P. Fleming. (2012). *Dead Man Working*. New Alresford: John Hunt Publishing.

Chatterjee, A., S. Dutta, & H. Rao. (2018). Fields of contention: Challengers, incumbents, and the use of boss-napping in Bengal. Academy of Management Proceedings, (Vol. 01).

Clarke, C. A. & D. Knights. (2015). Careering through academia: Securing identities or engaging ethical subjectivities? *Human Relations* 68(12), 1865–1888.

Clegg, S. R. (1989). *Frameworks of Power*. London: Sage.

Clegg, S. R., D. Courpasson, & N. Phillips. (2006). *Power and Organizations*. Newbury Park: Pine Forge Press.

Contu, A. (2008). Decaf resistance: On misbehavior, cynicism, and desire in liberal workplaces. *Management Communication Quarterly* 21(3), 364–379.

Courpasson, D. (2016). Impactful resistance: The persistence of recognition politics in the workplace. *Journal of Management Inquiry* 25(1), 96–100.

Courpasson, D. (2017). Beyond the hidden/public resistance divide: How bloggers defeated a big company. *Organization Studies* 38(9), 1277–1302.

Courpasson, D., F. Dany, & S. Clegg. (2012). Resisters at work: Generating productive resistance in the workplace. *Organization Science* 23(3), 801–819.

Courpasson, D., F. Dany, & R. Delbridge. (2017). Politics of place: The meaningfulness of resisting places. *Human Relations* 70(2), 237–259.

Dahl, R. A. (1957). The concept of power. *Behavioral Science* 2(3), 201–215.

Dawson, V. R. & N. Bencherki. (2022). Federal employees or rogue rangers: Sharing and resisting organizational authority through Twitter communication practices. *Human Relations* 75(11), 2091–2121.

De Rond, M. & A. N. Miller. (2005). Publish or perish: Bane or boon of academic life? *Journal of Management Inquiry* 14(4), 321–329.

Ditton, J. (1977). Perks, pilferage, and the fiddle: The historical structure of invisible wages. *Theory and Society* 4(1), 39–71.

Ezzamel, M., H. Willmott, & F. Worthington. (2001). Power, control and resistance in "the factory that time forgot." *Journal of Management Studies* 38(8), 1053–1079.

Fantasia, R. (1989). *Cultures of Solidarity: Consciousness, Action, and Contemporary American Workers*. Los Angeles: University of California Press.

Fleming, P. (2005). Metaphors of resistance. *Management Communication Quarterly* 19(1), 45–66.

Fleming, P. (2013). "Down with Big Brother!" The end of "corporate culturalism?" *Journal of Management Studies* 50(3), 474–495.

Fleming, P. (2016). Resistance and the "post-recognition" turn in organizations. *Journal of Management Inquiry* 25(1), 106–110.

Fleming, P. (2021). *Dark Academia: How Universities Die*. London: Pluto Press.

Fleming, P. & A. Spicer. (2007). *Contesting the Corporation: Struggle, Power and Resistance in Organizations*. London: Cambridge University Press.

Fleming, P. & A. Spicer. (2008). Beyond power and resistance: New approaches to organizational politics. *Management Communication Quarterly* 21(3), 301–309.

Fleming, P. & A. Spicer. (2014). Power in management and organization science. *Academy of Management Annals* 8(1), 237–298.

Ford, J. D., L. W. Ford, & A. D'Amelio. (2008). Resistance to change: The rest of the story. *Academy of Management Review* 33(2), 362–377.

Foucault, M. (1980). *Power/Knowledge: Selected Interviews and other Writings*. New York: Pantheon.

Foucault, M. (1990). The History of Sexuality: An Introduction (Vol.) I. 95, 1–160. Trans. Robert Hurley. New York: Vintage.

French, J. R. & B. Raven. (1968). The bases of social power. In D. Cartwright & A. Zander (eds.), *Group Dynamics*. New York: Harper and Row.

Gagnon, S. & D. Collinson. (2017). Resistance through difference: The co-constitution of dissent and inclusion. *Organization Studies* 38(9), 1253–1276.

Giroux, H. (2002). Neoliberalism, corporate culture, and the promise of higher education: The university as a democratic public sphere. *Harvard Educational Review* 72(4), 425–464.

Gouldner, A. W. (1954). *Patterns of Industrial Bureaucracy*. New York: Free Press.

Harding, N., S. Gilmore, & J. Ford. (2022). Matter that embodies: Agentive flesh and working bodies/selves. *Organization Studies* 43(5), 649–668.

Hardman, M., L. Chipungu, H. Magidimisha, P. J. Larkham, A. J. Scott, & R. P. Armitage. (2018). Guerrilla gardening and green activism: Rethinking the informal urban growing movement. *Landscape and Urban Planning* 170, 6–14.

Hirschman, A. O. (1970). *Exit, Voice, and Loyalty: Responses to Decline in Firms, Organizations, and States* (Vol. 25). Harvard: Harvard University Press.

Hyman, R. (1989). *Strikes*. London: Springer.

Inge, S. (2018). Pensions strike forces UK universities to reset examinations. *Times Higher Education*, 28th March 2018. Retrieved from https://www.timeshighereducation.com/news/pensions-strike-forces-uk-universities-reset-examinations

Jermier, J., D. Knights, & W. Nord. (1994). *Power and Resistance in Organizations*. London: Routledge.

Jones, D. R., M. Visser, P. Stokes, A. Örtenblad, R. Deem, P. Rodgers, et al. (2020). The performative university: "Targets," "terror" and "taking back freedom" in academia Management Learning, 51(4), 363–377.

Juris, J. S. & A. Khasnabish. (2013). *Insurgent Encounters: Transnational Activism, Ethnography, and the Political*. Durham: Duke University Press.

Kelley, R. D. (1993). "We are not what we seem:" Rethinking black working-class opposition in the Jim Crow south. *The Journal of American History* 75–112.

Kellogg, K. C., M. A. Valentine, & A. Christin. (2020). Algorithms at work: The new contested terrain of control. *Academy of Management Annals* 14(1), 366–410.

Korica, M. (2022). A hopeful manifesto for a more humane academia. *Organization Studies* 43(9), 1523–1526.

Korpi, W. (2018). *The Democratic Class Struggle* (Vol. 22). London: Routledge.

Lough, R. (2023). Paris police shooting: Why are there riots in France? *Reuters*, 29 June 2023. Retrieved from https://web.archive.org/web/20230630024903/https://www.reuters.com/world/europe/riots-shake-france-after-police-shoot-teenager-2023-06-29/.

Lukes, S. (1974/2021). *Power: A Radical View*. London: Bloomsbury Publishing.

McCabe, D., S. Ciuk, & M. Gilbert. (2020). 'There is a crack in everything:" An ethnographic study of pragmatic resistance in a manufacturing organization. *Human Relations* 73(7), 953–980.

McCann, L., E. Granter, P. Hyde, & J. Aroles. (2020). "Upon the gears and upon the wheels:" Terror convergence and total administration in the neoliberal university. *Management Learning* 51(4), 431–451.

McKay, G. A. (2011). *Radical Gardening: Politics, Idealism & Rebellion in the Garden*. London: Frances Lincoln.

Mechanic, D. (1962). Sources of power of lower participants in complex organizations. *Administrative Science Quarterly* 7(3), 349–364.

Mumby, D. K. (2005). Theorizing resistance in organization studies: A dialectical approach. *Management Communication Quarterly* 19(1), 19–44.

Mumby, D. K., R. Thomas, I. Martí, & D. Seidl. (2017). Resistance redux. *Organization Studies* 38(9), 1157–1183.

Norman, J. (2018). *Adam Smith: What He Thought, and Why it Matters*. UK: Penguin.

Parker, M. (2014). University, Ltd: Changing a business school. *Organization* 21(2), 281–292.

Paulsen, R. (2014). *Empty Labor: Idleness and Workplace Resistance*. Cambridge: Cambridge University Press.

Paulsen, R. (2015). Non-work at work: Resistance or what? *Organization* 22(3), 351–367.

Polsby, N. (1963). *Community Power and Political Theory*. Yale: Yale University Press.

Prasad, P. & A. Prasad. (2000). Stretching the iron cage: The constitution and implications of routine workplace resistance. *Organization Science* 11(4), 387–403.

Rao, H. & S. Dutta. (2012). Free spaces as organizational weapons of the weak: Religious festivals and regimental mutinies in the 1857 Bengal Native Army. *Administrative Science Quarterly* 57(4), 625–668.

Rintamäki, J. & M. Alvesson. (2023). Resisting whilst complying? A case study of a power struggle in a business school. *Academy of Management Learning & Education* 22(2), 257–273.

Robinson, S. L. & R. J. Bennett. (1995). A typology of deviant workplace behaviors: A multidimensional scaling study. *Academy of Management Journal* 38(2), 555–572.

Salih, K. E. O. (2013). The roots and causes of the 2011 Arab uprisings. *Arab Studies Quarterly* 35(2), 184–206.

Scott, J. C. (1985). *Weapons of the Weak: Everyday Forms of Peasant Resistance*. New Haven: Yale University Press.

Scott, J. C. (1990). *Domination and the Arts of Resistance: Hidden Transcripts*. New Haven: Yale University Press.

Shore, C. (2010). Beyond the multiversity: Neoliberalism and the rise of the schizophrenic university. *Social Anthropology/Anthropologie Sociale* 18(1), 15–29.

Spicer, A. & S. Böhm. (2007). Moving management: Theorizing struggles against the hegemony of management. *Organization Studies* 28(11), 1667–1698.

Taskin, L., D. Courpasson, & C. Donis. (2023). Objectal resistance: The political role of personal objects in workers' resistance to spatial change. *Human Relations* 76(5), 715–745.

Thomas, R. & A. Davies. (2005). Theorizing the micro-politics of resistance: New public management and managerial identities in the UK public services. *Organization Studies* 26(5), 683–706.

Thomas, R., L. D. Sargent, & C. Hardy. (2011). Managing organizational change: Negotiating meaning and power-resistance relations. *Organization Science* 22(1), 22–41.

Thompson, J. D. (1956). Authority and power in "identical" organizations. *American Journal of Sociology* 62(3), 290–301.

Thompson, P. (2016). Dissent at work and the resistance debate: Departures, directions, and dead ends. *Studies in Political Economy* 97(2), 106–123.

Thompson, P., P. McDonald, & P. O'Connor. (2020). Employee dissent on social media and organizational discipline. *Human Relations* 73(5), 631–652.

Valentine, M. A., S. M. Asch, & E. Ahn. (2023). Who pays the cancer tax? Patients' narratives in a movement to reduce their invisible work. *Organization Science* 34(4), 1400–1421.

Vardi, Y. & E. Weitz. (2003). *Misbehavior in Organizations: Theory, Research, and Management*. London: Psychology Press.

Vardi, Y. & Y. Wiener. (1996). Misbehavior in organizations: A motivational framework. *Organization Science* 7(2), 151–165.

Weiskopf, R. & Y. Tobias-Miersch. (2016). Whistleblowing, parrhesia and the contestation of truth in the workplace. *Organization Studies* 37(11), 1621–1640.

Weiskopf, R. & H. Willmott. (2013). Ethics as critical practice: The "Pentagon Papers," deciding responsibly, truth-telling, and the unsettling of organizational morality. *Organization Studies* 34(3), 469–493.

Wolfinger, R. E. (1971). Nondecisions and the study of local politics. *American Political Science Review* 65(4), 1063–1080.

Index

Tables and figures are indicated by an italic *t* and *f* following the page number

7-Eleven 77, 81

academic publications 256-7
Achaemenid Persians 5
action 208
Adler, P. S. 151
affect 208
Age of Reason 57-8
agency 238
agentic state theory 230-1
agro-pastoralism 21-3
Alcock, G. G. 92-3
alcohol industry 110
algorithmic management techniques 63
alienation
  bureaucracy and 153-4
  Marxism and 60-1
Alphabet 47
altruism 7-11, 82, 118
  behavioural norms 9-10
  competition 10-11
  cooperation 7
  dominance 10-11
  protection 8-9
  reward 8-9
  rise of 8-11
  socialization 9-10
Alvesson, M. 257-60
Amazon 47
American Academy of Management 185
Amnesty International 108
animals
  altruistic behavior 8
  social species 7
Antarctica 67
anthropology 6
Apple 47, 49-50, 54, 85, 88, 108
  News 5

apprenticeships 88
Arab Spring (2011) 250
archaeology 6
Arendt, H. 230, 251-2
Argentina 19
Arsenal of Venice 179-81, 180*f*, 205, 215, 226
Aurangzeb, Mughal Emperor 68
austerity 29, 35-6
Australia 37, 41
Austria 79, 80

backstreet manufacturers 78
Banality of Evil thesis 230
Bandinelli, C. 197, 201
Bangladesh 90, 95
banking 77, 94, 154-5
bankruptcy 50-1, 72
Barker, J. R. 254
Battle of Buxar (1764) 71
Battle of Plassey (1757) 70
Bauman, Z. 158-9, 162
BBC (British Broadcasting Corporation) 188
'Big Four' 11-13
Blake, W. 218
Blau, P. M. 13, 25, 34, 156, 240
bloggers 255
Boeing 737 MAX 55
  safety first culture 64
Boeing B17 'Flying Fortress' 166
  pre-flight checklist 167*f*
Bolivia 79, 98
Bouazizi, M. 250
Brandeis, L. D. 185, 188
Brazil 76
bribes 107

Bridgman, T. 13
Bristow, A. 249, 253
brotherhood, concept of 118
Bumble app 200
Burbidge, D. 82–4, 92
bureaucracy 139–70
  alienation and 153–4
  best practices 141
  bureaucrats, definition of 141
  concept of 140, 161
  context 139–40
  criminal organizations and 112
  criticisms of 157–8
  defence of 162
  definition of 140–3
  films and documentaries 162
  flawed system 152–60
  goal displacement 157
  historical origins of 14
  key characteristics of 142–3*t*
  location of 143–4
  Mesopotamians 25
  mock 248–9
  morality and 159, 162
  organic materials, record-keeping on 147
  organizational research 161
  origins of 144–50
  'out of sight, out of mind' 157–60
  preference for 151–2
  Qin empire (China) 24–6
  rationale for rule-following 157–60
  reading suggestions 161–2
  'real life' 154–7
  substantive rationality 160
  systemic rule 141
  universities 151–3
  writing systems 144–5
Burrow, R. 123
Business School of Economics (BSE) 257–60

Cadbury, E. 217
Cadburys 216
Cairo slums 76
call centers 195

Cambridge University 53
Canada
  marijuana market 110
  population size 19
  WHO Surgical Safety Checklist 169
Cannes Film Festival 162, 254
Cantor, N. 210
capitalism 206, 217
  alienation and 60–1
  free-market 29, 37
  laissez-faire 188
  Marxism and 57, 59–60
  shareholder ownership 49
  welfare 215
Caracas slums 76
carbon budget 65
Carrefour 77
cartels 113, 125
Catino, M. 124
CEOs (Chief Executive Officers) 55
Chantavanich, S. 90
charity 216–17
checklists
  helpfulness of 169
  see also surgical safety checklist (WHO)
Child, J. 68
child labor 223
Chile 48, 67
China 106
  ancient manufacturing 178
  ancient public organizations 175
  bureaucracy, origins of 14
  dating apps 198
  Great Wall 5, 139–40
  population size 19
  Qin army 26
  Qin civil service 26
  Qin empire 11, 24–5, 206
  Railway 19, 31
  Triads 116, 124
  Yakuza and 133
Chinese People's Liberation Army (PLA) 19
Churchill, W. 131
civil unrest 250

clan formula 119
climate crisis 55, 65, 97
Clive, R. 66, 69–72
clothing manufacturing 90
cobalt mining 108
cocaine 105, 109, 115
cognition, definition of 208
collective bargaining 59
collectivism 19, 29, 37, 57
college fraternities 116
Collinson, D. 252
Colombia
  cartels 113
  cocaine 109
commodification of education 255–6
communism 29
  totalitarian 57
Compartamos (microfinance provider) 96, 98
construction workers 78
contested space 14, 237
control
  concept of 206–7
  concertive forms of 254
  definition of 207
  ethnographic study of 254
  rational 254
Contu, A. 246–7
Cook, T. 50
cooperatives 12, 47, 47*t*
corporate immortality *see* immortality
corporations 12, 45, 47, 47*t*
  ancient origins of 51
  CEOs 55
  challenges of 46
  civic-orientated 53
  concept of 46
  corporate scandals 64
  critique of 56, 61–2
  definition 46–7, 49
  documentaries 64
  history of 51–4
  importance of 46
  Marxist critiques of 56, 59
  preference for 54–6
  profit maximisation 64
  rationale for study 47–9
  reading suggestions 63–4
  regulation of 52
  risky business 55–6
  trustworthiness of 64
  types 47*t*
Corrigan, J. M. 165
Cosa Nostra (mafia organization) 114, 118–19, 122, 124
Costa Coffee 113
Costello, F. 131
Courpasson, D. 246, 250
COVID-19 pandemic 4, 157, 165
Craig, D. 111
criminal economy 107
criminal organizations 12–13, 105–33
  bureaucracy, lack of 112
  context 105–6
  cooperation in 114–22
  definition 106–7
  documentaries 125
  dynamic capability 110
  Full Body Tattoo Suit (Anton Kusters) 117*f*
  functioning of 108–10
  Hands (Anton Kusters) 117*f*
  hierarchical structure of 113
  impact 108
  integration 107–8
  juvenile 119
  kinship and 115
  motivations for 114
  ritualized fraternity 123
  secrecy and 108–12
  size of 111
  violence and 115, 123
  see also Yakuza
Critical Management Studies (CMS) 253
Cuba 20
Cummings, S. 13
cuneiform writing 147, 149*f*

Daʻesh 105
Dahl, F. 239
Dale, D. 222–4
Dalrymple, W. 66, 68

Damon, M. 116
Dante Alighieri 181
dating apps 196–201
  self-branding and 194, 195
Davis, R. C. 226
De Niro, R. 116
deception *see* strategic deception
deep acting 192
Delbridge, R. 196
Democratic Republic of the Congo (DRC) 108, 145, 146f,
  Ishango Bone (DRC) 146f
Denmark 18
deregulation 29, 57
Deutsche Bank 109
developed nations 87
DeVoe, S. E. 209
Dhaka slums 76
Dionysius of Halicarnassus 51–2
discrimination 88
division of labor 140, 158–9, 177, 181–2
Donaldson, M. S. 165
Drucker, P. 64
drug trafficking 105, 107, 109–10
  see also cartels
Du Gay, P. 151
Dutch East India Company (VOC) 67
Dutta, S. 245

early career researchers (ECRs) 249–50
East India Company (EIC) case study 53, 59, 65–73
  Anglo-French war 69
  background 66–8
  context 65–6
  defeat 68
  establishment of 66
  fortified trading base 67
  governmental powers 70–2
  imperial ambitions 69–70
  inaugural voyages 67
  Madras, village of 67–8
  questions 73
  state-chartered enterprise 66–7
  treaty terms 67
  turning points 68–9
  winding-up of 66
Easterlin, R. 210
Eastland Company 53
eBay 5
Edu-factory case study 36–41
  concept of edu-factories 36–7
  context 36–7
  cost of education 39
  economic value 38
  education as big business 38
  education as a private commodity 38
  employability and education 39
  learning responsibilities 38–40
  neoliberalism 37–8, 40
  payment for education/student debt 38, 40
  pros and cons 40–1
  return on investment 39
efficiency 197
egalitarianism 21, 23
Egypt 6, 250
eHarmony 198
Eichmann, A. 230
Einstein, A. 256
Eisenhower, D. D. 131
electrification 219
Elizabeth I, queen of England 66–7
emotional labor
  concept of 191–4
  in practice 190
employment
  absenteeism 244
  contracts 48, 119
  CVs 259
  formal 48
  immigration and 87–8
  job insecurity 258
  job quality 63
  microfinance and 97
  normalized lying at work 196
  online forums 248
  overworking 209
  pilferage 244
  prisoners, prospects for 63
  private sector 48

self-employment 209
  strike action 251
  work-related stress and burnout 209
  worker's privacy 221
empty labor 245
energy
  renewables industry 179
  sector 31–2
Engels, F. 57–8
Enlightenment era 14, 28
escrow services 124
ethics 160, 162
  deceptive research 226
  unethical behavior 211–12
European Amalfi Prize for Sociology and Social Sciences 162
European monarchies 52–3
Evans, O. 183–4
  flour factory 184*f*
Exxon 65
ExxonMobil Corp 65

Factory magazine 220
factory system 222–3
  'modern' 181–4
fairness 152–7
fake goods 107–8
fear work 120–1, 123
FEDEX 5
feudalism 216–17
financial crisis (2008) 50
Five Dollar Day initiative 224
Fleming, P. 14, 28, 34, 36, 38, 40, 237
for-profit organizations 12, 30, 72–3
  see also private organizations
Ford Motor Company 113, 185, 188, 213–14, 224
Ford, H. 185, 189–90, 216, 221, 224
  'fully mechanized' moving assembly line 184–6
  Five Dollar Day 212–15
Fordism 186
  principles of 187–8*t*
formal economy 76, 86
formal organizations 12–13
  classification 84
  positive benefits of 89
  see also private organizations; public organizations
fossil fuels 65
Foucault, M. 238, 242
Fournier, V. 12
France riots (2023) 251
franchises 113
fraternity *see* ritualized fraternity
free markets 29
free trade 29, 37
free-riding 9–10
Friedman, M. 28–9, 31, 35
Frys 216
functional management 185

G20 107
Gagnon, S. 252
Gambetta, D. 121
Gandini, A. 197, 201
GAP 85
Garimperos ('cowboy' prospectors) 76
GDP (gross domestic product) 32, 79, 107, 109
gender 94, 98
genealogical kin 7
General Motors
  core principles of 64
Germany
  Federal Bundes Finanz Ministerium (BZSt) 77
  formalized economy 80
  Nazism 29
Gibbs, P. 200
gig economy 63
Gill, M. 123
Gino, F. 211–12
global warming 65
globalization 29, 64
Good Shepherd, The (film) 116
Gouldner, A. 154–5, 248
government
  definition of 140
  institutions, marketization of 30–3
  planning 29

Graeber, D. 24, 151, 160
Great Britain *see* United Kingdom (UK)
Grey, C. 160
Gruffudd ap Gwenwynwyn, prince of Wales 65
guarantees 124
Guerrilla Gardeners 248
gun crime 110

happiness 209–11, 220
happn app 197–8
Harappan Brick 178f
Harding, N. 257
Harvey, D. 56
Haslam, S. A. 230
Hassard, J. 13
Hawthorne Studies 114
Hayek, F. 28–9
health 218–24
  initiatives 218–19
healthcare
  adverse incidents 164–6
  Never 'Event', definition of 164–5
  organ trafficking 96
  organizations *see* National Health Service (NHS)
  retained foreign object post procedure 165
  shadow economy 96
  wrong implant/prosthesis 165
  wrong site surgery 165
Henry III, king of France 181
Hewlett-Packard (HP) 88
higher education
  adjunct teaching staff 39
  grade inflation 40
  group tutorials 39
  lectures 39–40
  student evaluations 40
  teaching, depersonalization of 39
Hochschild, A. 191–2, 194
hostage-taking 120, 124
human resources (HR) 109
human species
  organizations and 3–15
  organized species 4–6
human trafficking 105–7

hunger strikes 250, 255
Hyundai 113

I, Daniel Blake (film) 162
immigration, illegal 87, 93
immortality 50
  concept of 54
India 6, 48, 66
  ancient manufacturing 178
  Armed Forces 19, 67
  call centers 195
  manufacturing output 67
  microfinance 97–8
  population size 67
  Railways 19, 31
  street vending 81
  WHO Surgical Safety Checklist 169
  see also East India Company (EIC)
individualism 11, 19, 37, 57
industrial manufacturing 14
industrial paternalism 215
  concept of 216–18, 225
  global differences 216
  origins of 216
  paternal industrialists, focus of 217–18
industrial revolution 58, 144, 193
industrialization 223
industrialized civilization 175
informal economy 75–6, 92
  negative effects of 89–90
  positive benefits of 89
informal organizations 12–13, 75–99
  concept of 76
  context 75–6
  definition 76–9
  documentaries 92–3
  exploitation and modern slavery 90, 91
  'extremely' 80–4, 91, 93–9
  flexibility of 86
  functioning of 82–4
  identifying 80–2
  isolated 76
  key dimensions of 77, 78f
  multinationals, origin of 88
  rationale for study 79–80
  reading suggestions 92
  role of 88

informality
  key dimensions of 78f
  value of 87–8
information-checking 124
information-gathering 124
initial public offering (IPO) 54
insolvency 50
Instagram 5, 249
International Labour Organization (ILO) 79–80
International Monetary Fund (IMF) 95
internet dating *see* dating apps
Iran 6
Iraq 6, 105, 146
Italy 48
  mafia organizations 109, 112–14, 116, 118, 122, 124–6
  see also Roman Empire

Jack Daniels (beveridge brand) 110
Jafar, M. 70–1
Japan
  kinship rituals 116
  public sector 18, 20
  Yakuza clans 116, 117f, 119, 122, 124
Jenkins, J. 196
jobs *see* employment
Jobs, S. 50, 88
Jordan 169
Jung, G. 109
junk food 93

Kenya 19
kidnapping 251
knowledge economy 256
Kohn, L. T. 165
Korea 133

laissez-faire economics 35
Layer Cake (film) 111
LeBaron, G. 90
Lehman Brothers 50
leisure 220–2
LG 108
liberal economic policy 29
liberalism 206
  classic concept of 28–9, 37
  see also neoliberalism
libertarianism 57
Libya 250
life expectancy 55
lifestyle regulation 220–2
limited liability 50–1, 53
  concept of 50–1, 54–5, 73
  high-risk investment 55–6
logging, illegal 110
Lombe, Sir Thomas 183
  silk throwing mill Derby (UK) 182f
Lukes, S. 238–43, 252–4

Machiavelli, N. 120
mafia organizations 109, 114, 116, 118–19, 124–6
  commission, the 122
  Eastern European 120
  omertà (code of silence) 118, 126
  violence and 120–1
Magnuson, W. 51
Malmendier, U. 52
management science 185–8, 195
manufacturing 176–88
  ancient Persia 178–9, 179f
  bronze production 177
  fundamentals of 176–7
  origins of 176–9
  proto-industrial 179–88
  'satanic' factories 216
  supply chains 85
  see also Arsenal of Venice
marijuana 110
market-pricing mindset 209
marketization 30
Marx, K. 56–60
Marxism 56
  alienation and 60–1
  challenges of 56
  concept of 56–7
  historical context 57–8
  neoliberalism compared 61–2
  versions of 56–7
  wealth inequality and 58–9
Match.com 198
material aspirations 210

Mayo, E. 114
McChesney 28
McDonald's (corporation) 39, 109, 113
'McDonaldization' 194
McDonnell Douglas 64
McLove case study 196–201
  calculability 198–9
  control 200
  efficiency 197–8
  predictability 199–200
mercenary mentality 258–60
Merzouk, N. 251
Mesopotamians 25, 145
Meta 5
Mexico
  cartels 113, 125
  microfinance providers 96, 98
Meyer III, S. 213–14
microenterprises 91
microfinance
  agricultural businesses 97
  case study 94–9
  concept of 94–5
  context 94
  debt/loan repayments 97
  definition of 94
  employment and 97
  future of 98
  gender and 94, 98
  global institutions 95
  growth of 95
  history of 94
  negative effects of 98
  organ trafficking 96
  poor profitability of 96
  questions 99
  real-world impact 97–8
  subsidized capital 96
  suicide and 95
  sustainability and 95–6
  'win-win' scenario 94
Microsoft 5, 88
migration 105, 124
Milgram, S. 226–32
misbehavior 249
mobile phones 108

modernity 162, 174–6, 224
  concept of 174–5
  early 175
  late 175
  theoretical foundations 174–6
monarchy *see* European monarchies
money 207–12
  action and 211–12
  affect and 210–11
  cognition and 208–9
  happiness and 209–11
  organizational behavior and 225
  priming 212
  scarcity of 208–9
  unethical behavior and 211–12
Mongolia 95
Monsters University (film) 116
Monteiro, P. 151
moral responsibility 159
morality 159, 162
  paternal industrialists 216–17
  social class and 211
morbidity 163
Morocco 98
mortality 35–6, 163
motivation 14, 205–32
  concept of 206–7, 224
  context 205–6
  films 226
  psychology of 225
  reading suggestions 225
  theoretical foundations 206–7
  welfare-orientated approaches 206–7
  workforce 207
  see also control; power
moving production line, concept of 185
Mughal Empire 68, 71
Mullainathan, S. 208
Mumbai slums 76
Mumby, D. K. 244, 249–50, 253, 258
Muscovy Company 53
mutualism 11
mutualistic cooperation 7
my single friend app 198–9

Nairobi slums 76
National Health Service (NHS) 19, 26–7, 31–3
  adverse incidents 164
natural resources 188
Nazism 29
  Holocaust 158, 162, 230–1
Ndrangheta (mafia organization) 109, 113–14, 116, 119, 124
neoliberalism 37–8, 40, 217, 253
  concept of 28–9
  critical thinking about 32–3
  documentary 35
  Edu-factory case study 37–8
  higher education 34, 36, 40
  ideology 30
  importance of 28
  key proponents of 35
  Marxism and 56–7, 61–2
New Lanark experiment 222–4
New Zealand 37, 41, 169
NGOs *see* non-governmental organizations (NGOs)
Nicaragua 98
Nigeria 122
Nike 85
Nobel Peace Prize 95
Nobel Prize for Economics 28
nominated succession 52
non-governmental organizations (NGOs) 88, 94, 166
Norway 79, 80
  public sector 18

obedience experiments 226–32
  findings 229
  implications 229–30
  procedure 227–9
online businesses 78–9
organization(s)
  concept of 3
  definition of 3, 114
  functioning of 13–15
  origins of 6–8
  studies 34
Organization Science (journal) 256

organized crime 106, 116
  see also criminal organizations
Östlund, R. 254
Owen, R. 224
  workers' utopia 222–4
Oxford University 53

Pakistan 98
Palm Guixi 198
pandemic *see* COVID-19 pandemic
Paoli, L. 119
Parker, M. 12
partes (tradeable shares) 52
partnerships 12, 46–7, 47*t*, 49
pastoralism 21–3
paternal industrialists 215
  see also industrial paternalism
Persian vertical windmills 179*f*
Peru
  Amazonian Gold Rush 77*f*
  drug trafficking 105
  Gold Rush, Peruvian Amazon 77*f*
  poverty 95
  see also Garimperos ('cowboy' prospectors)
Pfeffer, J. 209
Philippines 169
Pierce, L. 211–12
poaching 110
police brutality 251
poverty 23, 87–8, 94–9
  alleviation of 94, 98
  exacerbation of 95, 97
  extreme 94
  see also microfinance
power 238–43
  absolute 252
  academic 257
  causal 239
  compliance and 243
  concept of 14, 206–7, 236–9, 251–2
  conflict and 242–3
  definition of 207
  direct 239
  episodic 239
  ideational domination 242

power (*Cont.*)
  intuitive idea of 239
  invisible forms of 242
  micro-physics of 242
  one-dimensional view of 239–40, 252
  radical view of 254
  reading suggestion 253–4
  shifting 254
  situational 239–40
  theoretical foundations 237–43
  thought control 242
  three-dimensional view of 238–9, 242–3, 253
  two-dimensional view of 240–1, 252
precocious bureaucratization 24
prisoners 63
private organizations 12, 45–73
  concept of 62
private sector 30, 32, 48, 55, 62–3
privatization 29
productivity 218–24
property rights 29, 37
prostitution 106
psychology 207
  of motivation 225
public organizations 12, 17–41, 45
  archaeological history 21–3
  austerity, effect of 35–6
  concept of 18, 33
  context 17–18
  criticisms of 27–8
  definition 18–19
  documentaries 33, 35
  functioning of 26–7
  history of 20–6
  modern 24–6
  rationale for study 19–20
  reading suggestions 33–5
  see also Edu-factory case study; neoliberalism; universities
public-private partnerships (PPP) 34
publicani (public contractors) 51–2
Pyramids (Giza, Egypt) 5, 11, 139–40

Quakers 217

racial discrimination 88
racism 251
Raistrick, A. 217
Rao, L. 245
rationality
  context 173
  definitions 174
  documentaries and dramas 195
  formal 173–201
  instrumental 160
  post-industrial services economy 188–93
  reading suggestions 194
  substantive 160
rationalized organizations 14
rationalized service 189–90
reciprocity 118
record-keeping *see* bureaucracy
redundancy payments 86
Reedy, P. 12
relaxation 220–2
resipliance 258–60
resistance 236–60
  concept of 14, 236–8, 244, 252
  context 236–7
  definition of 237
  direct action 249
  films 254
  forms of 244–51, 253
  hidden 244, 260
  macro-resistance, forms of 247–51
  micro-resistance, forms of 244–7, 249–50, 258, 260
  non-compliant behaviour 249
  overt 244
  physical acts of 249
  positive effects of 252
  risk and resistance case study 255–60
  theoretical foundations 237–43
Rintamäki, J. 257–60
riots 251
risk
  healthcare 27
  sharing 26
ritualized fraternity 115–20, 123
Ritzer, G. 194

Roger II, king of Sicily 24
Roland Calori Prize 196
Roman Empire 11, 48, 51
Romania
    Colectiv nightclub fire (2016) 35
Roosevelt, F. 29
Roser, C. 176
Rowlinson, M. 13
Royal Charter 53
Royal Society (UK) 257
rule of law 84
rules *see* bureaucracy
Russia
    communism 29
    mafia organizations 124
Ryanair 39

sabotage 249
Samsung 108
Sanderson, C. A. 210
satisfaction treadmill 210
Saudi Aramco 54–5
schizophrenia 110
scientific management, concept of 185–8, 195
Scott, W. R. 13
Seabright, P. 4
seasonal workers 78
Second World War *see* World War II
secrecy *see* criminal organizations
self-determination 247
self-interest *see* altruism
selfishness 11
semi-formal organizations 84–91, 93
    distorted markets 89–90
    functioning of 86–7
    identifying 84–6
    importance of 87–90
    informality, human cost of 90
    'race to the bottom' 89–90
    survival 87–8
    underground businesses 93
services economy 14
    definition of 188
    hyper-rationalization 195

    post-industrial 188–93
    virtual reception 196
shadow economy 79–80, 87–8
shadow factories 76, 85, 90
Shafir, E. 208
Shah Alam, Mughal Emperor 71
shareholder ownership 49–50, 54–5
shrimp farming 90
Siméon, O. 222
Singer, R. 56
Siraj ud-Daula 69–70
slavery 14, 140, 206, 224
    modern 90, 108
slums 76
small- and medium-sized organizations 85
smart phones 108
Smith, A. 256
smuggling 110, 124
social equality 23
social initiatives 221–3
social media 249
social security 8
social services 26
social venues 221
social welfare 217, 223
    see also welfare
socialism 222
societas publicanorum (society of publicans) 51–2
sole traders 12, 46, 47t, 49
South Africa 67
    informal economy 92
    Port Elizabeth 6
    private sector employment 48
    Townships 76
South Korea 18
Spain 19
specialization (labor) 177
Spice Islands 67
Spicer, A. 14, 237
Spinoza, B. 242
sports facilities 221
Starbucks 41, 239–40
Steinbeck, J. 59
Stiglitz, J. 28

strategic deception 196
street hawkers 78
street vending 76–7, 80–1, 93
strikes 251
subcontracting 90
   'first-tier' 85
substantive rationality *see* rationality
Sumerian 145–50
   bullae 147, 148*f*
   clay tokens 147*f*
   cuneiform writing 149*f*
   engraved tokens 148*f*
   taxation payments 149–50
surface acting 192
surgical safety checklist (WHO) 163–70
   idea for 166–8
   questions 169–70
   visual diagram 168*f*
surplus value theory 59
sustainable resources 105
Sweden 18, 106
Switzerland 79, 80, 106
Syria 6, 105

tacit skill 155–6
Tanzania
   Mwanza, illegal marketplaces 82–4, 92
   WHO Surgical Safety Checklist 169
Taylor, F. 185–6, 195
Taylorism 186–8
   principles of 187*t*
tea farming 90
Tell Sabi Abyad (Syria) 21–3
terrorism 105–6
Tesco 77
Thailand 90
timber 110
Tinder 196–9
totalitarianism 29, 57, 62
Toyota 113
trade unions 59, 156, 222, 225
training 88
Treaty of Alinagar (1757) 69
Treaty of Allahabad (1765) 71–2
Triangle of Sadness (film) 240, 254

Tribe, K. 141
trust
   anchor 83
   substitutes for 124
Tunisia 250
tunneling 208
Turkey 83–4

UK *see* United Kingdom (UK)
underground businesses 93
unionism 222
unions; unionization *see* trade unions
United Kingdom (UK)
   business start-ups 88
   Department for Work and Pensions (DWP) 77
   energy sector 31–2
   GDP 32
   Higher Education sector 251
   informal shadow economy 79
   manufacturing output 67
   mortality rates 35–6
   neoliberalism 37, 41
   Office for National Statistics (ONS) 48
   population size 67
   Powis Castle 65–6
   Royal Charter 53
   Royal Society 257
   student debt 41
   welfare state 29, 162
   WHO Surgical Safety Checklist 169
   see also National Health Service (NHS) 19
United Nations (UN) 95, 107
United Nations Educational, Scientific, and Cultural Organization (UNESCO) 224
United Nations Office on Drugs and Crimes (UNODC) 110
United States (US)
   American Revolution 53
   civilian defense groups 125
   corporate charters 53–4
   corporations, role of 53–4

culture training 195
Department of Defense 19
drug cartels 125
formalized economy 80
GDP 32
informal economy 93
informal workers 80–1
Internal Revenue Service (IRS) 144
military 105
neoliberalism 37, 41
New Deal 29
organized crime 111
privatized healthcare sector 32
prohibition on alcohol 110
salary figures 210–11
stock market 54
street vending 80–1
student debt 41
WHO Surgical Safety Checklist 169
Yakuza 133
universities
  bureaucracy 151–3
  financially orientated evaluations of 36
  as historic civic, institutions 36
  as public organizations 36
University and College Union (UCU) 251
unlicenced traders 81
US *see* United States (US)

Valentine, M. A. 256
Vanguard Group 50
Varcin, R. 83–4
Vardi, Y. 249
Vaughn, M. 111
vegan electricity 57
Venetian-style motivation 226
  see also Arsenal of Venice
violence 123
  shared experience of 121
volunteering 209, 212
von Mises, L. 29

Walmart 19, 77, 81
Watson, Admiral 69
Weber, M. 18, 34, 81, 141, 161, 174, 194, 254

WeChat 9
Weiner, Y. 249
welfare
  capitalism 215, 222
  initiatives 218–20
  services 216
  statism 222, 225
  work 215
wellbeing 210, 216, 218–24
  emotional health and 219–20
  initiatives 218–19
Wengrow, D. 24
WhatsApp 9
whistleblowing 250
wildlife 110
Williams, C. C. 92
Windsor, D. B. 217
workforce motivation *see* motivation
World Bank 84, 94–5
World Drug Report (2020) 107
World Health Organization
    (WHO) 166–7
  see also surgical safety checklist (WHO)
World Heritage sites 224
World War II 29, 64, 131
  see also Nazism
Worshipful Company of Saddlers 53

X (formerly Twitter) 249

Yakuza 126–33
  associate and freelance roles 132–3
  associations and societies 131
  black markets 131–2
  consolidation of 133
  context 126
  diversification of 133
  future prospects 132–3
  history of 133
  legal criminal organization 126–7
  mainstream organizations, infiltration of 126
  Major Yakuza crime syndicates (2001) 128–9*t*
  Office of the Kobe Yamaguchi-gumi in Awaji, Japan 127*f*

Yakuza (*Cont.*)
　offices 126, 127*f*
　origins 127–30
　positive image of 132
　post-war expansion 131
　pre-war boom 130
　questions 133
　rationale for study 107–8
　reading suggestions 123–4
　registered headquarters 126–7, 128–9*t*
　ritualized fraternity 115–20
　rule of 21 110–14
　scope and size of 107, 126
　social position 127–30
　summary 123
　'three no's policy' 132
　uneasy acceptance 131–2
　violence 120–2
Yemen 250
Yunus, M. 95, 99

Zimbabwe 79
Zonca, V. 183
Zoom 4